HEIRLOOMS

HEIRLOOMS

Edited by
Margaret T. Applegarth

author of TWELVE BASKETS FULL, *etc.*

HARPER & ROW, PUBLISHERS, NEW YORK, EVANSTON, AND LONDON

THESE HEIRLOOMS

ARE FOR

MARGARET SHANNON

⚜

ACKNOWLEDGMENTS

Acknowledgment is made to the following for permission to reprint copyrighted material:

ABINGDON PRESS for "Patterns of Delight" from *In Green Pastures* by Jane Merchant, copyright © 1959 by Abingdon Press.

CHRISTIAN CENTURY FOUNDATION for "Altars" by Edgar Frank; extract from "Spring Landscape" by Louis Ginsberg; "The Irresistible Intention" by Virgil A. Kraft; "In Prayer" and "The Picture" by Arthur B. Rhinow.

CITY BANK OF PORTAGE, WISCONSIN, for "Voice" by Zona Gale.

COWARD-MC CANN, INC., for extract from *The Little Locksmith* by Katharine Butler Hathaway.

CURTIS BROWN, LTD., for extract from *Father Malachy's Miracle* by Bruce Marshall, copyright 1931 by Bruce Marshall.

J. M. DENT & SONS, LTD., for extract from *The Adventures of a Mountaineer* by Frank S. Smythe.

DOUBLEDAY & COMPANY, INC., for extract from "The Explorer" from *Rudyard Kipling's Verse*, reprinted by permission of Doubleday & Company, Inc., The Mac-

Acknowledgments (*continued*)

millan Company of Canada, and Mrs. George Bambridge.

E. P. DUTTON & COMPANY, INC., for "Adoration" from *Bow Down in Jericho* by Byron Herbert Reece.

FIRST AND MERCHANTS NATIONAL BANK OF RICHMOND, VIRGINIA, for extract from *The Deliverance* by Ellen Glasgow.

GOOD HOUSEKEEPING for "The Villages" by Martha Haskell Clark.

HARCOURT, BRACE & WORLD, INC., for extract by W. H. Auden from *Poets at Work*, copyright 1948 by Harcourt, Brace & World, Inc.; "The Cambridge Ladies" and "May My Heart Always" by E. E. Cummings from *Poems: 1923–1954*, copyright © 1954 by E. E. Cummings; extract from *Reflections on the Psalms* by C. S. Lewis; extract from *Remembrance Rock* by Carl Sandburg; extract from *Unpopular Opinions* by Dorothy L. Sayers; "Prayer" by Louis Untermeyer from *Challenge* by Louis Untermeyer, copyright 1914 by Harcourt, Brace & World, Inc., renewed by Louis Untermeyer.

HARPER & ROW, PUBLISHERS, for extracts from *Man the Unknown* by Alexis Carrel; "The Way of Holiness" by Martin Buber in *The Eternal Light*, ed. by Charles L. Wallis; extract from *The Art of Loving* by Erich Fromm; extract from *The Gospel According to Thomas;* extract from *Prayers and Meditations* by Gerald Heard; extract from *Secretly Armed* by Allan A. Hunter; extracts from *A Testament of Devotion* by Thomas Kelly; extract from *The Gothic Image* by Émile Mâle; "Earth Is Enough"

by Edwin Markham from *Poems,* ed. by Charles L. Wallis; "God Is Here" by Madeleine Aaron, "To Mother" by Thomas W. Fessenden, and "My Name Is Legion" by Edward Sanford Martin in *Masterpieces of Religious Verse,* ed. by James Dalton Morrison; extracts from *The Dilemma of Modern Belief* by Samuel H. Miller; "Voice" by Zona Gale, "Indirection" by Richard Realf, and "ABC's in Green" by Lenora Speyer in *One Thousand Quotable Poems,* ed. by Thomas Curtis Clark; "A Little Te Deum" and "True Happiness" in *Selected Poems of John Oxenham,* ed. by Charles L. Wallis; extracts from *The Path of the Saint;* extracts from *Love Is a Spendthrift* by Paul Scherer; extract from Adlai E. Stevenson in *A Stevenson Sampler,* ed. by Alden Whitman; "A Prayer" by Marion Franklin Ham and "A Prayer" by Irene Rutherford McLeod in *A Treasury of Poems for Worship and Devotion,* ed. by Charles L. Wallis; extract from *Ethics* by Radoslav A. Tsanoff, rev. ed.; extract from *All the Plants of the Bible* by Winifred Walker; extract from *Our Town* by Thornton Wilder; extract from Roy A. Burkhart in *Worship Resources for the Christian Year,* ed. by Charles L. Wallis.

HOLT, RINEHART AND WINSTON, INC., for "Spring" by John Gould Fletcher in *Selected Poems,* copyright 1938 by John Gould Fletcher; "Stopping by Woods on a Snowy Evening" by Robert Frost in *Complete Poems,* copyright © 1923, 1930, 1939 by Holt, Rinehart and Winston, Inc.,

1936, 1942, 1951, 1958 by Robert Frost, 1964 by Lesley Frost Ballantine; "Loveliest of Trees" from *A Shropshire Lad* (Authorized Edition) in *The Collected Poems of A. E. Housman,* copyright 1940 by Holt, Rinehart and Winston, Inc.; "Sometimes" by Thomas S. Jones, Jr., in *Shadow of the Perfect Rose,* copyright 1937 by John L. Foley.

HOUGHTON MIFFLIN COMPANY for "Music and Drum" by Archibald MacLeish in *Poems: 1924–1933.*

ALFRED A. KNOPF, INC., for extract from *The Prophet* by Kahlil Gibran, copyright © 1923 by Kahlil Gibran, 1951 by Administrators C.T.A. of Kahlil Gibran Estate and Mary G. Gibran; "Mother to Son" from *The Dream Keeper* by Langston Hughes, copyright 1932 by Alfred A. Knopf, Inc.; "The Excesses of God" by Robinson Jeffers in *Selected Poems,* copyright © 1941 by Robinson Jeffers, 1962, 1964 by Donnan Jeffers and Garth Jeffers; "The Pine-Trees in the Courtyard" by Po-Chü-i in *Translations from the Chinese,* ed. by Arthur Waley, copyright 1919, 1941 by Alfred A. Knopf, Inc.

THE MACMILLAN COMPANY for "The Spider" by Robert P. Tristram Coffin in *Collected Poems;* "A Song in Humility" in *Proud Horns* by Carleton Drewry; extract from *The Journal of Mary Harvey Russell* by Storm Jameson; extract from *The Primacy of Faith* by Richard Kroner; extract from "The Widow in the Bye Street" and extract from "The Everlasting Mercy" in *Poems* by John

Acknowledgments (*continued*)

Masefield, reprinted by permission of The Macmillan Company, The Macmillan Company of Canada, and the Society of Authors; "In Remembrance" by James Stephens in *Collected Poems,* reprinted by permission of The Macmillan Company, The Macmillan Company of Canada, and Mrs. Stephens; extracts from *Collected Poems and Plays* by Rabindranath Tagore; "The Voice" by Sara Teasdale in *Collected Poems;* extract from "A Prayer for Old Age" by William Butler Yeats in *Collected Poems.*

NEW DIRECTIONS for extract from *Seeds of Contemplation* by Thomas Merton, copyright 1949 by Our Lady of Gethsemani Monastery.

OXFORD UNIVERSITY PRESS for "Leisure" from *Poems of William Henry Davies;* extract from *The Sea Around Us* by Rachel L. Carson.

OXFORD UNIVERSITY PRESS, LTD., for extract from *A Sleep for Prisoners* by Christopher Fry.

G. P. PUTNAM'S SONS for extract from *Alone* by Richard E. Byrd, copyright 1938 by Richard E. Byrd; extract from *A Book of Hours* by Donald Culross Peattie, copyright 1937 by Donald Culross Peattie.

RANDOM HOUSE, INC., for extract from *A Man for All Seasons* by Robert Bolt; extract from "For the Time Being" in *The Collected Poems of W. H. Auden,* copyright 1945 by W. H. Auden.

SATURDAY REVIEW for "Migrations" by Elsa Gidlow.

CHARLES SCRIBNER'S SONS for extract from "A Natural History of the Dead" in *The Short Stories of Ernest Hemingway;* extracts from *Cry, the Beloved Country* by Alan Paton; extract from *Cross Creek* by Marjorie Kinnan Rawlings; extract from "Earth" by John Hall Wheelock in *Poems: 1911–1936.*

SIDGWICK & JACKSON, LTD., for "Morning Thanksgiving" by John Drinkwater in *Poems: 1908–1919.*

SIMON AND SCHUSTER for extracts from *The Art of Living* by Wilferd A. Peterson, copyright © 1960, 1961 by Wilferd A. Peterson.

A. P. WATT & SON AND EXECUTORS OF THE ESTATE OF H. G. WELLS for extract from *Joan and Peter* by H. G. Wells.

WILLIAMSON MUSIC, INC., for extract from *South Pacific,* copyright 1949 by Oscar Hammerstein II, Richard Rodgers, and Williamson Music, Inc.

Acknowledgment is also made to the following persons for permission to reprint materials from their writings: Mortimer J. Adler, Harry Emerson Fosdick, Winfred Ernest Garrison, Glenn Frank, Sara Henderson Hay, Herman Hagedorn, Helen Keller, Robert Lee, Lin Yutang, Clare Boothe Luce, Herbert V. Prochnow, Nathan M. Pusey, David H. C. Read, Archibald Rutledge, Ralph W. Seager, Massey H. Shepherd, Jr., Ralph W. Sockman, Douglas V. Steere, John Wallace Suter, Edwin Way Teale, Nancy Byrd Turner, Henry Pitney Van Dusen, Wernher Von Braun, Leslie D. Weatherhead, E. B. White.

Acknowledgment is also made to the estates of the following for permission to reprint materials: Karle Wilson Baker, Leslie Savage Clark, Catherine Cate Coblentz, Arthur Guiterman, M. K. W. Heicher, Harry Kemp, Angela Morgan, William Alexander Percy, Edwin McNeill Poteat, Rolland W. Schloerb, Samuel M. Shoemaker, Abba Hillel Silver, Joseph R. Sizoo, Evelyn Underhill.

PICTURE CREDITS

AMERICAN AIRLINES: pages 180, 290
CORNING GLASS MUSEUM, Corning, N.Y.: frontispiece
EWING GALLOWAY, N.Y.: pages 106, 160, 252
JACKSON & PERKINS: page 98
LEONARD KAMSLER: page 270
GEORGE LAESSIG: page 60
LUFTHANSA: page 134
METROPOLITAN MUSEUM OF ART, N.Y.: page

PHILADELPHIA MUSEUM OF ART, PHILADELPHIA, PA.: page 76
RELIGIOUS NEWS SERVICE, N.Y.: pages 200, 300
KOSTI RUOHOMAA, FROM BLACK STAR: pages 10, 18, 26, 32, 42, 50, 70, 82, 92, 140, 188, 232, 242, 258, 280
STANDARD OIL CO. (N.J.): pages 38, 122, 146, 152, 170, 210, 216, 226

CONTENTS

A LETTER TO THE READER

_I_ n rather a charming way we are all magpies! For don't you often find yourself saving strange scraps of this or that because some dear and inescapable memory is wrapped up in them? Ask your next dinner partner what he carries in his wallet besides money, and out will come his curious assortment: "See this old yellow Time Table? Well, there used to be a punk little old train to a pokey place where I went fishing, Saturdays . . . and look at this old clipping . . . as for this theater ticket stub, let me tell you. . . ." You do this, too; for it is precious stuff, the secret treasure of your heart.

Yet all the time you are also a millionaire in matchless major Heirlooms, inherited from all the earlier members of your family. Every Bible ever printed certain relatives have loved to "read, mark, and inwardly digest." Other ancestors had a part in every Hymnbook. And as for Nature —just recall the tradition that your Number One great-great-great-great-grandparents set up housekeeping in a Garden, given as a wedding gift, actually, with one famous tree "Posted." You have imagined all your life what a thrill to have been allowed to name all the animals, watch all the birds, find all the flowers, sample all the meals, try on those first clothes, mimic all the music of water and wind and wild creatures. It is about such delightful Heirlooms that this album comes to awaken your imagination.

You will welcome the occasional appearance of dates placed beside the names of certain authors from whose pens there can come no future heirlooms. Yet surely you agree that these writers, no longer here, seem as modern as tomorrow morning. And why not? since they also had the same sort of divine-human inheritance as yours now is.

Out of my wallet, therefore, into your hands—with God's richest blessing on your reading.

Margaret T. Applegarth

NEW YORK
1967

ADORATION

Think magnificently of God!

SIR THOMAS BROWNE, 1605–1682

Where shall we find strength to praise
  him?
  For he is greater than all his works.
Terrible is the Lord and very great,
  and marvelous is his power.
When you praise the Lord, exalt him as
  much as you can;
  for he will surpass even that.
When you exalt him, put forth all your
  strength,
  and do not grow weary, for you cannot praise him enough.
Who has seen him and can describe
  him?
  Or who can extol him as he is?
Many things greater than these lie hidden,
  for we have seen but few of his
  works.
For the Lord has made all things,
  and to the godly he has granted wisdom.

ECCLESIASTICUS 43:28–33

God expects only one thing of you:
that you come out of yourself as far as
you are a created being, and let God be
God within you.

MEISTER ECKHART, 1260–1328

From PAULINE

My God, my God, let me for once look
  on Thee
As though naught else existed, we
  alone!
And as creation crumbles, my soul's
  spark
Expands till I can say,—"Even from
  myself
I need Thee and I feel Thee and I love
  Thee.
I do not plead my rapture in Thy works
For love of Thee, nor that I feel as one
Who cannot die: but there is that in me
Which turns to Thee, which loves or
  which should love."

ROBERT BROWNING, 1812–1889

SPIRITUAL JOURNEY

As a man journeys in the Spirit he finds
that "Spirit with Spirit can meet."
Then he becomes conscious that this
higher part of himself is co-terminous
with and continuous with a *more* of the
same quality which is operative in the
universe outside of him, and which he
can keep in working touch with and in
a fashion get on board of.

WILLIAM JAMES, 1842–1910

INNER CHAMBER

Up now, slight man! Flee, for a little while, thy occupation; hide thyself, for a time, from thy disturbing thoughts.

Cast aside thy burdensome cares, and put away thy toilsome business.

Yield room for some little time to God, and rest for a little time with Him.

Enter the inner chamber of thy mind; shut out all thoughts save that of God and such as can aid thee in seeking Him; close thy door and seek Him.

ST. ANSELM, 1034–1109

Not to me
The unmoved mover of philosophy
An absolute still sum of all that is,
The God whom I adore—not this!
Nay, rather a great moving nave of bliss,
A surging torrent of dynamic love
In passionate swift career,
That down the sheer
And fathomless abyss
Of being ever pours,
His ecstasy to prove.

EVELYN UNDERHILL, 1875–1941

From STARTING FROM PAUMANOK

I say the whole earth and all the stars in the sky are for religion's sake.

I say no man has ever yet been half devout enough,
None has ever yet adored or worship'd half enough,
None has begun to think how divine he

himself is, and how certain the future is.

I say that the real and permanent grandeur of these States must be their religion,
Otherwise there is no real and permanent grandeur;
(Nor character nor life worthy the name without religion,
Nor land nor man or woman without religion).

WALT WHITMAN, 1819–1892

FRAMER OF THE WORLD

Essence beyond essence,
Nature increate,
Framer of the world,
I set Thee, Lord, before my face,
and I lift up my soul unto Thee.
I stretch forth my hands unto Thee.
My soul is as a thirsty land towards Thee.
O Lord, Thou knowest, and canst, and willest
the good of my soul.
Thou, O Lord, I beseech Thee,
in Thine unspeakable love,
so order concerning me,
and so dispose,
as Thou knowest
to be most pleasing to Thee,
and most good for me.

LANCELOT ANDREWES, 1555–1625

DIVINE ORIGIN

There is surely a piece of divinity in us, something that was before the elements, and owes no homage to the sun.

SIR THOMAS BROWNE, 1605–1682

GOD GLORIFIED

The motto of the Benedictine Order is the four letters: I.O.G.D.—*In omnibus gloridicetur Deus,* "That God may be glorified in everything."

AWARENESS

Perhaps, for many of us, all experience merely defines, so to speak, the shape of that gap where our love of God ought to be. It is not enough.

If we cannot "practice the presence of God," it is something to practice the absence of God, to become increasingly aware of our unawareness till we feel like men who should stand beside a great cataract and hear no noise, or like a man in a story who looks in a mirror and finds no face there, or a man in a dream who stretches out his hand to visible objects and gets no sensation of touch.

To know that one is dreaming is to be no longer perfectly asleep.

C. S. LEWIS, 1898–1963

I think about God, yet I talk of small
    matters,
Now isn't it odd how my idle tongue
    chatters
Of quarrelsome neighbors,
Fine weather and rain,
Indifferent labors,
Indifferent pain,
Some trivial style
Fashion shifts with a nod,
And yet all the while
I am thinking of God.

GAMALIEL BRADFORD, 1863–1932

WHO CAREST FOR EACH

O thou good Omnipotent, who so carest for each of us, as if Thou carest for him alone; and so for all, as if all were one! Blessed is the man who loveth Thee, and his friend in Thee, and his enemy for Thee. I behold how some things pass away, that others may replace them, but Thou dost never depart. O God, my Father, O Thou most supreme, most good, most potent, most omnipotent, most merciful yet most just, most secret yet most present, beauty of all things beautiful, what have I said now, my God, my life, my holy Joy? Or what says any man when he speaks of Thee? To Thee I entrust whatsoever I have received from Thee, and so shall I lose nothing.

ST. AUGUSTINE, 354–430

If Shakespeare should come into the room, we should all rise up to meet him; but if that Person were to come into it, we should all fall down and try to kiss the hem of His garment.

WILLIAM HAZLITT, 1778–1830

INCARNATION

He became what we are that He might make us what He is.

ST. ATHANASIUS, 295–373

I see clearly that God reserved for Himself those who serve in secret. For He said to Elias: I love the unknown adorers in the world.

BLAISE PASCAL, 1623–1662

ABOVE ALL GLORY
AND HONOR

Grant me, O most sweet and loving Jesus, to rest in Thee above every creature, above all health and beauty, above all glory and honor, above all power and dignity, above all knowledge and subtlety, above all richness and arts, above all joy and gladness, above all fame and praise, above all mirth and exuberation that the mind can receive or feel.

Because Thou, O Lord my God, art above all things the best, Thou alone art most noble and glorious above all things, in whom all things together perfectly are, and ever have been, and shall be.

And therefore, it is too small and unsatisfying, whatsoever Thou bestowest on me besides Thyself. For surely my heart cannot truly rest, unless it rest in Thee.

THOMAS A KEMPIS, 1379–1471

From FATHER MALACHY'S
MIRACLE

Now when Father Malachy pronounced the Sacred Name he did not, like many priests, articulate It as though It were "Ramsey MacDonald"; but he spoke It slowly and reverently so that the syllables seemed to be printed before the eyes in scarlet and gold, as indeed they are in illuminated mediaeval missals. And Canon Geoghegan and the Reverend Humphrey Hamilton, hearing him, knew, each in his own way, that here was a man to whom the practise of religion was as important as the theory.

BRUCE MARSHALL

LIFE OF LIFE

Religion's all or nothing; it's no mere
  smile
O' contentment, sigh of aspiration,
  sir—
No quality o' the finelier-tempered clay
Like its whiteness or its lightness;
  rather, stuff
O' the very stuff, life of life, and self
  of self.

ROBERT BROWNING, 1812–1889
From MR. SLUDGE, "THE MEDIUM"

Some people want to see God with their eyes as they see a cow, and to love Him as they love their cow. They love their cow for the milk and cheese and profit it makes them.

This is how it is with people who love God for the sake of outward wealth or inward comfort. They do not rightly love God when they love Him for their own advantage.

Indeed, I tell you the truth. Any object you have in your mind, however good, will be a barrier between you and the inmost truth.

MEISTER ECKHART, 1260–1328

IN SUN OR SHADOW

Whenever the sun shines brightly
I arise and say,
"Surely it is the shining of His face."
And when a shadow falls
across the window of my room
where I am working at my appointed
  task,
I lift my head to watch the door,
and ask if He is come.

SECOND-CENTURY MYSTIC

EXPETANS EXPECTAVI

From morn to midnight, all day
   through,
I laugh and play as others do,
I sin and chatter, just the same
As others with a different name.

And all year long upon the stage,
I dance and tumble and do rage
So vehemently, I scarcely see
The inner and eternal me.

I have a temple I do not
Visit, a heart I have forgot,
A self that I have never met,
A secret shrine—and yet, and yet

This sanctuary of my soul
Unwitting I keep white and whole,
Unlatched and lit, if Thou should'st
   care
To enter or to tarry there.

With parted lips and outstretched
   hands
And listening ears Thy servant stands,
Call Thou early, call Thou late,
To Thy great service dedicate.

               CHARLES HAMILTON SORLEY

OUR COMMON SPIRIT

I am sure there is a common Spirit that
plays within us, yet makes no part of
us and that is the Spirit of God, the
fire and scintillation of that noble and
mighty Essence, which is the life and
radical heat of Spirits, and those essences which know not the virtue of the
Sun; a fire quite contrary to the fire of
Hell.

This is that gentle heat that brooded
on the waters; and in six days hatches
the World. This is that irradiation that
dispels the mists of Hell, the clouds

of horror, fear, sorrow, despair; and
preserves the region of the mind in
serenity.

Whoever feels not the warm gale
and gentle ventilation of this Spirit,
though I feel his pulse, I cannot say
he lives; nor heat under the Tropic;
nor any light, though he dwell in the
body of the Sun.

        SIR THOMAS BROWNE, 1605–1682

PRAYER FOR
DIVINE INSTRUCTION

Teach us, O God, that silent language
which says all things.

Teach our souls to remain silent in
Thy presence, that we may adore Thee
in the depth of our being and await all
things from Thee, whilst asking of
Thee nothing but the accomplishment
of Thy will.

Teach us to remain quiet under Thy
action and produce in our souls that
deep and simple prayer which says
nothing and expresses everything,
which specifies nothing and expresses
everything.

      JEAN NICOLAS GROU, 1731–1803

THE HANDS OF GOD

It is not easy to fall out of the hands
of the living God for they are so large
and they cradle so much of a man. It
is a long time before a man can get
himself away; even through the greatest blasphemies the hand of the living
God still continues to cradle him.

       D. H. LAWRENCE, 1885–1930

THE LIGHT WITHIN

Deep within us all is an amazing inner sanctuary of the soul, a holy place, a Divine Center, a speaking Voice, to which we can continuously return. Eternity is at our hearts, pressing upon our time-torn lives, warming us with intimations of an astounding destiny, calling us home unto Itself.

It is a Light Within which illumines the face of God and casts new shadows and new glories upon the face of men. It is a seed stirring, if we do not choke it. It is the Shekinah of the soul, the Presence in the midst.

The basic response of the soul to the Light is internal adoration and joy, thanksgiving and worship, self-surrender and listening.

The secret places of the heart cease to be our noisy workshop. They become a holy sanctuary of adoration, if our minds are stayed on Him.

Begin now, as you read these words, as you sit in your chair, to offer your whole selves, utterly and in joyful abandon, in quiet glad surrender to Him who is within. In secret ejaculations of praise, turn in humble wonder to the Light.

Formulate them spontaneously: "Thine only, Thine only!" Or seize upon a fragment of the Psalms: "So panteth my soul after Thee, O God." Repeat them inwardly, over and over again.

All we can say is, prayer is taking place, and I am given to be in the orbit. In holy hush we bow in Eternity, and know the Divine Concern tenderly enwrapping us and all things within His persuading love.

THOMAS KELLY, 1893–1941

ADORATION

If I but had a little coat,
A coat to fit a no-year-old,
I'd button it close about His throat
To cover Him from the cold,
   The cold,
To cover Him from the cold.

If my heart were a shining coin,
A silver coin or a coin of gold,
Out of my side I'd it purloin
And give it to Him to hold,
   To hold,
And give it to Him to hold.

If my heart were a house also,
A house also with room to spare,
I never would suffer my Lord to go
Homeless, but house Him there,
   O there,
Homeless, but house Him there.

BYRON HERBERT REECE

BEFORE THE EUCHARIST

I proclaim Thee great and wonderful,
Not because Thou hast made the sun to
   avail by day
And the stars to avail by night;
Not because Thou hast made the earth
   and all that is therein,
The fruits of the field, the flowers, the
   cinemas, the locomotives;
Not because Thou hast made the sea
   and all that is therein,
The animals and plants, submarines
   and sirens;
I proclaim Thee great and eternally
   wonderful
Because Thou makest Thyself tiny in
   the Eucharist,
So tiny that I, weak and wretched, am
   able to contain Thee.

MURILLO MENDES
Tr. DUDLEY POORE

PRAYER OF
DIVINE DISCOVERY

Eternal Spirit, most awful, most gentle, most patient, most wise; most loving, least possessive; more pervasive than the air, less noticed, more needed. Let us, perceiving Thy gentleness, conceive of that awfulness; realizing Thy patience, estimate Thy power; experiencing Thy unpossessiveness, come to understand the nature of Thy love.

GERALD HEARD

❧

From THE MEETING

And so I find it well to come
For deeper rest to this still room,
For here the habit of the soul
Feels less the outer world's control;
The strength of mutual purpose pleads
More earnestly our common needs;
And from the silence multiplied
By these still forms on either side,
The world that time and sense have
known
Falls off and leaves us, God, alone.

JOHN GREENLEAF WHITTIER,
1807–1892

❧

DYNAMIC ACTIVITY

In Christianity God is not a static *thing* —not even a person—but a dynamic, pulsating activity, a life, almost a kind of drama. Almost, if you won't think me irreverent, a kind of dance. The union between the Father and the Son is such a live concrete thing that this union itself is also a Person.

C. S. LEWIS, 1898–1963

A PERPETUAL SENSE

My God, give me a perpetual sense of Your Presence, of Your Presence in me and all around me, and at the same time that living fear one feels in the presence of him one loves passionately, and which makes one, in the presence of one's Beloved, keep one's eyes upon him with great desire and firm purpose to do all that may please him and be for his good, and greatly fear to do or think anything that may displease or harm him. In You, by You, and for You. Amen.

CHARLES DE FOUCAULD

❧

CLAD IN THE GOODNESS
OF GOD

As the body is clad in the cloth,
and the flesh in the skin,
and the bones in the flesh,
and the heart in the whole,
so are we, soul and body,
clad in the goodness of God,
and enclosed.
Yea, and more homely,
for all these may waste and wear away,
but the goodness of God is ever whole,
and more near to us.
For our kindly will is to have God,
and the good will of God is to have us;
and we may never cease from willing
nor for longing,
till we have Him in fullness of joy.

JULIANA OF NORWICH, 1343–1413

❧

God can no more do without us than we can do without Him.

MEISTER ECKHART, 1260–1328

ANIMALS

A mouse is miracle enough to
stagger sextillions of infidels.

WALT WHITMAN, 1819–1892

Why so impatient, my heart?
He who watches over birds, beasts and
    insects,
He who cared for you while you were
    yet unborn,
Think you He will not care for you now
    that you have come forth?
O my heart, how could you turn away
    from the smile of your Lord,
And wander so far from Him?

KABIR, FIFTEENTH CENTURY
Tr. RABINDRANATH TAGORE

THE HOLY CARELESSNESS
The bliss of the animals lies in this,
that, on their lower level, they shadow
the bliss of those—few at any moment
on the earth—who do not "look before
and after, and pine for what is not"
but live in the holy carelessness of the
eternal now.

GEORGE MACDONALD, 1824–1905

EPITAPH FOR HIS DOG
Near this spot are deposited the remains of one who possessed beauty
without vanity, strength without inso-
lence, courage without ferocity, and
all the virtues of man without his vices.
This praise, which would be unmean-
ing flattery if inscribed over human
ashes, is but a just tribute to the memory of Boatswain, a dog.

GEORGE GORDON BYRON, 1788–1824

ALL CREATURES OF OUR GOD
Lord, may I love all Thy creation, the
whole and every grain of sand in it.
May I love every leaf, every ray of Thy
light.

May I love the animals. Thou hast
given them the rudiments of thought
and joy untroubled. Let me not trouble
it, let me not harass them, let me not
deprive them of their happiness, let me
not work against Thine intent.

For I acknowledge unto Thee that
all is like an ocean, all is flowing and
blending, and that to withhold any
measure of love from anything in Thy
universe is to withhold that same measure from Thee.

FEODOR DOSTOEVSKI, 1821–1881

REMEMBRANCE

Remember the spider weaving a square,
And that you did it everywhere.
Remember the cat tormenting a bird,
And that you did it in thought and in
    word.
Remember the fool mistreating the
    good,
And that you did it whenever you
    could.
Remember the devil and treachery,
And that you did it when you were he.
And then remember not to forget,
That you did it, and do it yet.

JAMES STEPHENS, 1882–1950

GRAND EMBODIMENT
OF ADORATION

Standing at the masthead of my ship
during a sunrise that crimsoned sky
and sea, I once saw a large herd of
whales in the east, all heading towards
the sun, and for a moment vibrating in
concert with peaked flukes.

As it seemed to me at the time, such
a grand embodiment of adoration of
the gods was never beheld, even in
Persia, the home of the fire worship-
pers.

As Ptolemy Philopator testified of
the African elephant, I then testified of
the whale, pronouncing him the most
devout of all beings. For according to
King John, the military elephants of
antiquity often hailed the morning
with their trunks uplifted in the pro-
foundest silence.

HERMAN MELVILLE, 1819–1891
From MOBY DICK

INNATE

The hen lifts up her head toward
heaven when swallowing her grain.

AFRICAN PROVERB

The camel always kneels when drinking from the streams of Allah, and
kneels also to receive his burden for
the day.

ARABIAN PROVERB

Lambs have the grace to kneel when
nursing.

CHINESE PROVERB

Even Buddha was once a carthorse, and
carried the loads of others.

INDIAN PROVERB

The saddles are changed, the donkeys
remain the same.

TURKISH PROVERB

If God wishes to rejoice the heart of
a poor man, He makes him lose his
donkey and then find it.

ARMENIAN PROVERB

PROVIDENCE

God is a tailor who makes for the deer
a coat that will last for a thousand
years.

He is a shoemaker who provides
boots for the deer that the deer will not
outlive.

God is the best cook, because the
heat of the sun supplies all the heat
there is for cooking.

God is a butler who sets forth a feast
for the sparrows and spends on them
annually more than the total revenue
of the King of France.

MARTIN LUTHER, 1483–1546

THE DIFFERENCE

Granted that man is only a more highly developed animal; that the ring-tailed monkey is a distant relative who has gradually developed acrobatic tendencies; and the humpbacked whale is a far-off connection who in early life took to the sea—granted that back of these lie the vegetables and is still subject to the same laws as plants, fishes, birds, and beasts.

Yet there is this difference between man and all other animals—he is the only animal whose desires increase as they are fed; the only animal who is never satisfied. The wants of every other living thing are uniform and fixed.

The ox of today aspires to no more than did the ox when man first yoked him. The sea gull of the English Channel, who poises himself above the swift steamer, wants no better food or lodging than the gulls who circled round as the keels of Caesar's galleys first grated on a British beach.

Of all that nature offers them, be it ever so abundant, all living things save man can take, and care for, only enough to supply wants which are definite and fixed.

HENRY GEORGE, 1839–1897

IN LINE OF DUTY

When Emily Dickinson thought of a line for a poem, "In the name of the bee and the butterfly and the breeze, Amen," she was not linking unrelated things. For people have noticed for centuries that before the first man dreamed of his first bridge over impassable precipices to a further shore, bees and butterflies had been doing it daily in their line of duty. And spiders, even more tangibly, of course.

Distances meant nothing. A breeze could carry them across, if only they could get caught up in an air current going their way. And curiously enough, for fertilization of fruits and flowers and grains, God has depended upon such inconsequential creatures—seemingly so frivolous, dancing their days away haphazardly. Yet actually like clockwork in keeping all their dates on time, with more than 100,000 species of plants which could never form seeds without bee, butterfly, or breeze.

THE BRUTE CREATION

You cannot go to Bethlehem "and see this thing which is come to pass," without going past the camels, the mules, the dogs, the oxen. The animals of the stable heard the first cry of our Lord.

Have you ever thought that Christ came, among other things, to alleviate the sufferings of the brute creation?

Not a camel in all the centuries, not a bird's nest, not a worn-out horse on the tow-path, not a herd freezing in the poorly built cow-pen, not a freight car in summer-time bringing the cattle to market without water through a thousand miles of agony, but has an interest in the fact that Christ was born in a stable, surrounded by animals.

THOMAS DE WITT TALMAGE,
1832–1902

None preaches better
than the ant,
and she says nothing.

BENJAMIN FRANKLIN, 1706–1790

From AURORA LEIGH

And truly, I reiterate, nothing's small!
No lily-muffled hum of a summer-bee,
But finds some coupling with the spin-
    ning stars;
No pebble at your foot, but proves a
    sphere;
No chaffinch, but implies the cherubim.

ELIZABETH BARRETT BROWNING,
1806–1861

❧

CONSIDER THE BEE

Consider this bee: five eyes—three simple ones on top of the head, two com-
pound ones with thousands of lenses;
five thousand nostrils—enough to smell
an apple tree half a mile away; two sets
of wings—which can be hooked together in flight, so that they flap as one:
16,000 times each moment, twenty
miles an hour, seven miles, nonstop.

No matter how zigzag the dizzy
dance, always that beeline straight
home to the all-important hive and the
next big job to be done there. Acting
as street cleaners, water carriers, nurses,
sentries, masons, engineers, air condi-
tioners, electric fans—often fanning
twelve hours at a stretch, indoors; on
top of twelve hours of gathering honey,
outdoors. All that dipping into dandelions and blossoms in obedience to
God's holy ordinance that "while the
earth remaineth, seedtime and harvest
shall not cease." This is a beautiful
business, expertly done.

A mere mortal feels almost a heart-
break, however, over the discovery that
to make one pound of honey one bee
would need to travel 50,000 miles,
more than twice the distance round the
globe. And, actually, a single teaspoon-
ful of honey in six weeks is a bee's entire life quota. But his buzz is not a
grumble, merely his motor working
overtime.

And all this labor without being
spoken to twice—no reminders, no
reproaches from a foreman. For mystical reasons the liturgical Church has always prescribed that candles used at
Holy Communion be made from beeswax; and without any hesitation even
the most nonliturgical is touched by
this lovely tribute paid to such a pure
and faithful "worker in the vineyard,"
filling out Emerson's statement that
"the air is full of sounds, the sky is full
of tokens; the ground is all memoranda
and signatures, and every object covered over with hints that speak to the
intelligent."

❧

From SONG OF MYSELF

I think I could turn and live with ani-
    mals, they are so placid and self-
    contain'd,
I stand and look at them long and long.
They do not sweat and whine about
    their condition,
They do not lie awake in the dark and
    weep for their sins,
They do not make me sick discussing
    their duty to God,
Not one is dissatisfied, not one is de-
    mented with the mania of owning
    things,
Not one kneels to another, nor to his
    kind that lived thousands of years
    ago,
Not one is respectable or unhappy over
    the whole earth.

WALT WHITMAN, 1819–1892

HERITAGE

I remain, and seem likely to remain, a somewhat altered fish, a slightly remodeled ape.

GEORGE R. STEWART

NEW TOGETHERNESS

I beg to choose by what road I shall go
To Paradise, where the clear stars shine by day.
I'll take my walking-stick and go my way,
And to my friends the donkeys I shall say;
"I am Francis Jammes, and I'm going to Paradise,
For there is no hell in the land of the living God."
And I'll say to them: "Come, sweet friends of the blue skies,
Poor creatures who with a flip of the ears or a nod
Of the head shake off the buffets, the bees, the flies . . ."
Let me come with these donkeys, Lord, into Your land,
These beasts who bow their heads so gently, and stand
With their small feet joined together in a fashion
Utterly gentle, asking Your compassion.
I shall arrive, followed by their thousands of ears,
Followed by those with baskets at their flanks,
By those who lug the carts of montebanks,
Or loads of feather-dusters and kitchenwares,
By those with humps of battered watercans,
By bottle-shaped she-asses who halt and stumble,
By those tricked out in little pantaloons
To cover their wet, blue galls where flies assemble
In whirling swarms, making a drunken hum.
Dear Lord, let it be with these donkeys that I come,
And let it be that angels head us in peace
To leafy streams where cherries tremble in air,
In that haven of souls let it be that leaning above
Your divine waters, I shall resemble these donkeys,
Whose humble and sweet poverty will appear
Clear in the clearness of Your eternal love.

FRANCIS JAMMES
Tr. RICHARD WILBUR

FOR ALL CREATURES

As far back as I can remember I was saddened by the amount of misery I saw in the world around me. One thing that especially saddened me was that unfortunate animals had to suffer so much pain and misery. It was quite incomprehensible to me why in my evening prayers I should pray for human beings only. So when my mother had prayed with me and kissed me good night, I used to add silently a prayer that I had composed myself for all living creatures:

"O heavenly Father, protect and bless all things that have breath, guard them from all evil, and let them sleep in peace."

ALBERT SCHWEITZER, 1875–1965

A CHRISTMAS PRAYER

Loving looks the large-eyed cow,
Loving stares the long-eared ass,
At Heaven's glory in the grass!
Child, with added human birth
Come to bring the child of earth
Glad repentance, tearful mirth,
And a seat beside the hearth
At the Father's knee—
Make us peaceful as Thy cow;
Make us patient as Thine ass;
Make us quiet as Thou art now;
Make us strong as Thou wilt be.
Make us always know and see
We are His, as well as Thou.

GEORGE MACDONALD, 1824–1905

From THE GARDENER

I often wonder where lie hidden the boundaries of recognition between man and beast whose heart knows no spoken language.

Through what primal paradise in a remote morning of creation ran the simple path by which their hearts visited each other?

Those marks of their constant tread have not been effaced though their kinship has been long forgotten.

Yet suddenly in some wordless music the dim memory wakes up and the beast gazes into the man's face with a tender trust, and the man looks into its eyes with amused affection.

It seems that the two friends meet masked, and vaguely know each other through the disguise.

RABINDRANATH TAGORE, 1861–1941

FROM A SERMON BY AN AFRICAN PREACHER

It has been told me once, and twice have I seen this with my own eyes, how the rhinoceros is accompanied by a little bird which ever gives a shrill cry of warning at the imminent approach of danger.

And this is wonderful! Since the rhinoceros is so curiously made in his head that he can only see what is straight in front of him, and so would otherwise be at the mercy of what approaches him from the side. Who else but God could let so small a creature guide so large a one?

Also I have seen it once, and also twice, how that a small bird rides upon the back of our water buffalo; but should he ever hop off, then this is a signal for alarm. Has not God put such a little signal inside each of us to warn us at all times when we do that which is wrong?

My children, have you not noticed how the herds of antelopes graze near one or two giraffes? And have you not asked your hearts why this should be so?

I am the one who can tell you truly. It is because the antelope may have better sight and hearing; but the giraffe, by ever turning his tall and delicate head on his long neck, has the better sight and wider range of view. So that when the wind is away from the antelopes, they watch the behavior of the giraffes, whether they be uneasy and apprehensive of danger. And when the wind is toward them, the giraffes rely on the antelopes. As God's other family, even so do ye, my children.

REJOICE IN THE LAMB

Rejoice in God, O ye Tongues,
   give glory to the Lord and the Lamb.
Nations, and languages, and every
   Creature in which is the breath of
   Life.
Let man and beast appear before Him
   and magnify His name together.
Let Nimrod, the mighty hunter, bind a
   leopard to the altar and consecrate
   his spear to the Lord.
Let Ishmail dedicate a Tyger, and give
   praise for the liberty in which the
   Lord has let him at large.
Let Balaam appear with an ass, and
   bless the Lord, His people, and His
   creatures for a reward eternal.
Let Daniel come forth with a lion, and
   praise God with all his might
   through faith in Jesus Christ.
Let Ithamar minister with a chamois,
   and bless the name of Him that
   cloatheth the naked.
Let Jakim with the Satyr bless God in
   the dance.
Let David bless with the Bear the beginning of victory to the Lord—to
   the Lord the perfection of excellence.
Hallelujah from the heart of God, and
   from the hand of the Artist inimitable, and from the echo of the
   heavenly harp in sweetness magnif-
   icabe and mighty, Hallelujah.
For I will consider my cat Geoffry.
   For he is the servant of the living
   God, duly and daily serving Him.
For at the first glance of the glory of
   God in the East he worships Him in
   his way.
For this is done by wreathing his body
   seven times round with elegant
   quickness.

For he knows that God is his Saviour.
For God has blessed him in the variety
   of his movements.
For there is nothing sweeter than his
   peace when at rest.
For I am possessed of a cat surpassing
   in beauty from whom I take occasion
   to bless Almighty God.

        CHRISTOPHER SMART, 1722–1771

THE SPIDER

With six small diamonds for his eyes
He walks upon the Summer skies,
Drawing from his silken blouse
The laceworks of his dwelling house.

He lays his staircase as he goes
Under his eight thoughtful toes
And grows with the concentric flower
Of his shadowless, thin bower.

His back legs are a pair of hands,
They can spindle out the strands
Of a thread that is so small
It stops the sunlight not at all.

He spins himself to threads of dew
Which will harden soon into
Lines that cut like slender knives
Across the insects' airy lives.

He makes no motion but is right,
He spreads out his appetite,
Into a network, twist by twist,
This little ancient scientist.

He does not know he is unkind,
He has a jewel for a mind
And logic deadly as a dry bone,
This small son of Euclid's own.

      ROBERT P. TRISTRAM COFFIN,
             1892–1955

ARTS

A poet, a painter, an architect, a musician—the man or woman who is not one of these is not a Christian.

WILLIAM BLAKE, 1757–1827

Raphael paints wisdom,
Handel sings it,
Phidias carves it,
Shakespeare writes it,
Christopher Wren builds it,
Luther preaches it,
Washington arms it,
Watts mechanizes it.

RALPH WALDO EMERSON, 1803–1882

FOR LOVE OF HIM

There is little or no doubt that the mind of Christ finds a more congenial environment in the studio where beauty is loved for its own sake and not because it pays, on the ship's bridge in a gale where duty is loved for its own sake and not because it pays, in the science laboratory where truth is loved for its own sake and not because it pays, than in the modern church where the preacher is busy with the sorry argument *ad hominem* in behalf of a Christianity commended to moral investors because it offers large material returns on the spiritual venture.

WILLARD L. SPERRY, 1882–1954

From FRA LIPPO LIPPI

For, don't you mark, we're made so
  that we love
First when we see them painted, things
  we have passed
Perhaps a hundred times nor cared to
  see;
And so they are better, painted—better
  to us,
Which is the same thing. Art was given
  for that;
God uses us to help each other so,
Lending our minds out.

ROBERT BROWNING, 1812–1889

PERPETUAL PARENTAGE

Religion has had a perpetual parentage. All the arts of common life owe their present status and vitality to some sojourn within the historic body of religion; there is little that we call culture which was not at some time a purely religious function.

WILLIAM ERNEST HOCKING,
1873–1966

All great art is the expression of man's delight in God's work, not his own.

JOHN RUSKIN, 1819–1900

❧

THE GREATEST ART

The Incarnation may be said to have for its object the drawing of men from misery to happiness.

Being the act of God, it is the greatest of all rhetorical acts and therefore the greatest of all works of art. And as from the fatherhood of God, all paternity is named in heaven and earth, so from His creative power all art is named.

In the Incarnation we do not only know a fact of history or a truth of religion, we behold a work of art, a thing made.

As a fact of history it is the most interesting and illuminating of all historical happenings. As a truth of religion it is of primary and fundamental importance. But it is as a work of art that it has saving power to persuade, power to heal, power to rescue, power to redeem.

ERIC GILL, 1882–1940

❧

To me it seems that when God conceived the world,
that was poetry;
He formed it,
and that was sculpture;
He varied and colored it,
and that was painting;
and then, crowning all,
He peopled it with living beings,
and that was the grand, divine,
eternal drama.

CHARLOTTE CUSHMAN, 1816–1876

SELF-MADE ARTIST

Every man is the sculptor and the painter of his own life.

ST. JOHN CHRYSOSTOM, 347–407

❧

FUSED IN THE SOUL OF MAN

I am the reality of things that seem:
The great transmuter, melting loss to gain,
Languor to love, and finding joy from pain;
I am the waking, who am called the dream;
I am the sun, all light reflects my gleam;
I am the altar fire within the fane;
I am the force of the refreshing rain;
I am the sea which flows to every stream.
I am the utmost height there is to climb;
I am the truth mirrored in fancy's glass;
I am stability, all else will pass;
I am eternity, encircling time;
Kill me, none may; conquer me, nothing can,—
I am God's soul, fused in the soul of man.

ELLA CROSBY HEATH

❧

APHORISM

Poetry is vocal painting, just as painting is silent poetry.

SIMONIDES OF CEOS, 556–468? B.C.

❧

MOTHER OF THE ARTS

Christianity has borne one after another of the arts—not only music and painting and sculpture and drama and architecture, but also dancing, legislation, science, philosophy, moral control; has given them birth and nurtured them through their critical infancy.

Then, as they attained maturity and sufficient strength to exist independently, religion has sent them forth to continue their development as secular enterprises—often not without the struggle and hard feeling so characteristic of adolescents' break from home.

Hospitals, schools, colleges, institutions for the unfortunate and the outcast, general philanthropy—all had their birth within the life of the Church.

HENRY PITNEY VAN DUSEN

APPROPRIATE LIBERATOR

Everything in creation has its appointed painter or poet, and remains in bondage like the princess in the fairy tale, till its appropriate liberator comes to set it free. The story of the Sleeping Beauty is more than a fairy tale; it is an allegory of the life of every human being who fights his way through life.

RALPH WALDO EMERSON, 1803–1882

From AURORA LEIGH

I stood up straight and worked
My veritable work. And as the soul
Which grows within a child, makes the
child grow,—

Or as the fiery sap, the touch from God,
Careering through a tree, dilates the bark,
And roughs with scale and knob, before it strikes
The summer foliage out in a green flame—
So life, in deepening with me, deepened all
The course I took, the work I did.

ELIZABETH BARRETT BROWNING,
1806–1861

MYSTERIOUS WITHHOLDING

A poet's pleasure is to withhold a little of his meaning, to intensify by mystification. He unzips the veil from beauty, but does not remove it. A poet utterly clear is a trifle glaring.

The subject is a fascinating one. I think poetry is the greatest of the arts.

It combines music and painting and story-telling and prophecy and the dance.

It is religious in tone, scientific in attitude.

A true poem contains the seed of wonder.

E. B. WHITE

GIFT OF ECSTASY

A disciplined ecstasy
is the finest gift
of God to man.
It is likewise
the best an artist
can give
to the work
of his hands.

WILLIAM ROTHENSTEIN, 1872–1945

THROUGH A BARN DOOR

Often, as I have walked along a country road, idly pleased with the world about me, I have passed an old barn, with great doors flung wide open, front and back, so that one could look through them to the meadows behind.

It is the same country I have been passing—fields, bushes, fence-lines, a bit of hill and sky—but the great doorways framing it in timbers and shadow create thereby a certain enhancement of its values, so that invariably, looking through, one gets one's impression with something added—a heightening of perception that is strangely arresting.

What is it that the big barn doors do? They limit, of course, they cut a little piece out from the wholeness of things, they say to us, "Never mind the rest, take just this, look at it in just this way—and now see how beautiful it is!"

They play the artist to us for a moment, forcing upon us our point of view, selecting our subject, adjusting the lights, and—perhaps greatest service of all—suggesting to us, or rather, imposing upon us, that sense of distance that is so necessary a part of the aesthetic experience.

THE ATLANTIC MONTHLY

AMBITION ACCOMPLISHED

I want to paint humanity and again humanity. I love nothing better than this series of bipeds, from the smallest baby in long clothes to Socrates.

VINCENT VAN GOGH, 1853–1890

From CLEON

I have not chanted verse like Homer,
  no—
Nor swept string like Terpander, no—
  nor carved
And painted men like Phidias and his
  friend:
I am not great as they are, point by
  point.
But I have entered into sympathy
With these four, running these into
  one soul,
Who, separate, ignored each other's
  art.
Say, is it nothing that I knew them all?
    ROBERT BROWNING, 1812–1889

Poetry is the grouping of words, phrases, and ideas that have always loved each other but have never gotten into that combination before.

AUTHOR UNKNOWN

ARTISTIC HIBERNATION

The poet is he that hath fat enough, like bears and marmots, to suck his claws all winter. He hibernates in this world, and feeds on his own marrow.

Alas, the poet too is, in one sense, a sort of dormouse gone into winter quarters of deep and serene thoughts, insensible to surrounding circumstances. His words are the relation of his oldest and finest memory, a wisdom drawn from the remotest experience.

Other men live a starved existence, meanwhile, like hawks that would fain keep on the wing and trust to pick up a sparrow now and then.

HENRY DAVID THOREAU, 1817–1862

THE FIRST ARTISTS

When for the first time a human being was able to separate himself from an object—animal or idea—and so to re-invent it, why had he an impulse to paint it on the wall of a cave or make a song of it?

Why was he not content simply to embrace it with his thoughts?

It was perhaps because he was a failure in other ways: not a clever hunter, he impresses himself on the men he despised with their invariable luck as lords, by drawing the horses they tamed and the bears they killed; or he was blind and sang to prove how brightly he saw.

With the achievement of happiness for all, there may be no artists. All will be content simply to live, with grace, energy, reason, and when they are old, sit still.

STORM JAMESON

AMAZEMENT EXPLORED

Poetry is the language in which man explores his own amazement.

It is the language in which he says heaven and earth in one word.

It is the language in which he speaks of himself and his predicament as though for the first time.

It has the virtue of being able to say twice as much as prose in half the time, and the drawback, if you do not give it your full attention, of seeming to say half as much in twice the time.

CHRISTOPHER FRY

JOURNEY TO REASONABLE MEN

A good poem goes about the world offering itself to reasonable men, who read it with joy and carry it to their reasonable neighbors.

RALPH WALDO EMERSON, 1803–1882

MADE FROM THE HAND OF GOD

There is no adventure in the world more thrilling than that of coming un-expectedly upon some vision of splen-dor or beauty when one least expects it.

In the days before I knew Rodin's sculpture very well I came suddenly upon one of his masterpieces standing at the end of a corridor in the Metro-politan Art Museum. As one ap-proached it there seemed to be merely a great block of white unhewn marble, but as one came nearer there emerged from the rough marble a great, beauti-ful, shapely hand. The hand seemed to grow right out of the marble, a device which Rodin was fond of employing.

Drawing closer, one saw that this hand held certain shapes—the half-formed bodies of a man and woman, curled up in the great hand. Finally one was near enough to read the in-scription carved beneath: "The Hand of God."

There they were—man and woman carved from the same piece of marble as the Hand of God itself!

Suddenly there flashed upon my mind a sentence from the Old Testa-ment: "Look to the rock whence ye are hewn."

WILLIAM L. STIDGER, 1885–1949

BIRDS

*Oh, the little birds sang east, and the
little birds sang west,
And I smiled to think God's greatness
flowed around our incomplete-
ness—
Round our restlessness, His rest.*

ELIZABETH BARRETT BROWNING,
1806–1861

God is a huge mountain of grain, from which we take our thoughts, little separate grains such as sparrows pick up in their feeding.

ST. FRANCIS OF ASSISI, 1182–1226

MATINS

It is the way of chimney swifts, one hour before the dawn, to arise in utter darkness, ascending in faith to seek a light they cannot see; up and up they spiral, attaining unthinkable altitudes. Aviators find them at six thousand feet, flying at one hundred miles an hour in realms above our dust. For they have business with the dawn. They take one bath of glory and, if you like to think of it that way, dance once before the Lord. Skimming back on the tilted planes of their wings, one after the other, they hover over the chimney-stacks, and then lifting wings that seem to touch as those of angels are said to do, each bird drops quietly down into the dingy darkness of its home.

DONALD CULROSS PEATTIE

If I were a nightingale I would pour out my life in song to God, but being just an old man, what can I do but praise and bless Him as I can?

EPICTETUS, A.D. C. 60

OVERTONES

I heard a bird at break of day
  Sing from the autumn trees
A song so mystical and calm,
  So full of certainties,
No man, I think, could listen long
  Except upon his knees;
Yet, this was but a simple bird,
  Alone, among the trees.

WILLIAM ALEXANDER PERCY,
1885–1942

FROM A SIXTEENTH-CENTURY YORKSHIRE PRAYERBOOK

The storke shee rose on Christmasse
  Eve
And sayd unto her broode,
"I now must fly to Bethlehem
To viewe the Sonne of God."
Shee gave to each his dole of meat,
Shee stowed them fairlye in,
And far shee flewe, and fast shee flewe,
And came to Bethlehem.
"Now where is Hee of David's line?"
Shee asked in house and halle.
"Hee is not here," they spake hardlye,
"But in the maungier stalle."
Shee found Hym in the maungier stalle
With that most Holy Mayd,
The gentyl storke shee wept to see
The Lord so rudlye layd.
Then from her pauntyng breast shee
  plucked
The feathers soft and warme,
She strawed them in the maungier bed
To keep the Lord from harme.
"Nowe blessed be the gentyle storke
Forevermore," quothe Hee,
"In that shee sawe my sadde estate
And showed such pitie.
Full welcome shall shee be
Full welcome shall shee be
In hamlet and in halle
And hight henceforth the blessed byrd,
And friend of babies alle."

DISTINCTION

I once had a sparrow alight upon my
shoulder for a moment while I was
hoeing in a village garden, and I felt
that I was more distinguished than I
should have been by any epaulet I
could have worn.

    HENRY DAVID THOREAU, 1817–1862

OVERHEARD IN AN ORCHARD

Said the Robin to the Sparrow:
  "I should really like to know
Why these anxious human beings
  Rush about and worry so."

Said the Sparrow to the Robin:
  "Friend, I think that it must be
That they have no heavenly Father
  Such as cares for you and me."

    ELIZABETH CHENEY

may my heart always be open to little
birds who are the secret of living
whatever they sing is better than to
  know
and if men should not hear them men
  are old

may my mind stroll about hungry
and fearless and thirsty and supple
and even if it's sunday may i be wrong
for whenever men are right they are
  not young

and may myself do nothing usefully
and love yourself so more than truly
there's never been quite such a fool
  who could fail
pulling all the sky over him with one
  smile.

    E. E. CUMMINGS, 1894–1962

BEAUTY

The most beautiful things
in the world
are the most useless;
peacocks and lilies,
for example.

    JOHN RUSKIN, 1819–1900

ST. FRANCIS' SERMON
TO THE BIRDS

St. Francis lifted up his eyes and beheld some trees by the wayside whereon were an infinite multitude of birds. He marvelled and said to his companions, "Tarry here for me and I will go and preach to my little sisters the birds."

He entered into the field and began to preach to the birds that were on the ground. Anon those that were on the trees flew down to hear him, and all stood still the while St. Francis made an end of his sermon. Even then they departed not until he had given them his blessing.

The substance of the sermon St. Francis preached was this: "My little sisters the birds, much are ye beholden to God your Creator, and always and in every place ye ought to praise Him for He hath given you a double and a triple vesture.

"He hath given you freedom to go into every place, and also did preserve the seed of you in the ark of Noah, in order that your kind might not perish from the earth.

"Again, ye are beholden to Him for the element of air which He hath appointed for you.

"Moreover, ye sow not, neither do you reap, and God feedeth you and giveth you the rivers and fountains for your drink.

"He giveth you the mountains and the valleys for your refuge, and the tall trees wherein to build your nest. Forasmuch as ye can neither spin nor sew, God clotheth you, you and your children.

"Wherefore your Creator loveth you much, since He hath dealt so boun-

teously with you. Therefore beware, little sisters mine, of the sin of ingratitude, but ever strive to praise God."

While St. Francis was uttering these words, all those birds began to open their beaks, and stretch their necks, and spread their wings, and reverently to bow their heads to the ground, showing by their gestures and songs that the holy father's words gave them greatest joy.

St. Francis was glad and rejoiced with them, and marveled much at so great a multitude of birds and at their manifold loveliness, and at their attention and familiarity; for which things he devoutly praised the Creator in them.

Finally, his sermon ended, St. Francis made the sign of the holy cross over them and gave them leave to depart. All those birds soared up into the air in one flock with wondrous songs, dividing themselves, singing, among the four quarters of the globe, so preaching Christ's cross, renewed by St. Francis and his friars to be borne throughout the whole world.

The same friars, possessing nothing of their own in this world, after the manner of birds, committed their lives wholly to the providence of God.

From HOME THOUGHTS
FROM ABROAD

That's the wise thrush; he sings each
    song twice over,
Lest you should think he never could
    recapture
The first fine careless rapture!
ROBERT BROWNING, 1812–1889

QUERY

People of Orphalese,
you can
muffle the drum,
and you can
loosen the strings
of the lyre,
but who shall
command the skylark
not to sing?

KAHLIL GIBRAN, 1883–1931

YOUR FATHER KNOWS

Of eight hundred American varieties
of birds, one hundred and twenty-five
varieties migrate.

Their inborn urge to make this long
uncomfortable trip, their awaiting
some almost mystical signal to start, is
one of Emerson's "hints" that all life
proceeds on God's spiritual basis.

Why should all the shy birds fly by
night? Warblers, sparrows, vireos,
juncos, finches, thrushes, wrens, hum-
ming-birds? To be safer from capture,
of course. But—in Don Quixote's
happy phrase: "The little birds of the
field have God for their Caterer"—
their uncomfortable night flight ends
on a branch, for they are berry eaters
and can nibble at their leisure.

The bold and strong-winged birds
are insect eaters and fly by day. Orioles,
bluebirds, robins, grackles, swallows,
swifts, larks, crows, bobolinks.

"Your heavenly Father knows." Just
as Jesus knew, the day He told the
parable of the sower, where some seed
fell by the wayside, "but the birds were
fed"! The Father, who knows when a
sparrow falls, knows when a seed falls
and a bird spots it.

INCLINED TOWARD LOVE

With partridges, it often occurs that
some steal the eggs of others, in order
to brood, and it is a strange but nevertheless well-attested fact that when the
chick hatched and nourished under the
wing of the thievish partridge first
hears the cry of its true mother, it
forthwith quits its thievish partridge,
and hurries to meet and follow its
own parent, drawn by its correspondence with her, which had remained hidden and as though sleeping
in the depth of its nature, until the encounter of each with each.

Thus it is with our heart, for although hatched, nourished, and
brought up among the temporal, low,
and transitory, yet at the first look it
casts toward God, at the first consciousness inspired by Him, the natural inborn inclination to love Him, slumber-
ing and imperceptible till now, awakes
in an instant unawares, as a spark
among ashes, and affecting the will,
gives it an impulse of the supreme love
due to the Sovereign and First Principle
of all things.

ST. FRANCIS DE SALES, 1567–1622

From TO A SKY-LARK

Up with me! up with me into the
    clouds!
  For thy song, Lark, is strong;
Up with me, up with me into the
    clouds!
  Singing, singing,
With clouds and sky about thee ring-
    ing,
  Lift me, guide me till I find
That spot which seems so to thy mind!

WILLIAM WORDSWORTH, 1770–1850

MOTHER LOVE

The eagle builds a hard and hostile
  nest
To house her fledglings, lining it with
  stones
And sticks and thorns. Her little, stir-
  ring ones
Do not know cradled comfort, downy
  rest—
But all about, the breath of heaven
  sings;
The lifting mountains beckon to the
  heights;
The sun allures them, and the sky in-
  vites,
And soon the feathered eaglets find
  their wings!
She knows the way that eagle wings
  must go,
That only from untender nurturing
In rugged nests do strong young eagles
  spring—
She will not let them rest content below
When it is time for winged ones to
  rise,
No mother-softness robs them of their
  skies!
　　ROSELLE MERCIER MONTGOMERY,
　　　　　　　　　　1874–1933

From TRICO'S SONG

What bird so sings, yet so does wail?
O, 'tis the ravish'd nightingale.
Jug, jug, jug, jug, tereu! she cries,
And still her woes at midnight rise,
Brave prick-song! Who is't now we
  hear?
None but the lark so shrill and clear;
How at heaven's gates she claps her
  wings,
The morn not waking till she sings.

Hark, hark, with what a pretty throat
Poor robin redbreast tunes his note!
Hark how the jolly cuckoos sing
Cuckoo! to welcome in the spring!
Cuckoo! to welcome in the spring!
　　JOHN LYLY, 1554?–1606

From THE HUMMINGBIRD

And all it lends to the sky is this—
A sunbeam giving the air a kiss.
　　　　　　　　HARRY KEMP

A NATURAL COLORATURA

Nightingales pour out a ceaseless gush
of song for fifteen days and nights on
end when the buds of the leaves are
swelling—a bird not in the lowest rank
remarkable.

In the first place there is so loud a
voice and so persistent a supply of
breath in such a tiny little body.

Then there is the consummate
knowledge of music in a single bird.
The sound is given out with modula-
tions, and now is drawn out into a
long note with one continuous breath,
now varied by managing the breath,
now made staccato by checking it, or
linked together by prolonging it, or
carried on by holding it back.

Or it is suddenly lowered, and at
times sinks into a mere murmur, loud,
low, bass, treble, with trills; with long
notes, modulated when this seems good
—soprano, mezzo, baritone; and
briefly all the devices in that tiny throat
which human science knows with all
the elaborate mechanism of the flute.
　　　　　PLINY, A.D. 62?–C. 113

BOOKS

A book is a garden, an orchard, a storehouse, a party, a company by the way, a counsellor, a multitude of counsellors.

HENRY WARD BEECHER, 1813–1887

GOOD COMPANY

Consider what you have in the smallest chosen library.

A company of the wisest and wittiest men that could be picked out of all civilized countries in a thousand years have set in the best order the results of their learning and wisdom.

The men themselves were hid and inaccessible, solitary, impatient of interruption, fenced by etiquette; but the thought which they did not uncover to their bosom friend is here written out in transparent words to us, the strangers of another age.

RALPH WALDO EMERSON, 1803–1882

For hym was levere have at his beddes
   heed
Twenty bookes, clad in blak or redd,
Of Aristotle and his philosophie,
Than robes riche, or fithele, or gay
   sautrie,
But al be that he was a philosophre,
Yet hadde he but litel gold in cofre.

GEOFFREY CHAUCER, 1340?–1400

WITH BOTH HANDS!

I only wish that I could write with both hands, so as not to forget one thing while I am saying another.

ST. TERESA, 1515–1582

From DON JUAN

But words are things, and a small
   drop of ink,
   Falling like dew, upon a thought,
    produces
That which makes thousands, per-
   haps millions, think;
   'Tis strange, the shortest letter which
    man uses
Instead of speech, may form a last-
   ing link
   Of ages; to what straits old Time re-
    duces
Frail man, when paper—even a rag
   like this,
Survives himself, his tomb, and all
   that's his!

GEORGE GORDON BYRON, 1788–1824

PUBLIC LIBRARY

It was from my own early experience that I decided there was no use to which money could be applied so productive of good to boys and girls who have good within them, and ability and ambition to develop it, as the founding of a public library.

ANDREW CARNEGIE, 1835–1919

From FOR AN AUTOGRAPH

Life is a sheet of paper white
Whereon each one of us may write
His word or two, and then comes night.

Greatly begin! though thou have time
But for a line, be that sublime—
Not failure, but low aim, is crime.

JAMES RUSSELL LOWELL, 1819–1891

BOOK BROTHERS

Except a living man there is nothing more wonderful than a book!

A message to us from the dead, from human souls we never saw, who lived, perhaps, thousands of miles away.

And yet there, in those little sheets of paper, they speak to us, arouse us, terrify us, teach us, comfort us, open their hearts to us as brothers.

CHARLES KINGSLEY, 1819–1875

BOOKS WISELY USED

To use books rightly, is to go to them for help; to appeal to them when our own knowledge and power fail; to be led by them into wider sight and purer

conception than our own, and to receive from them the united sentence of the judges and councils of all time, against our solitary and unstable opinion.

JOHN RUSKIN, 1819–1900

ENTHUSIASTIC STUDY

Education is the enthusiastic study of subjects for the love of them and without any ulterior motive.

CHARLES W. ELIOT, 1834–1926

AMERICANA

I

A lady may visit a public library unattended by a gentleman escort without the slightest breach of decorum.

This custom is in general use in Washington, and to some extent in other cities, which are day by day getting rid of the provincialism that suggested its impropriety.

In Boston, New York, Philadelphia, and Baltimore the principal libraries are arranged with an eye to the visits of ladies.

A concert or a theatre is another matter.

ETIQUETTE IN WASHINGTON (1850)

II

The perfect hostess will see to it that the works of male and female authors be properly separated on her bookshelves.

Their proximity, unless they happen to be married, should not be tolerated.

BOOK OF ETIQUETTE (1863)

READER ANALYSIS

There are only four kinds of readers.

The first is like the hour-glass; their reading being as the sand, it runs in and runs out, and leaves no vestige behind.

The second is like the sponge, which imbibes everything, and returns it in nearly the same state, only a little dirtier.

A third is like a jelly-bag, allowing all that is pure to pass away, retaining only the refuse and dregs.

And the fourth is like the slaves in the diamond mines, who, casting aside all that is worthless, retain only pure gems.

SAMUEL T. COLERIDGE, 1772–1834

Some books
are to be tasted,
others to be swallowed,
and some few
to be chewed and digested;
that is,
some books
are to be read
only in parts;
others to be read,
but not curiously;
and some few
to be read wholly,
and with diligence
and attention.

FRANCIS BACON, 1561–1626

COMPANIONSHIP

No man can be called friendless when he has God and the companionship of good books.

ELIZABETH BARRETT BROWNING,
1806–1861

TASTE FOR READING

If I were to pray for a taste which should stand me under every variety of circumstances, and be a source of happiness and cheerfulness to me through life, and a shield against its ills, however things might go amiss and the world frown upon me, it would be a taste for reading. Give a man this taste, and the means of gratifying it, and you can hardly fail of making him happy. You make him a denizen of all nations, a contemporary of all ages.

JOHN HERSCHEL, 1792–1871

RECEPTIVENESS

They are there, waiting and silent.

They neither urge nor call, nor press their claims.

Mutely they are ranged along the wall.

They seem to be asleep and yet from each one a name looks at you like an open eye.

If you direct your glances their way or move your hands over them, they do not call out to you in supplication, nor do they obtrude themselves upon you.

They make no demands.

They wait until you are receptive to them; only then do they open up.

First, there has to be quiet about us, peace within us; then we are ready for them.

STEFAN ZWEIG, 1881–1942

My book and heart
Shall never part.

NEW ENGLAND PRIMER

CHARACTER

*Every act leaves upon the world
a greater or lesser impress of God.*

ALFRED NORTH WHITEHEAD,
1861–1947

LINE DRAWING

While waiting for her mother to come downstairs, the small daughter of the house walked round and round the waiting visitor with such obvious curiosity that finally the lady asked: "What on earth are you looking for?"

"I'm looking for a word! For my mother says that if ever a woman had the word 'character' written all over her, it is you!"

GROWING EDGE

Conscience is the growing edge of God in the world.

WILLIAM ERNEST HOCKING,
1873–1966

From IMPROVISATIONS

Fame is what you have taken,
  Character's what you give:
When to this truth you waken,
  Then you begin to live!

BAYARD TAYLOR, 1825–1878

SELF-REVEALING

Men best show their character in trifles, when they are not on their guard. It is in insignificant matters and in the simplest habits that we often see the boundless egotism which pays no regard to the feelings of others and denies nothing to itself.

ARTHUR SCHOPENHAUER,
1788–1860

EVOLUTION

Whatever we come on that is great, beautiful, significant, cannot be recollected.

It must from the first be evolved from within us, be made and become a part of us developing into a new and better self, and so continually created in us, live and operate as part of us.

There is no past that we can bring back by longing for it. There is only an eternally now that builds and creates out of the past something new and better.

JOHANN WOLFGANG VON GOETHE,
1749–1832

THREE JOHNS

There are three Johns.

The real John, known only to his Maker.

John's ideal John, never the real one, and often very unlike him.

Thomas' ideal John, never the real John, nor John's John, but often very unlike either.

OLIVER WENDELL HOLMES,
1809–1894

❧

ABOVE OURSELVES

Enable us to rise
above ourselves to Thee,
and from Thee
to move below
ourselves in love,
and always to remain
in Thee, and in love.

MARTIN LUTHER, 1493–1546

❧

MENDING

Man is born broken.
He lives by mending.
The grace of God
 is the glue!

EUGENE O'NEILL, 1888–1953

❧

RECOMMENDATION

The best advertisement of a workshop is first-class work. The strongest attraction to Christianity is a well-made Christian character.

THEODORE L. CUYLER, 1822–1900

❧

ETHICAL MOVEMENT

Civilization can only revive when there shall come into being in a number of individuals a new tone of mind, independent of the prevalent one among the crowd, and in opposition to it—a tone of mind which will gradually win influence over the collective one, and in the end determine its character. Only an ethical movement can rescue us from barbarism, and the ethical comes into existence only in individuals.

ALBERT SCHWEITZER, 1875–1965

❧

SEVEN DEADLY VIRTUES

Respectability
Childishness
Mental timidity
Dullness
Sentimentality
Censoriousness
Depression of spirits

DOROTHY L. SAYERS, 1891–1957

❧

O the blindness and perversity of man!

All that he has he wants to be good, but himself he does not want to be good.

Who wants to have a farm that is not good?

Or a wife that is not good?

Or a house that is not good?

Or even a pair of shoes that are not good?

As though bad shoes could hurt you more than a bad life!

When your shoes are worn, you mend them or throw them away and get a new pair.

Your life you will not mend.

ST. AUGUSTINE, 354–430

From BISHOP APOLOGY
BLOUGRAM'S

When the fight begins within himself,
A man's worth something. God stoops
   o'er his head,
Satan looks up between his feet—both
   tug—
He's left, himself, i' the middle: the
   soul wakes
And grows.

     ROBERT BROWNING, 1812–1889

HIGHEST CHARACTER

The highest of characters is his who is
ready to pardon the moral errors of
mankind as though he were every day
guilty of some himself, and at the same
time as cautious of committing a fault
as though he never forgave one.

     PLINY THE YOUNGER, 62?–C. 113

From GITANJALI

I came out alone on my way to my tryst.
But who is this that follows me in the
silent dark?

I move aside to avoid his presence
but I escape him not.

He makes the dust rise from the
earth with his swagger; he adds his
loud voice to every word that I utter.

He is my own little self, my lord, he
knows no shame; but I am ashamed to
come to thy door in his company.

     RABINDRANATH TAGORE, 1861–1941

LATIN MOTTO

Esse quam videri.
To be rather than to seem to be.

I wish a greater knowledge, than to
   attain
The knowledge of myself; a greater
   gain
Than to augment myself; a greater
   treasure
Than to enjoy myself; a greater pleas-
   ure
Than to content myself. How slight
   and vain
Is all self-knowledge, pleasure, treas-
   ure, gain;
Unless my better knowledge could re-
   trieve
My Christ; unless my better gain could
   thrive
In Christ; unless my better wealth grow
   rich
In Christ; unless my better pleasure
   pitch
On Christ; or else my knowledge will
   proclaim
To my own heart, how ignorant I am:
Or else my gain, so ill improved, will
   shame
My trade, and show me how much de-
   clined I am;
Or else my treasure will but blur my
   name
With bankrupt, and divulge how poor
   I am;
Or else my pleasures, that so much
   inflame
My thoughts, will blab how full of
   sores I am.
Lord, keep me from myself. 'Tis best
   for me,
Never to own myself, if not in Thee.

     FRANCIS QUARLES, 1592–1644

Only forgiveness with reason can match
sin without excuse.

     EDWIN A. ROBINSON, 1869–1935

MATURITY IN CHARACTER

Faith without credulity,
Conviction without bigotry,
Charity without condescension,
Courage without pugnacity,
Self-respect without vanity,
Humility without obsequiousness,
Love of humanity without sentimental-
ity,
Meekness with power.

CHARLES EVANS HUGHES, 1862–1948

LESSON IN MATHEMATICS

Subtract from the great man
all that he owes to opportunity,
all that he owes to chance,
and all that he has gained
by the wisdom of his friends
and the follies of his enemies,
and the giant will often be seen
to be a pigmy.

CHARLES CALEB COLTON

Sin is enmity against God. It is as though we said:

"Lord, I know full well that this action displeases Thee, yet I shall do it nonetheless.

"I am aware that Thy eyes see it.

"I know perfectly well that Thou dost not want it, but I will rather follow my bent and fancy than follow Thy will."

Some people are full of the best resolutions, but never carry them out.

They resemble the soldiers in a painting of a battle, who are in the attitude of striking the enemy but never really strike.

ST. TERESA, 1515–1582

Sin is a brat nobody will own.

MATTHEW HENRY, 1662–1714

INSIGHT

If every year we would root out one vice, we should soon become perfect men. But now oftentimes we perceive it goeth contrary, and that we were better and purer at the beginning of our entrance into religious life. It is accounted a great matter if a man can retain but some part of his first zeal.

Endeavor to be patient in bearing the defects and infirmities of others; for that thou hast also many failings which must be borne by others. If thou canst not make thyself such a one as thou wouldst, how wilt thou be able to have another in all things to thy liking?

For occasions do not make a man frail, but they show of what he is made.

Why doth a little matter spoken against thee make thee sad? Even although it had been much more, thou ought not to have been moved. But now let it pass; it is not the first that has happened, nor is it anything new; neither shall it be the last, if thou live long. Put it out of thy heart the best thou canst. Bear it at least patiently, if thou canst not joyfully.

All is not lost, although thou do feel thyself very often afflicted or grievously tempted. Thou art a man, and not God; thou art flesh, not an angel.

If there be any good in thee, believe better things of others, that so thou preserve humility. It doth no hurt to thee to set thyself lower than all men, but it hurteth thee exceedingly if thou set thyself above even one man.

THOMAS A KEMPIS, 1379–1471

HEAVENLY ART

In Heaven, the only art of living
Is forgetting and forgiving.

WILLIAM BLAKE, 1757–1827

PARTIAL VIEWS

Prejudice is the beginning of self-inflicted blindness. Men choose to take partial views of life to suit their whim and fancy. Catholicity has nothing to recommend it unless it is the condition in which everything is measured and considered in terms of the whole. There is no graver offence than to use a catholic garment to hide a sectarian heart.

CHARLES H. BRENT, 1862–1929

TIMETABLE

It is never
too late
to give up
your prejudices.

HENRY DAVID THOREAU, 1817–1862

INDWELLING

In these two things the greatness of man consists: to have God so dwelling in us as to impart His character to us, and to have Him so dwelling in us that we recognize His presence and know that we are His, and He is ours. The one is salvation; the other the assurance of it.

FREDERICK W. ROBERTSON,
1816–1853

A PRAYER FOR PURGING

Burn up, like thorns, all my transgressions.

Purge Thou my soul and hallow my imagination.

Knit firm my bones and joints withal.

Shine into all five senses of my body.

Fasten me wholly in the fear of Thee.

Guard, shield, and shelter me evermore from every deed and word that stains the soul.

Cleanse, wash, and adorn me.

Set me right.

Give me understanding.

MEISTER ECKHART, 1260–1328

THE REAL HEATHEN

The only real heathen and heretics are the purely selfish. It is for our sakes as well as theirs that we desire their conversion. For while they are losing all life has to give, we are losing the share they might contribute.

WILFRED T. GRENFELL, 1865–1940

From SONNET TO JEFFRIES WYMAN

The wisest man could ask no more of fate
Than to be simple, modest, manly, true,
Safe from the many, honored by the few;
To count as naught in world, or church, or state,
But inwardly in secret to be great.

JAMES RUSSELL LOWELL, 1819–1891

THE EVILS OF THE AGE

1. A wise man without good works.
2. An old man without religion.
3. A young man without obedience.
4. A rich man without charity.
5. A woman without modesty.
6. A lord without virtue.
7. A quarrelsome Christian.
8. A poor man who is proud.
9. An unjust king.
10. A negligent bishop.
11. A populace without discipline.
12. A people without law.

THIRTEENTH-CENTURY BOOK

COMPANIONSHIP

Go with mean people and you will think life is mean. Then read Plutarch, and the world is a proud place, full of heroes and demi-gods standing around us, who will not let us sleep.

RALPH WALDO EMERSON, 1803–1882

When wealth is lost, nothing is lost;
When health is lost, something is lost;
When character is lost, all is lost.

ST. AUGUSTINE, 354–430

From A GRAMMARIAN'S FUNERAL

That low man seeks a little thing to do,
  Sees it and does it:
This high man, with a great thing to pursue,
  Dies ere he knows it.
That low man goes on adding one to one,

His hundred's soon hit:
This high man, aiming at a million,
  Misses a unit.

ROBERT BROWNING, 1812–1889

SELF-RESPECT

Rightly or wrongly, I conceive self-respect to be belief in one's own worth—worth to God and worth to man.

It may, of course, abnormally develop until it becomes pride, conceit, or arrogance; or it may be minimized, making a man slack, careless, and shabby in character as in dress.

But we can all echo the prayer of the old Edinburgh weaver, "O God, help me to hold a high opinion of myself."

"The first thing to be done to help a man to moral regeneration," says MacDougall, the great psychologist, "is to restore if possible his self-respect."

LESLIE D. WEATHERHEAD

THE ANVIL

No man can dream
character into himself;
he must
hammer and forge
himself
into a man.

JOHN WANAMAKER, 1838–1922

BLESSING

I wish you then, a very rich, deep, true, straight, and simple growth in the love of God, accepted and willed gently but greatly, at the daily hourly cost of self.

FRIEDRICH VON HÜGEL, 1852–1925

ALWAYS REMEMBER

To change one's disposition is greater than to change one's dress.

ST. JEROME, C. 347–419?

LOOKING-GLASS

If thy heart were sincere and upright, then every creature would be unto thee a looking-glass of life and a book of holy doctrine.

THOMAS A KEMPIS, 1379–1471

CONFESSION

I wish there were some one
Who would hear confession.
Not a priest—I do not want to be told
of my sins;
Not a mother—I do not want to give
sorrow;
Not a friend—she would not know
enough;
Not a lover—he would be too partial;
Not a God—He is far away;
But someone who would be friend,
lover, mother, priest, God all in one,
And a stranger besides—who would
not condemn or interfere;
Who, when everything is said from be-
ginning to end
Would show the reason for it all
And tell you to go ahead
And work it out your own way.

JEANNE D'ORGE

My business is not to remain myself, but to make the absolute best of what God made.

ROBERT BROWNING, 1812–1889

COUNSEL

Be very circumspect in the choice of thy company. In the society of thine equals, thou shalt enjoy more pleasure; in the society of thy superiors, thou shalt find more profit.

FRANCIS QUARLES, 1592–1644

The tragedy is not that things are broken. The tragedy is that they are not mended again.

ALAN PATON

THE REAL COMFORT

O Lord, Thou in Thyself remainest, but I am rolled about in experiments.

Woe to the rash soul which hopes by forsaking Thee to find something better. It tosses and turns; but the bed is hard; and Thou alone art rest. And lo! Thou art near, and settest free from the misery of wandering and plantest our feet in Thy road, and comfortest us, saying, "Run, I will carry you, and I will bring you home, and then I will set you free."

It is not by feet or change of place that men leave Thee or return to Thee; rather in lustful darkened affections is the true distance from Thy face, O my God.

ST. AUGUSTINE, 354–430

ECONOMY

Superfluous money can buy superfluities only. Money is not required to buy one necessity of the soul.

HENRY DAVID THOREAU, 1817–1862

CHILDHOOD

And children's faces looking up
Holding wonder like a cup.

SARA TEASDALE, 1884–1933

What is it to be a child?

It is to have a spirit yet streaming from the waters of baptism.

It is to believe in love, to believe in loveliness, to believe in belief.

It is to be so little that the elves can whisper in your ear.

It is to turn pumpkins into coaches, mice into horses, lowness into loftiness, and nothing into everything, for each child has his own fairy godmother in his own soul.

It is to live in a nutshell and count yourself king of infinite space. It is, in William Blake's words,

To see a world in a grain of sand,
And a heaven in a wild flower;
Hold infinity in the palm of your
hand,
And eternity in an hour.

AUTHOR UNKNOWN

The dreams of childhood—its airy fables, its graceful, beautiful, humane, impossible adornments of the world beyond: so good to be believed in once, so good to be remembered when outgrown.

CHARLES DICKENS, 1812–1870

From THE EVERLASTING MERCY

Each one could be a Jesus mild,
Each one has been a little child,
A little child with laughing look,
A lovely white unwritten book;
A book that God will take, my friend,
As each goes out at journey's end.
The Lord Who gave us Earth and
Heaven
Takes that as thanks for all He's given.
The book He lent is given back
All blotted red and smutted black.

JOHN MASEFIELD, 1878–1967

GLANCE OF WISDOM

Sometimes looking deep into the eyes of a child, you are conscious of meeting a glance full of wisdom. The child has known nothing yet but love and beauty. All this piled-up world knowledge you have acquired is unguessed at by him. And yet you meet this wonderful look that tells you in a moment more than all the years of experience have seemed to teach.

HILDEGARDE HAWTHORNE

WHOSE CHILD?

A child cried one night
Outside,
And I said, That is my child.
But I found him to be another lad,
So I went back to my room and said,
There is nothing for me to do;
Now I can sleep.

The child cried again
And I went out and looked into his
    face
And said, Why this is my child!
And brought him in
And gave him something to eat
And put him in a warm bed;
And I slept.

A child laughed
And I followed the sweet laughter
Out to a place called the Kingdom of
    God,
Where many children were.
The Lord of the place asked me,
Which child did you help?
And I could not tell!

HERBERT S. WHITING

NEW GENERATION

How wise of God every twenty years to
give us a new generation of children in
the Church.

MARTIN LUTHER, 1483–1546

INHERITANCE

I think it must somewhere be written
that the virtues of the mothers, as well
as the sins of the fathers, shall be
visited on their children.

CHARLES DICKENS, 1812–1870

GOD WAITING

When God wants an important thing
done in this world, or a wrong righted,
He goes about it in a very singular way.

He doesn't release His thunderbolts
nor stir up His earthquakes.

He simply has a tiny, helpless baby
born, perhaps in a very obscure home,
perhaps of a very humble mother.

And He puts the idea or purpose
into a mother's heart.

And she puts it in the baby's mind.
And then God waits!

EDWARD T. SULLIVAN

TO MOTHER

You painted no Madonnas
    On chapel walls in Rome,
But with a touch diviner
    You lived one in your home.

You wrote no lofty poems
    That critics counted art,
But with a nobler vision
    You lived them in your heart.

You carved no shapeless marble
    To some high soul design,
But with a finer sculpture,
    You shaped this soul of mine.

You built no great cathedrals
    That centuries applaud,
But with a grace exquisite
    Your life cathedraled God.

Had I the gift of Raphael,
    Or Michelangelo,
Oh, what a rare Madonna
    My mother's life would show!

THOMAS W. FESSENDEN

A LITTLE CHURCH

Every Christian family ought to be a little church, consecrated to Christ, and wholly influenced and governed by His rules.

Family education and order are some of the chief means of grace.

If these fail, all other means are likely to prove ineffectual.

If these are duly maintained, all the means of grace will be likely to prosper and be successful.

JONATHAN EDWARDS, 1703–1758

HOPE

Families when a child is born
Hope it will turn out intelligent.
I, through intelligence,
Having wrecked my whole life,
Only hope that the baby will prove
Ignorant and stupid.
Then he will be happy all his days
And end as a cabinet minister.

SU TUNG PO, A.D. 1036

MIRACULOUS MULTIPLICATION

To teach each child the miraculous multiplication of mercy sealed into every church envelope every Sunday! To help him visualize his own feet soon walking to strange doors; his own hands giving food; his own eyes shocked by so much misery on earth; his own heart troubled by human despair. This is the very least any mother can do in describing each week what utter excitement it is to fill an offering envelope. Kindling a divine imagination; awakening a divine response.

MOTHER OF THE WESLEYS

Susannah Wesley, the twenty-fifth child of her father, had nineteen children of her own. On an income always pitiably small, she cared for her vast family, making herself Father Confessor and Mother Superior to each separate child.

When asked how she ever found time to do this, she asked: "There is no mystery about the matter. I just took Jacky alone with me into my room every Monday night, and Charley every Tuesday night, and Molly every Wednesday, and so on, all through the week."

She allotted just so much time for teaching each of them the alphabet and primer, as well as Bible stories. Because this method expected them to learn a certain matter in a certain time, they generally did.

When her husband on one occasion said to her, "How can you have the patience to tell the little dolt the same thing twenty times?" her reply was: "If I had told him but nineteen times, I should have lost all of my labor!"

It was out of such patient methods that John and Charles Wesley formed the Methodist Church.

As a pattern for behavior, they adopted their mother's early motto: "Whatever obscures your own sense of God, whatever impairs the tenderness of your own conscience, and whatever destroys your own relish for spiritual things, that is sin to you, however innocent it may be in itself. Do not obscure your radiant ecstasy!"

God could not be everywhere, and so He made mothers.

JEWISH PROVERB

From THERE WAS A CHILD WENT FORTH

There was a child went forth every day,
And the first object he look'd upon,
that object he became,
And that object became part of him for
the day or a certain part of the day,
Or for many years or stretching cycles
of years.

The early lilacs became part of this
child,
And grass and white and red morning-
glories, and white and red clover,
and the song of the phoebe-bird,
And the third-month lambs and the
sow's pink-faint litter, and the
mare's foal and the cow's calf,
And the noisy brood of the barnyard
or by the mire of the pond-side,
And the fish suspending themselves so
curiously below there, and the beautiful curious liquid,
And the water-plants with their graceful flat heads, all became part of
him.
And the schoolmistress that pass'd on
her way to the school,
And the friendly boys that pass'd, and
the quarrelsome boys.

His own parents, he that had father'd
him and she that had conceiv'd him
in her womb and birth'd him,
They gave this child more of themselves than that,
They gave him afterward every day,
they became part of him.

The mother at home quietly placing
the dishes on the supper-table,
The mother with mild words, clean her
cap and gown, a wholesome odor
falling off her person and clothes as
she walks by,
The father, strong, self-sufficient,
manly, mean, anger'd, unjust,
The blow, the quick loud word, the
tight bargain, the crafty lure.
The family usages, the language, the
company, the furniture, the yearning
and swelling heart,
Affection that will not be gainsay'd,
the sense of what is real, the thought
if after all it should prove unreal,
The doubts of day-time and the doubts
of night-time, the curious whether
and how,
Whether that which appears so is so,
or is it all flashes and specks?
These all become part of that child
who went forth every day, and who
now goes, and will always go forth
every day.

WALT WHITMAN, 1819–1892

PATTERN

The parent's life is
the child's copy-book.

BRAID SCOTS TRANSLATION

Ye bairns be dutiful to yere ain parents
in the Laird, for this is bonnie.

EPHESIANS 6:1

Archbishop William Temple once said
that a child's earliest knowledge of
prayer should be the discovery of a person praying; its earliest knowledge of
worship, the beholding of a person
worshiping.

Religion will become real to the
child because that child has seen its reality in adults whom he trusts and loves.

TO HIS SAVIOUR, A CHILD, A PRESENT, BY A CHILD

Go pretty child, and bear this flower
Unto thy little Saviour;
And tell Him, by that bud now blown,
He is the Rose of Sharon known:
When thou hast said so, stick it there
Upon His bib, or stomacher:
And tell Him, (for good handsel too)
That thou hast brought a whistle new,
Made of a clean straight oaten reed,
To charm His cries, (at time of need:)
Tell Him, for coral, thou hast none;
But if thou hadst, He should have one;
But poor thou art, and known to be
Even as moneyless, as He.
Lastly, if thou canst win a kiss
From those mellifluous lips of His,
Then never take a second one,
To spoil the first impression.

ROBERT HERRICK, 1591–1674

From ODE: INTIMATIONS OF IMMORTALITY

Our birth is but a sleep and a forgetting;
The soul that rises with us, our life's star,
    Hath had elsewhere its setting,
    And cometh from afar;
    But not in entire forgetfulness,
    And not in utter nakedness,
But trailing clouds of glory do we come
    From God, who is our home.

WILLIAM WORDSWORTH, 1770–1850

If a man thinks well of you, make his thought come true.

ARABIAN PROVERB

OMAHA INDIAN PRAYER

Ye Sun, Moon, Stars, all ye that move in the heavens, I bid you hear me! Into your midst has come a new life. Make its path smooth, that it may reach the brow of the first hill.

WE HAVE SEEN HIS STAR AND ARE COME

We were all cross in the Christmas hurry
(Lord forgive us!), the wear and worry,
Things gone wrong without reason or rhyme,
Too much bustle and too little time.
Some were restless, and some beset
By last-minute duties they mustn't forget;
All but the youngest, the five-year-old,
There by the hearth in a pool of gold.
Still, so still, in her little chair
We had forgotten she was there,
The firelight on her.
            A knock at the door,
Sudden and loud, and we fretted some more:
Was it a guest, or a beggarman,
Or a last-minute message changing a plan?
Something, no doubt, to harry and push,
And all so tired with Christmas rush!
All but the youngest. She came to her feet
Caught by a wonder wild and sweet,
Starry-eyed, breathless, with lifted head:
"Listen! The Wise Men have come!" she said.

NANCY BYRD TURNER

WHEN THEY WERE VERY YOUNG

When Martin Luther was a boy in school, Herr Trebonius, his teacher, used to lift his hat to his pupils, in salutation to their future greatness.

When William Carey was a boy, he sat up in a tree imitating Captain Cook going off to the South Sea islands.

When St. Teresa was a small girl, she and her brother, stunned by the word "Eternity," would say to each other: "What? Forever?" "Yes, forever and ever and ever!"

When James Watt was a boy, the lid of his mother's teakettle fascinated him: steam, rising and falling. What else could it do? He longed to find out.

When Albert Schweitzer was a boy in Alsace-Lorraine, he passed the statue of a French colonel in uniform staring down at a naked African captive kneeling before him, and thought, "Someone must atone for all the sins of all the white people against all the black people!" Eventually he said: "I, Albert Schweitzer, will atone!" Although, in his own rare phrase, he and his friends "grew up like a bunch of wild roses," this reverence for life became the motif of all his days.

❧

A few years ago in the Harvard graduation processional the Freshman class carried a banner which read: "This College Has Been Waiting 250 Years for Us!"

From THE UNSEEN PLAYMATE

When children are playing alone on
   the green,
In comes the playmate that never is
   seen.
When children are happy and lonely
   and good,
The Friend of the Children comes out
   of the wood.
Nobody heard him and nobody says,
His is a picture you never could draw,
But he's sure to be present, abroad or
   at home,
When children are happy and playing
   alone.

ROBERT LOUIS STEVENSON,
1850–1894

❧

HIGHER MATHEMATICS

You save an old man and
you save a unit, but you
save a boy and you save
a multiplication table.

GYPSY SMITH, 1797–1874

ANCIENT JUDGMENT

The children love luxury.
They have bad manners
and contempt for authority.
They show disrespect for their elders.
They love chatter in place of exercise.
They are now tyrants,
not servants of their households.
They no longer rise
when elders enter the room.
They contradict their parents,
gobble up dainties at the table,
cross their legs,
and tyrannize over their teachers.

SOCRATES, 469–399 B.C.

A BOY

He is a person who is going to carry on what you have started.

He is to sit right where you are sitting, and attend, when you are gone, to those things you think are so important.

You may adopt all the policies you please, but how they will be carried out depends upon him.

Even if you make leagues and treaties, he will have to manage them.

He will assume control of your cities, states, and nation.

He is going to move in and take over your churches, schools, universities, and corporations.

All your work is going to be judged and praised or condemned by him.

Your reputation and your future are in his hands.

All your work is for him, and the fate of the nation and of humanity is in his hands.

AUTHOR UNKNOWN

MOTHER TO SON

Well, son, I'll tell you:
Life for me ain't been no crystal stair.
Ise had tacks in it,
And splinters,
And boards torn up,
And place with no carpet on the
    floor—
Bare.

But all the time
It's been a-climbin' on,
And reachin' landin's
And turnin' corners,
And sometimes goin' in the dark
Where there ain't been no light.
So, boy, don't you turn back.

Don't you set down on the steps
'Cause you finds it kinder hard.
Don't you fall now—
For I'se still goin', honey,
I'se still climbin',
And life for me ain't been no crystal
    stair.

LANGSTON HUGHES, 1902–1967

TWO MOTHERS TALKING

"Are you sending your children to dancing school?"

"Indeed, I am. I feel it is totally necessary to develop social graces as early as possible."

"But do they like to go?"

"No, I must admit they detest it! So I practically drag them there once a week by the hair of their heads; but I am determined they shan't grow up awkward and ill-at-ease."

"And how about Sunday school?"

"Well, y-e-s; if it doesn't rain—as it has so many Sundays this past year. I think it's too risky to sit with wet feet."

"But don't they go to weekday school, rain or shine?"

"Oh, but that's different, isn't it? Their total number of absences might be a mark against their graduation."

"And music lessons?"

"Oh, yes! yes! My husband doesn't agree; but I think maybe a spot of culture won't hurt them. Yet you know how it is. By the time you get their teeth straightened, and their eyeglasses fitted, and orthopedic shoes, then practicing seems like the last straw! But I always think music adds something so cultural, later on in life, don't you?"

From SOUTH PACIFIC

You've got to be taught to hate and
    fear,
You've got to be taught from year to
    year,
It's got to be drummed in your dear
    little ear—
You've got to be carefully taught!

You've got to be taught to be afraid
Of people whose eyes are oddly made,
And people whose skin is a different
    shade—
You've got to be carefully taught.

You've got to be taught before it's too
    late,
Before you are six or seven or eight,
To hate all the people your relatives
    hate—
You've got to be carefully taught.

OSCAR HAMMERSTEIN II, 1895–1960

❧

Children are a poor man's wealth.

DANISH PROVERB

❧

This year, America, I bring you my son,
My baby son,
He comes with little heritage,
But his eyes are clear, his body strong,
He is ready for you to do with him
    what you will.

What will you?
Will you use him hurriedly for your
    quick ends,
And will you then discard him because
    he is worn out and still a foreigner?
Or will you teach him, watch him
    grow, and help him to be one of you,
To work with you for those great
    things you seek?

He is my son, America.
And all my treasure.
I bring him here to you—
And you, what will you do with him?

HELEN DWIGHT FISHER

❧

From THE CHILDREN

They are idols of the hearts and of
    households;
    They are angels of God in disguise;
The sunlight still sleeps in their tresses,
    His glory still gleams in their eyes;
These truants from home and from
    heaven—
    They have made me more manly and
    mild;
And I know now how Jesus could liken
    The Kingdom of God to a child.

CHARLES M. DICKINSON

❧

COMPENSATION

A mother has, perhaps,
the hardest earthly lot.
Yet no mother
worthy of the name
ever gave herself thoroughly
for her child
who did not feel that,
after all,
she reaped what
she had sown.

HENRY WARD BEECHER, 1813–1887

❧

FULFILLMENT

As each one wishes his children to be,
so they are.

TERENCE, 185–159 B.C.

TOUCH ME!

In one of her dreams Olive Schreiner saw a woman, soon to become a mother, wandering out over the African veldt and lost in the mist.

After a time a shape appears out of the mist. "If I touch you," it says, "your child will find wealth." The woman shakes her head and the shape disappears.

A second shape speaks: "If I touch you, your child will have fame." Again the woman shakes her head.

A third shape promises power, and so they kept coming, until a last shape appears. "And if I touch you, your child shall have neither fame, nor power, nor success; but he will always see a light beyond the horizon, and he will always hear a voice calling him from behind the hills, and he will set out after the voice and the vision; but as he reaches them, lo! beyond the horizon a new light, and in his ears a new voice. And he must leave all and go."

And the woman murmured, "But what gift will my child receive?"

"This," answered the strange shape. "When he looks at the dust, he will always see the beautiful in it. In the real he will see the dream!"

And the woman cried, "Touch me! Touch me!"

So the shape touched her and vanished.

⚜

The little child
is the only
true democrat.

HARRIET BEECHER STOWE,

1811–1896

AS TOLD BY EVELYN UNDERHILL

A Brownie lived in a wood. He had a little wheelbarrow, and passed his time in a very moral and useful manner picking up slugs and snails. Yet there was something lacking in his life.

The King of the World passed through that wood very early every morning, and made all things beautiful and new, but the Brownie had never seen him. He longed to, but something prevented it.

He had one cherished possession, a lovely little green blanket which had fallen out of the fairy queen's chariot and which he had not been able to help keeping for himself.

It was cold in the wood at night, but the blanket kept him so warm and cosy that he never woke up to see the King of the World.

One day there came a Shepherd who looked deep into the soul of the Brownie and said to him, "Haven't you seen the King of the World?" and the Brownie said, "No, I do so want to, but somehow I can't manage it."

Then the Shepherd replied, "But I seem to see something in your soul that keeps you from the vision, something that looks rather like a blanket."

At that a terrible fight began in the heart of the Brownie, a battle between wanting to go on being warm and comfortable in his blanket and longing to see the King of the World.

Perhaps the ultimate choice which lies before us may turn out to be the Brownie's choice between the Heavenly Vision and the blanket.

MARGARET CROPPER

⚜

CLOCKS

Quiet minds cannot be perplexed or frightened, but go on in fortune or misfortune at their own private pace like the ticking of a clock during a thunderstorm.

ROBERT LOUIS STEVENSON,
1850–1894

WE ARE MOVING DIALS

We are tomorrow's past. Even now we slip away like the pictures painted on the moving dials of antique clocks . . . a ship, a cottage, sun and moon, a nosegay. The dial turns, the ship rides up and sinks again, the yellow painted sun has set; and we that were the new things gather magic as we go.

MARY WEBB, 1881–1927

It comforts me to hear the hour strike, for I feel that I have drawn a little nearer to God.

ST. TERESA, 1515–1582

POINTS OF DEVOTION

When the clock strikes, or however else you shall measure the day, it is good to say a short ejaculation every hour, that the points and returns of devotion may be the measure of your time; and so do in all the breaches of thy sleep, that those spaces which have in them no direct business of the world may be filled with religion.

JEREMY TAYLOR, 1613–1667

CARVED ON THE DOOR
OF A GRANDFATHER CLOCK

When, as a child, I laughed and wept,
> Time crept.

When, as a youth, I dreamed and talked,
> Time walked.

When I became a full-grown man,
> Time ran.

And later, as I older grew,
> Time flew.

Soon I shall find, while travelling on,
> Time gone.

Will Christ have saved my soul
> By then?

CHESTER CATHEDRAL, ENGLAND

DAILY CARE

However good a clock may be, we must wind it up daily, and he who takes good care of his heart, will, as it were, wind it up toward God night and morning.

ST. FRANCIS DE SALES, 1567–1622

MOTTO ON A SUNDIAL

Today is
the Tomorrow
you worried
about
Yesterday.

ETERNITY

A state but of one day, because no night shall over-take or determine it, but such a day, as is not of a thousand years, which is the longest measure in the Scriptures, but of a thousand millions of millions of generations.

Yesterday doth not usher it in, nor tomorrow shall not drive it out.

Methuselah, with all his hundreds of years, was but a mushroom of a night's growth to this day.

And all the four monarchies, with all their thousands of years, and all the powerful kings, and all the beautiful queens of this world, were but as a bed of flowers, some gathered at six, some at seven, some at eight, all in one morning, in respect of this day.

And in all those which God may be pleased to add, in this House of His Fathers, there was never heard quarter clock to strike, never seen minute glass to turn.

JOHN DONNE, 1572–1631

SPRING

At the first hour, it was as if one said, "Arise."

At the second hour, it was as if one said, "Go forth."

And the winter constellations that are like patient ox-eyes

Sank below the white horizon at the north.

At the third hour, it was as if one said, "I thirst";

At the fourth hour, all the earth was still:

Then the clouds suddenly swung over, stooped, and burst;

And the rain flooded valley, plain and hill.

At the fifth hour, darkness took the throne;

At the sixth hour, the earth shook and the wind cried;

At the seventh hour, the hidden seed was sown;

At the eighth hour, it gave up the ghost and died.

At the ninth hour, they sealed up the tomb;

And the earth was then silent for the space of three hours.

But at the twelfth hour, a single lily from the gloom

Shot forth, and was followed by a whole host of flowers.

JOHN GOULD FLETCHER, 1886–1950

A HUNDRED POCKETS

When one has much to put into them, a day has a hundred pockets.

FRIEDRICH NIETZSCHE, 1844–1950

SEVENTY-YEAR CLOCKS

Our brains are seventy-year clocks. The Angel of Life winds them up once for all, then closes the case, and gives the key into the hand of the Angel of the Resurrection.

OLIVER WENDELL HOLMES,
1809–1894

A ROOF FOR A SUNDIAL

An American visited an African village which had neither clocks nor watches. He responded to the obvious need of the people for some way to measure time by presenting to them a handsome sundial.

Later the villagers began to worry about the gift. Would the hot sun warp it? Would the torrential rains wear it away?

To protect such an important possession, they raised a wide straw roof over the sundial. They made certain that the gift would be preserved for their children's children, but in the meantime they continued without any way of measuring time.

As the mother's womb holds us for nine months, making us ready, not for the womb itself, but for life, just so, through our lives we are making ourselves ready for another birth. Look forward without fear to that appointed hour, the last hour of the body but not of the soul. That day, which you fear as being the end of all things, is the birthday of your eternity.

SENECA, C. 3 B.C.–A.D. 65

Tomorrow is never.

TURKISH PROVERB

MEASUREMENT

Every day is a little life.
Every waking and rising
is a little birth.
Every fresh morning
is a little youth.
Every going to rest and sleep
is a little death.

ARTHUR SCHOPENHAUER, 1788–1860

TO GIVE ONE'S LIFE

To give one's life through eighty years
    is harder
      Than to give it in one moment gloriously;
To make each instant a brown willow
    basket
      Heaped with fresh flowers and
      ferns; to ever be
A cup of never-failing cool spring
    water
      To those who walk a dusty road
      alone;
To succor with life-giving bread, regardless,
      Those who expect a stone;
To give one's life, on weary days and
    hopeless;
      To give one's life, hour after hour,
      and be
Ready to give again, again, is harder
    Than to give it in a moment, gloriously.

MARY CAROLYN DAVIES

RESOLUTIONS

Resolved: To live with all my might while I do live.

Resolved: Never to lose one moment of time, but improve it in the most profitable way I possibly can.

Resolved: Never to do anything which I should despise or think meanly of in another.

Resolved: Never to do anything out of revenge.

Resolved: Never to do anything which I should be afraid to do if it were the last hour of my life.

JONATHAN EDWARDS, 1703–1758

OPPORTUNITY

A man must not complain of his "element," or of his "time," or the like; it is thriftless work doing so. His time is bad; well then, he is there to make it better.

THOMAS CARLYLE, 1795–1881

Every man is the prisoner of his date.

JAMES RUSSELL LOWELL,
1819–1891

STUPENDOUS FACT

One moment of a man's life is a fact so stupendous as to take the lustre out of all fiction.

RALPH WALDO EMERSON,
1803–1882

From A TALE OF TWO CITIES

It was the best of times, it was the worst of times, it was the epoch of belief, it was the epoch of incredulity, it was the season of Light, it was the season of Darkness, it was the spring of hope, it was the winter of despair, we had everything before us, we had nothing before us, we were all going direct to Heaven, we were all going direct the other way—in short, the period was so far like the present period, that some of its noisiest authorities insisted on its being received, for good or for evil, in the superlative degree of comparison only.

There were a king with a large jaw, and a queen with a plain face, on the throne of England; there were a king with a large jaw, and a queen with a fair face, on the throne of France. In both countries it was clearer than crystal to the lords of the State preserves of loaves and fishes, that things in general were settled for ever.

It was the year of Our Lord one thousand seven hundred and seventy-five. . . .

It is likely enough that, rooted in the woods of France and Norway, there were growing trees . . . already marked by the Woodman, Fate, to come down and be sawn into boards, to make a certain movable framework with a sack and a knife in it, terrible in history. It is likely enough that, in the rough outhouses of some tillers of the heavy lands adjacent to Paris, there were sheltered from the weather, that very day, rude carts, bespattered with rustic mire, snuffed about by pigs and roosted in by poultry, which the Farmer, Death, had already set apart to be his tumbrels of the Revolution.

CHARLES DICKENS, 1812–1870

SOMETHING TOO BIG TO CARRY

Whenever anyone gives something too big to something too small to carry it —too big sails to too small a ship, too big meals to too small a body, too big powers to too small a soul—the result is bound to be a complete upset.

PLATO, 427–347 B.C.

ABREAST OF ALL THE CENTURIES

Son of Man, whenever I doubt of life, I think of Thee. Nothing is so impossible as that Thou shouldest be dead. I can imagine the hills to dissolve in vapor and the stars to melt in smoke and the rivers to exhaust themselves in sheer exhaustion. Thou never growest old to me. Last century is old, last year is obsolete fashion, but Thou art not obsolete. Thou art abreast of all the centuries.

GEORGE MATHESON, 1842–1906

NEW WORLD

God creates the world anew in each moment.

JAN VAN RUYSBROECK, 1293–1381

MEMORIES OR HOPES?

A man is old
when his memories
have become
more precious to him
than his hopes.

RUFUS WASHINGTON WEAVER

THE CHRISTIAN YEAR

It comes as a surprise to many people, upon opening the Book of Common Prayer for the first time, to discover that it begins with an almanac.

The introductory portion contains some fifty pages filled with calendar notes, time tables, and schedules.

Again, in the very heart of the Book, almost one-third of its contents are given over to specific prayers and lessons assigned to every Sunday and other stated days of the year.

Closer scrutiny of the Prayer Book will reveal that its entire contents are laid out according to an ordered time-sequence of rites and observances.

The liturgy takes time seriously because the Christian faith takes time seriously.

Philosophers may tell us that time is only an illusion, a glimpse of that eternity which God alone knows as an everlasting present.

The scientist may define it as man's device to measure the repeated courses of the heavenly bodies or of the heart's beat.

Yet no definition can enable us to escape it. For time is an inevitable condition of our creatureliness. It is part of the givenness of our human existence.

God has set us within the mysterious ordering of time that we may grow with it in His grace and spend it to His glory.

MASSEY H. SHEPHERD, JR.

It is magnificent to grow old if one keeps young.

HARRY EMERSON FOSDICK

THREE DAYS

There are two days in the week upon which and about which I never worry —two carefree days kept sacredly free from fear and apprehension.

One of these days is yesterday. Yesterday, with its cares and frets and all its pains and aches, all its faults, its mistakes and blunders, has passed forever beyond my recall.

It was mine.

It is God's.

And the other day that I do not worry about is tomorrow. Tomorrow, with all its possible adversities, its burdens, its perils, its large promise and poor performance, its failures and mistakes, is as far beyond my mastery as its dead sister, yesterday.

Tomorrow is God's day.

It will be mine.

There is left for myself, then, but one day in the week—today. Any woman can carry the burdens of just one day. Any man can resist the temptations of today.

It is only when we add the burdens of those two awful eternities, yesterday and tomorrow, that we break down.

ROBERT J. BURDETTE

EXASPERATION

Assigned to an unswept abandoned school building, as part of a teaching team at a writer's conference in Assam, one of the tired young men exclaimed at nightfall: "There are some days to have lived through which is to have done more than one's duty!"

MARION VAN HORNE

FIRST COMMUNION

Mary Moffat, wife of Robert Moffat, worked ten long years in Africa without a single convert. Ten years, and each year having 365 days, and each day having twenty-four hours, and each hour having sixty minutes. Moments and days of waiting. Yet Mary Moffat wrote to England: "Do send us a communion service; it will be wanted." And on the very day before the first company of converts were to partake of their first communion, a box containing the silver service for the Lord's Supper reached Kuruman!

From MACBETH

Tomorrow, and tomorrow, and tomor-
            row
Creeps in this petty pace from day to
            day,
To the last syllable of recorded time,
And all our yesterdays have lighted
            fools
The way to dusty death. Out, out, brief
            candle.
Life's but a walking shadow, a poor
            player
That struts and frets his hour upon the
            stage
And then is heard no more. It is a tale
Told by an idiot, full of sound and
            fury,
Signifying nothing.

WILLIAM SHAKESPEARE, 1564–1616

We cannot speak with any truth or realism about our faith in the future unless we understand the past.

PETER MARSHALL, 1903–1949

DAILY TREASURE

You wake up in the morning, and lo! your purse is magically filled with twenty-four hours of the unmanufactured tissue of the universe of your life. It is yours. It is the most precious of possessions. No one can take it from you. It is unstealable. And no one receives either more or less than you receive.

ARNOLD BENNETT, 1867–1931

OF TIMES AND SEASONS

To every thing there is a season, and a time to every purpose under the heaven:
A time to be born,
and a time to die;
a time to plant,
and a time to pluck up
that which is planted;

A time to kill,
and a time to heal;
a time to break down,
and a time to build up;

A time to weep,
and a time to laugh;
a time to mourn,
and a time to dance;

A time to cast away stones,
and a time to gather stones
together;
a time to embrace,
and a time to refrain
from embracing;

A time to get,
and a time to lose;
a time to keep,
and a time to cast away;

A time to rend,
and a time to sew;
a time to keep silence,
and a time to speak;

A time to love,
and a time to hate;
a time of war,
and a time of peace.

ECCLESIASTES 3:1–8

YESTERDAY

I am Yesterday.
I am gone from you forever.

I am the last of a long procession of days, streaming behind you, away from you, pouring into mist and obscurity, and at last into the ocean of oblivion.

I depart from you, yet I am ever with you.

Once I was called Tomorrow and was virgin pure; then I became your bride and was named Today; now I am Yesterday and carry upon me the stain of your embrace.

I am one of the leaves of a growing book. There are many pages before me.

Some day you will turn us all over, and read us, and know what you are.

I am rich, for I have wisdom.

I bore you a child and left him with you. His name is Experience.

I am Yesterday. Yet I am the same as Today and Forever, for I am you, and you cannot escape from yourself.

FRANK CRANE

Lincoln was equal to his hour. . . .
Cromwell was equal to his hour. . . .

RUPERT BROOKE, 1887–1915

THE SALUTATION OF
THE DAWN

Listen to the exhortation of the dawn!
Look to this day!
For it is life, the very life of life.
In its brief course lie all
The verities and realities of your ex-
   istence:
   The bliss of growth,
   The glory of action,
   The splendor of beauty,
For yesterday is but a dream,
And tomorrow is only a vision:
But today well lived makes
Every yesterday a dream of happiness,
And every tomorrow a vision of hope.
Look well therefore to this day!
Such is the salutation of the dawn!

FROM THE SANSKRIT

TWO QUESTIONS

Ignatius Loyola once asked himself
two pointed questions.

First, "When I am at the point of
death, what should I wish I had done
here and now? Precisely that is what
I should be doing."

Second, "When I am called before
the Divine tribunal, what will I wish
that I had done with all my worldly
goods? For this certainly is what I
ought to do at the present moment."

Concerning the New Society of
Jesus, which he started, he said: "In
this school we are taught to acquire a
rich poverty, a free slavery, a glorious
humility."

When he was being carried away to
his martyrdom, he said with conviction, "Now, I am beginning to be a
Christian!"

CURE

Time is an herb
that cures all diseases.

BENJAMIN FRANKLIN, 1706–1790

From THE WINDOW IN THE
BYE STREET

Man cannot call the brimming instant
   back;
Time's an affair of instants spun to
   days;
If man must make an instant gold, or
   black,
Let him, he may, but Time must go his
   ways.
Life may be duller for an instant's
   blaze.
Life's an affair of instants spun to
   years,
Instants are only cause of all these
   fears.

JOHN MASEFIELD, 1878–1967

The great mystery of Time,
were there no other;
the illimitable, silent,
never-resting thing called Time,
rolling, rushing on, swift, silent,
like an all-embracing ocean-tide,
on which we
and all the Universe swim
like exhalations, like apparitions
which are, and then are not:
this is forever very literally
a miracle:
a thing to strike us dumb—
for we have no word
to speak about it.

THOMAS CARLYLE, 1795–1881

FIVE MINUTES LONGER

The Duke of Wellington once said of the Battle of Waterloo that the British Army won, not because his men were braver than French soldiers, but simply because they had had courage enough to hold out five minutes longer.

Such a spirit of extended endurance is one of the wonders of Christianity—that something superb grips a man, and neither death, nor life, nor angels, nor principalities, nor powers, nor things present, nor things to come, nor height, nor depth, nor any other creature is able to separate that man from Jesus Christ.

This is more than a letter written by Paul to the Romans.

It is Martin Luther facing the entire religious hierarchy five hundred years ago.

It is John Calvin, who for twenty-three years of his life had a price on his head if he dared to return to France, and so turned the whole city of Geneva into a sanctuary of God where thousands upon thousands of Frenchmen were safe as religious refugees. The symbol which Calvin used on his seal explains his secret—a palm held upturned, with a heart on it in flames, the words around it reading: "My heart I give thee, Lord, eagerly and sincerely."

This eagerness lasted five minutes longer. This sincerity added another five minutes. On and on for twenty-three years.

You cannot kill time without injuring eternity.

HENRY DAVID THOREAU, 1817–1862

From THE GATE OF THE YEAR

And I said to the man who stood at the
  gate of the year:
"Give me a light, that I may tread
  safely into the unknown!"
And he replied:
"Go out into the darkness and put
  thine hand into the Hand of God.
That shall be to thee better than light
  and safer than a known way."
So, I went forth, and finding the Hand
  of God, trod gladly into the night.
And he led me toward the hills and the
  breaking of the day in the lone East.
So, heart, be still!
What need our little life,
Our human life, to know,
If God hath comprehension?
In all the dizzy strife
Of things both high and low
God hideth his intention.

MINNIE LOUISE HASKINS

DAYS

Daughters of Time, the hypocritic
  Days,
Muffled and dumb like barefoot der-
  vishes,
And marching single in an endless file,
Bring diadems and fagots in their
  hands,
To each they offer gifts after his will,
Bread, kingdoms, stars, and sky that
  holds them all.
I, in my pleachèd garden, watched the
  pomp,
Forgot my morning wishes, hastily
Took a few herbs and apples, and the
  Day
Turned and departed silent. I, too late,
Under her solemn fillet saw the scorn.

RALPH WALDO EMERSON, 1803–1882

CONVERSATION

The magic of the tongue is that
most dangerous of all spells.

EDWARD BULWER-LYTTON,
1803–1873

PROPRE PLEASAUNTE TALKING

A mery talk with a frende refresheth a man much, and without any harme lyghteth hys mynde, and amendeth his courage and hys stomake, so that it semeth but well done to take suche recreacion. And Solomon sayeth I trowe that men should in heavines geve the sory man wine to make hym forgeat his sorowe. And saynct Thomas saieth that propre pleasaunte talking which is called conversation is a good vertue serving to refreshe the minde, and make it quicke and lusty to labor and study againe, where continuall fatigacion would make it dull and deadly.

THOMAS MORE, 1478–1535

BEST ENJOYMENT

The world is best enjoyed
and most immediately
while we converse
blessedly and wisely
with men.

THOMAS TRAHERNE, 1637–1674

DRUID KING OF THE PICTS: What difference will it make if I become Christ's man?

BRENDAN, A CELTIC MONK: If you become Christ's man, you will behold wonder on wonder, and every wonder true.

ANCIENT SCOTTISH ANNALS

CONQUERED WORDS

They were cruel words
To crush and sting.
Unspoken, now they form a ring
Of laughing flowers.
I can sing!

They were harsh words
Of rush and hate.
Unsaid, they now swing wide the gate
To life's abundance.
I can wait!

Where once such words
Cast love away,
And made my heart a thing of clay
They now are mastered.
I can pray.
Thank God for conquered words!

CAROL MC AFEE MORGAN

EARLY CHRISTIAN TESTIMONY

In the early days of Christianity, Pliny, the Roman governor of Bithynia, attempted desperately to destroy all Christians.

PLINY: I will banish thee.

CHRISTIAN: Thou canst not, for the whole world is my Father's house.

PLINY: I will slay thee.

CHRISTIAN: Thou canst not, for my life is hid with Christ in God.

PLINY: I will take away thy treasures.

CHRISTIAN: Thou canst not, for my treasure is in heaven.

PLINY: I will drive thee away from men, and thou wilt have no friends left.

CHRISTIAN: Thou canst not, for I have a Friend from whom thou canst never separate me.

ZOROASTER REVEALS THE SECRET OF YOUTH

CYPRUS THE GREAT, KING OF PERSIA: Please tell me how I can retain my youth?

ZOROASTER: Nobody grows old by merely living a number of years. People grow old by deserting their ideals. Years wrinkle the skin, but the giving up of enthusiasm wrinkles the soul. Worry, doubt, self-distrust, fear, and despair— these are the long years that bow the head and turn the growing spirit back to dust. You are as young as your faith, as old as your doubt, as young as your self-confidence, as old as your fears, as young as your hope, as old as your despair.

COLLABORATION

It takes two to speak truth: one to speak, another to hear.

HENRY DAVID THOREAU, 1817–1862

MARTYR'S WITNESS

CARDINAL WOLSEY TO HUGH LATIMER: Latimer, Latimer, thou art going to speak before the high and mighty King Henry the Eighth, who is able, if he think fit, to take thy life away. Be careful what thou sayest. But Latimer, Latimer, remember also thou art about to speak before the King of Kings and Lord of Lords. Take heed that thou dost not displease Him.

BE OF GOOD CHEER

In the year 1555, Hugh Latimer and Nicholas Ridley were sentenced to die by burning for their Christian beliefs.

An old chronicle records their last words:

"When Master Latimer stood at the stake and the tormentors were about to set fire upon him and that most Reverend Doctor Ridley, he lifted up his eyes to heaven with a most amiable and comfortable countenance, saying these words: 'God is faithful who does not suffer us to be tempted above our strength.'

"And addressing himself to Master Ridley he said: 'Be of good comfort, Master Ridley, and play the man; we shall this day light such a candle by God's grace in England as I trust shall never be put out.'"

INADEQUACY

AFRICAN ENVOY TO THE UNITED NATIONS: You fly through the air like birds and you swim in the sea like fish, but how to walk on the earth like brothers you do not know.

ANNO DOMINI 1676

JUDGE: Why can't you give up public meetings? The law does not stop you from talking to people one by one!

JOHN BUNYAN: But if I may talk to one, why not to two? And if to two, why not to three? And if to three, why not to four? And we shall soon have a meeting!

FOOLISH WORDS

When Denis Diderot, an eighteenth-century French philosopher, visited Russia by invitation of Empress Catherine the Great, he greeted Archbishop Platon with the words, "Non est Deus" ("There is no God").

The Archbishop's instant reply was a verse from Psalm 14 which he quoted in Latin: "The fool hath said in his heart there is no God."

ROAD OR NO ROAD

MISSION BOARD EXECUTIVE: Dr. Livingstone, is there a good road to where you are? If so, we have a couple of men who would like to come and help you.

DAVID LIVINGSTONE: If they need a good road, don't send them. I need men who can come, road or no road.

MOUNTAIN PILGRIMAGE

SIR EDMUND HILLARY (*the New Zealander when he had reached the top of Mt. Everest in 1953*): Damn good feeling!

TENZING NORKAY (*Sherpa herdsman and expedition guide*): I thought of God and the greatness of His work. I have a feeling for climbing to the top and there making worship closer to God. Not the same feeling of English Sahib who wants only to conquer the mountain. I feel more like making pilgrimage.

FRIEND: What would be a good thing for me to do every day to improve my inner life?

GOETHE: Read a stirring poem, look upon a marvelous picture, listen to some superior soul, and speak some useful, sensible words to the people you meet.

ANGEL'S SONG

Kind words are the music of the world. They have a power which seems to be beyond natural causes, as though they were some angel's song which had lost its way and come to earth.

FREDERICK WILLIAM FABER,
1814–1863

DAVID LIVINGSTONE: What is holiness?

AFRICAN CHIEFTAIN: When showers have fallen in the night and the earth is washed clean, and when the sun sparkles on every leaf and the air is fresh—that is holiness.

DIALOGUE BETWEEN PETER AND GOD

Why do you suffer all these cruel and unclean things? asked Peter.

You don't like it? said the Lord God, without any sign either of apology or explanation.

No, said Peter.

Then change it, said the Lord God.

But how are we to change it?

If you have no will to change it, you have no right to criticize it, said the Lord God, leaning back with the weariness of one who had to argue with each generation from Job onward—precisely the same arguments.

H. G. WELLS, 1866–1946
In JOAN AND PETER

From A CHRISTMAS CAROL

SCROOGE: Dreadful apparition, why do you trouble me?

MARLEY'S GHOST: It is required of every man that the spirit within him should walk abroad among his fellow-men, and travel far and wide; and, if that spirit goes not forth in life, it is condemned to do so after death. It is doomed to wander through the world—oh, woe is me! —and witness what it cannot share, but might have shared on earth, and turned to happiness!

SCROOGE: You are fettered. Tell me why?

GHOST: I wear the chain I forged in life. I made it link by link, and yard by yard; I girded it on of my own free-will, and of my own free-will I wore it. Is its pattern strange to *you?* Or would you know the weight and length of the strong coil you bear yourself?

SCROOGE: Speak comfort to me, Jacob!

GHOST: I have none to give. It comes from other regions, Ebenezer Scrooge, and is conveyed by other ministers, to other kinds of men.

CHARLES DICKENS, 1812–1870

THE REAL SECRET

ELIZABETH BARRETT BROWNING: What is the secret of your life? Tell me, that I may make my life beautiful, too.

CHARLES KINGSLEY: I had a friend.

POSTMAN NEEDED

BISHOP NATHAN SÖDERBLOM: Your Majesty, there is a little island off the coast of Sweden. One little church, only one main street, and only a few hundred people on the island. I want you to release me of my burdens here in Stockholm and send me to that little church!

KING OF SWEDEN: Ah, yes, I know that little island. It is so very lovely. The people there need a postman to take the mail through town once a day. Bishop, I would like to be that postman!

FIRST PLACE

FRIEND: The secret of living is to put yourself in second place.

IVAN TURGENEV: No! The secret of living is to know what to put in first place!

SOLILOQUY

LAUNCELOT GOBBO (*a clown and servant to Shylock*): Certainly my conscience will serve me to run from [Shylock] my master. The fiend is at mine elbow and tempts me, saying to me, "Gobbo, Launcelot Gobbo, good Launcelot," or "good Gobbo," or "good Launcelot Gobbo, use your legs, take the start, run away." My conscience says, "No, take heed, honest Launcelot, take heed, honest Gobbo," or, as aforesaid, "honest Launcelot Gobbo, do not run, scorn running with thy heels." Well, the most courageous fiend bids me pack. "Via!" says the fiend, "away!" says the fiend, "for the heavens, rouse up a brave mind," says the fiend, "and run." Well, my conscience, hanging about the neck of my heart, says very wisely to me, "My honest friend Launcelot, being an honest man's son"—or rather an honest woman's son, for indeed my father did something smack, something grow to, he had a kind of taste—well, my conscience says, "Launcelot, budge not." "Budge," says the fiend. "Budge," says the fiend. "Budge not," says my conscience. "Conscience," say I, "you counsel well." "Fiend," say I, "you counsel well." To be ruled by my conscience, I should stay with [Shylock] my master, who, God bless the mark, is a kind of devil; and to run away from him, I should be ruled by the fiend, who, saving your reverence, is the Devil himself. Certainly [Shylock] is the very Devil incarnation, and, in my conscience, my conscience is but a kind of hard conscience to offer to counsel me to stay with [Shylock]. The fiend gives me the more friendly counsel. I will run, fiend, my heels are at your command. I will run.

WILLIAM SHAKESPEARE, 1564–1616
In THE MERCHANT OF VENICE

⚜

LET HER IN!

Magdalen at Michael's gate
  Tirled at the pin;
On Joseph's thorn sang the blackbird,
  "Let her in! Let her in!"

"Hast thou seen the wounds?" said Michael,
  "Knowest thou thy sin?"
"It is evening, evening," sang the blackbird,
  "Let her in! Let her in!"

"Yes, I have seen the wounds,
  And I know my sin."
"She knows it well, well, well," sang the blackbird,
  "Let her in! Let her in!"

"Thou bringest no offerings?" said Michael,
  "Nought save sin."
And the blackbird sang, "She is sorry, sorry, sorry!
  Let her in! Let her in!"

When he had sung himself to sleep,
  And night did begin,
One came and open'd Michael's gate,
  And Magdalen went in.

HENRY KINGSLEY, 1830–1876

⚜

I have never been hurt by anything I didn't say.

CALVIN COOLIDGE, 1872–1933

COURTESY

*We must be as courteous to a man as
to a picture, which we are willing to
give the benefit of a good light.*

RALPH WALDO EMERSON, 1803–1882

SISTER OF CHARITY

Courtesy is one of the properties of
God, who gives His sun and rain to
the just and the unjust by courtesy; and
courtesy is the sister of charity, by
which hatred is extinguished and love
is cherished.

ST. FRANCIS OF ASSISI, 1182–1226

PRACTICAL ADVICE

When you go forth from your door, behave to all you meet as though you
were meeting some distinguished
guest. When employing the people,
be as though you were taking part in a
religious ceremony. For what you
would not wish done to yourself, do
not unto others.

CONFUCIUS, 500 B.C.

NURSERY RHYME

Hearts, like doors, will ope with ease
To very, very little keys,
And don't forget that two of these
Are "I thank you" and "If you please."

OPEN THE DOOR

Hail! ye small sweet courtesies of life;
for smooth do ye make the road of it,
like grace and beauty, which beget inclination to love at first sight. It is ye
who open the door and let the stranger
in.

LAURENCE STERNE, 1713–1768

GENTLY WITH LOVE

Politeness has been defined as love in
trifles.

Courtesy is said to be love in little
things.

And the one secret of politeness is
to love.

Love cannot behave itself unseemly.

You can put the most untutored
persons into the highest society, and
if they have a reservoir of love in their
hearts, they will not behave themselves
unseemly. They simply cannot do it.

The word "gentleman" means a
gentle man, a man who does things
gently with love. And that is the whole
art and mystery of it.

HENRY DRUMMOND, 1851–1897

SOMETHING SO SIMPLE

Goodness is something so simple: always to live for others, never to seek one's own advantage.

DAG HAMMARSKJÖLD, 1905–1961

BROTHERS AND SISTERS

Francis had pets, a lamb, a pheasant, a rabbit, a cicada, a dog, a wolf, but upon honest and unsentimental terms. For he was as polite and considerate to an earthworm, a slug, a bird, a beetle, or a mole, as amusedly tolerant and withal, understanding and warmly loving as one would be to one's brothers and sisters.

Indeed, they were his brothers and sisters. He called them so, not with the pious emptiness the words have come to connote in modern times, but with the deep conviction of kinship.

It is told of him that he would stop to remove an earthworm from his path so as not to crush it. One feels that with Francis it was a personal as well as symbolic courtesy to something living he happened to encounter.

There appears to be a touch of the child's world in this, but it is really an intensely practical way of life aboard an overpopulated planet, and what is more, it has the great advantage of beauty over ugliness.

Looking back to the daily joy and happiness that Francis managed to crowd into the forty-four years of his life, it is not difficult to understand that it is better to be kind than unkind and to be generous and accommodating instead of rude and possessive. This is not childish. It is one of the most adult discoveries ever made.

And one notes with equal satisfaction that Francis expected a full return of courtesies and what is more, he got it. For in that state of Nature which exists in the faith that all is divinely created with love and delight in beauty —and who shall say that a maggot, a spider, a rat or a hippopotamus is not beautiful in the eyes of God—there must be give as well as take.

Thus there is no difficulty in understanding his request to the noisy swallows—wheeling, looping, twittering in the late afternoon sky, drowning out Francis's attempt to preach with their chatter. "My brothers and sisters, the swallows, it is now time for me to speak. You have been speaking enough all the time. Give me leave to be heard."

It is recorded that the swallows piped down.

CLARE BOOTHE LUCE

MY DAILY CREED

Let me be a little kinder,
    Let me be a little blinder
To the faults of those about me;
    Let me praise a little more;
Let me be, when I am weary,
    Just a little bit more cheery;
Let me serve a little better
    Those that I am striving for.

Let me be a little braver
    When temptation bids me waver;
Let me strive a little harder
    To be all that I should be;
Let me be a little meeker
    With the brother that is weaker;
Let me think more of my neighbor
    And a little less of me.

AUTHOR UNKNOWN

Children in America used to reply to their elders, "Yes'm" and "No, Sir."

But they don't often do it anymore.

Maybe it's because their elders themselves rarely say "Thank you" or "Excuse me."

Has basic politeness gone the way of the biplane and the nickel cigar?

Has Sir Walter Raleigh's cloak given way to a poke in the ribs as a man races a woman for a seat on the bus?

Someone once said, "Rudeness is a weak man's imitation of strength."

Now that technology has surpassed the gentle art of human relations, perhaps a return to modest simple politeness could lead to a better understanding among all people.

It is inconceivable that a man thoughtful enough to answer his mail promptly, or return a fallen mop to a charwoman, or teach a child to be mannerly, would ever want to press the button marked "Cobalt-bomb."

NEWSWEEK

From MACBETH

The king-becoming graces—
As justice, verity, temperance, stableness,
Bounty, perseverance, mercy, lowliness,
Devotion, patience, courage, fortitude.

WILLIAM SHAKESPEARE, 1564–1616

DESIGNATION

God appoints our graces
to be nurses
to other men's weaknesses.

HENRY WARD BEECHER, 1813–1887

Small kindnesses, courtesies, considerations, habitually practiced in our social intercourse, give a greater charm to the character than the display of great talents and accomplishments.

MARY ANN KELTY

COURTESY

Of courtesy, it is much less
Than Couarge of Heart or Holiness,
Yet in my Walks it seems to me
That the Grace of God is in Courtesy.

On Monks I did in Storrington call,
They took me straight into their Hall;
I saw Three Pictures on a wall,
And Courtesy was in them all.

The first the Annunciation;
The second the Visitation;
The third the Consolation,
Of God that was Our Lady's Son.

The first was of St. Gabriel;
On wings a-flame from Heaven he fell;
And as he went upon one knee
He shone with Heavenly Courtesy.

Our Lady out of Nazareth rode—
It was her month of heavy load;
Yet was her face both great and kind,
For Courtesy was in her Mind.

The third it was Our Little Lord,
Whom all the Kings in arms adored;
He was so small you could not see
His large intent of Courtesy.

Our Lord, that was Our Lady's Son,
God bless you, People, one by one,
My Rhyme is written, my work is done.

HILAIRE BELLOC, 1870–1953

Gratitude is the mother of all the virtues.

CICERO, 106–43 B.C.

From IN MEMORIAM

The churl in spirit, howe'er he veil
His want in forms for fashion's sake,
Will let his coltish nature break
At seasons thro' the gilded pale;

For who can always act? but he,
To whom a thousand memories call,
Not being less but more than all
The gentleness he seem'd to be,

Best seem'd the thing he was, and join'd
Each office of the social hour
To noble manners, as the flower
And native growth of noble mind.

ALFRED TENNYSON, 1809–1892

MORAL FOUNDATION

There is no outside sign of true courtesy that does not rest on a deep moral foundation.

JOHANN WOLFGANG VON GOETHE,
1749–1832

Gratitude is the praise we offer God:
    for teachers kind,
benefactors never to be forgotten,
for all who have advantaged me,
by writings, sermons, converse,
prayers, examples, for all these
    and all others
which I know, which I know not, open,
    hidden,
remembered, and forgotten.

LANCELOT ANDREWES, 1555–1626

OUR LORD'S COURTESY

Christian women should take considerable comfort from our Lord's constant courtesy in recognizing the equal worth and equal necessity of women in every relationship.

All women should read the Gospel of Luke with keen appreciation of the alternation of the stories about men and women through his text, even in the arrangement of the parables: a shepherd's lost sheep balanced by a housewife's lost coin; the Kingdom likened to a farmer's mustard seed and to a cook's leaven.

Indeed the choice of bread and wine for one permanent memorial meant selecting elements in which the hands of men and women were equally needed in vineyard and kitchen.

Actually the choice of water and fruit would have seemed more literally Divine. But no, the Lord was and is dependent on human help.

BEHAVIOR

Always behave as if nothing had happened no matter what has happened.

ARNOLD BENNETT, 1867–1931

All doors open to courtesy.

THOMAS FULLER, 1608–1661

SEVEN WORDS

Good manners may in Seven
    Words be found:
Forget yourself and think of
    Those around.

ARTHUR GUITERMAN, 1871–1943

In all the affairs of life,
social as well as political,
courtesies of a small
and trivial character
are the ones
which strike deepest
to the grateful
and appreciating heart.

HENRY CLAY, 1777–1852

THE SAINT'S COURTESY

Many of us are capable of outstanding acts of courtesy—we call them "gestures," as though they were offhand superficialities—and forget the small ones.

The saint's courtesy is marked by never forgetting them. Their lives are no continuous display of heroic acts, of breath-taking self-belittlement, but rather a routine of small courtesies, often almost unobservable.

They can only proceed from those striving humbly to follow in the footsteps of Him who patiently accepted the discourtesies of the world and prayed that they be not laid up to its charge.

RICHARDSON WRIGHT

A gentleman is someone who puts in more than he takes out.

GEORGE BERNARD SHAW, 1856–1950

The small courtesies sweeten life; the greater, ennoble it.

CHRISTIAN NESTELL BOVEE,
1820–1904

No one is useless in this world who lightens the burden of it to anyone else.

CHARLES DICKENS, 1812–1870

GREETING THE DAY

To awaken each morning with a smile
brightening my face;
To greet the day with reverence for the
opportunities it contains;
To approach my work with a clean
mind;
To hold ever before me, even in the
doing of little things, the Ultimate
Purpose toward which I am working;
To meet men and women with laughter
on my lips and love in my heart;
To be gentle, kind, and courteous
through all the hours;
To approach the night with weariness
that ever woos sleep, and the joy that
comes from work well done—
This is how I desire to waste wisely
my days.

THOMAS DEKKER, 1572–1632

Drop a pebble in the water,
  And its ripples reach out far;
And the sunbeams dancing on them
  May reflect them to a star.

Give a smile to some one passing,
  Thereby make his morning glad;
It will greet you in the evening
  When your own heart may be sad.

Do a deed of simple kindness;
  Though its end you may not see,
It may reach, like widening ripples,
  Down a long eternity.

JAMES W. FOLEY

DELIGHT

Joy is the most infallible
sign of the presence of God.

LEON BLOY, 1846–1917

EXPLANATION

It is a comely fashion to be glad,
Joy is the grace we say to God.

JEAN INGELOW, 1820–1897

COUNTLESS INFINITESIMALS

The happiness of life is made up of minute fractions—the little soon-forgotten charities of a kiss or smile, a kind look, a heartfelt compliment, and the countless infinitesimals of pleasurable and genial feeling.

SAMUEL T. COLERIDGE, 1772–1834

THE TEST

The real test of a happy life is to see how much pain and loss and frustration can be endured and absorbed without spoiling the joy of it.

RUFUS M. JONES, 1863–1948

GIFT FOR A FRIEND

If, instead of a gem
or even a flower,
we could cast the gift
of a lovely thought
into the heart of a friend,
that would be giving
as angels give.

GEORGE MACDONALD, 1824–1905

A MEDIEVAL PRAYER

Help us this day, O God, to serve Thee devoutly, and the world busily. May we do our work wisely, give succour secretly, go to our meat appetitely, sit thereat discreetly, arise temperately, please our friend duly, go to bed merrily, sleep surely; for joy of our Lord Jesus Christ.

He who bends to himself a Joy
Does the wingèd life destroy;
But he who kisses the Joy at it flies
Lives in Eternity's sunrise.

WILLIAM BLAKE, 1757–1827

Happiness and Trouble stand at everyone's gate. Yours is the choice which you will invite in.

CHINESE PROVERB

There is no duty
we so underrate
as the duty
of being happy.
A happy man or woman
is a better thing
to find
than a five-pound note.

ROBERT LOUIS STEVENSON,
1850–1894

ABSURDLY HAPPY

In the Sermon on the Mount, Jesus promised His disciples three things— that they would be entirely fearless, absurdly happy, and that they would get into trouble. They did get into trouble, and found to their surprise, that they were not afraid. They were absurdly happy, for they laughed over their own troubles and only cried over other people's.

W. H. MALTBY

THE CELESTIAL SURGEON

If I have faltered more or less
In my great task of happiness;
If I have moved among my race
And shown no glorious morning face;
If beams from happy human eyes
Have moved me not; if morning skies,
Books, and my food, and summer rain
Knocked on my sullen heart in vain:
Lord, Thy most pointed pleasure take
And stab my spirit broad awake;
Or, Lord, if too obdurate I,
Choose Thou, before that spirit die,
A piercing pain, a killing sin,
And to my dead heart run them in!

ROBERT LOUIS STEVENSON,
1850–1894

THE OPEN WORLD

If I were to choose the sights, the sounds, the fragrances I most want to see and hear and smell—among the delights of the open world—on a final day on earth, I think I would choose these:

the clear, ethereal song of a white-throated sparrow singing at dawn;

the smell of pine trees in the room;

the lonely calling of Canada geese;

the sight of a dragon-fly glinting in the sunshine;

the voice of a hermit thrush far in a darkening woods at evening;

and—most spirited and moving of sights—the white cathedral of a cumulus cloud floating serenely in the blue of the sky.

EDWIN WAY TEALE

TRIFLES MATTER

Since trifles make the sum of human
    things,
And half our miseries from our foibles
    springs;
Since life's best joys consist in peace
    and ease;
And though but few can serve yet all
    can please;
O! let the ungentle spirit learn from
    hence
A small unkindness is a great offence.
To spread large bounties, though we
    wish in vain,
Yet all may shun the guilt of giving
    pain.

HANNAH MORE, 1745–1831

I want what God wants. That's why I am so merry.

ST. FRANCIS OF ASSISI, 1182–1226

DIVINE CONCERT

We are all strings in the concert of
His joy.

JACOB BOEHME, 1575–1624

WITTY GAIETY

List the things which delight you in
another person, and how often it is
actually Aristotle's ancient phrase, "the
virtue of witty gaiety." Juliana of Norwich in the year 1200 was blithe and
laughter-loving as she wrote about "our
dearworthie Lord": "Then was my
herte right merrie."

ATTITUDE

The attitude of unhappiness is not only
painful, it is also mean and ugly.

What can be more base and unworthy than the pining, puling, mump-
ing mood, no matter by what outward
ills it may have been engendered?

What is more injurious to others?

What less helpful as a way out of
difficulty?

It but fastens and perpetuates the
trouble which occasioned it, and increases the total evil of the situation.

WILLIAM JAMES, 1842–1910

SUCCESS

If the day and the night are such that
you greet them with joy, and life emits
a fragrance like flowers and sweet-
scented herbs, is more elastic, more
starry, more immortal—that is your
success.

HENRY DAVID THOREAU, 1817–1862

SEVENTEENTH-CENTURY GERMAN CAROL

The whole bright world rejoices now,
  Hilariter, hilariter;
The birds do sing on every bough,
  Alleluya, Alleluya.

Then shout beneath the racing skies,
  Hilariter, hilariter;
To him who rose that we might rise,
  Alleluya, Alleluya.

And all you living things make praise,
  Hilariter, hilariter;
He guideth you on all your ways,
  Alleluya, Alleluya.

He, Father, Son, and Holy Ghost,
  Hilariter, hilariter;
Our God most high, our joy and boast,
  Alleluya, Alleluya.

From A LITTLE TE DEUM

For all things beautiful, and good, and
  true;
For things that seemed not good, yet
  turned to good;
For all the sweet compulsions of Thy
  will
That chased, and tried, and wrought us
  to Thy shape;
For things unnumbered that we take of
  right,
For value first when first they are
  withheld;
For light and air; sweet sense of sound
  and smell;
For ears to hear the heavenly har-
  monies;
For eyes to see the unseen in the seen;
For vision of The Worker in the work;
For hearts to apprehend Thee every-
  where;
    We thank Thee, Lord!

JOHN OXENHAM, 1852–1941

TO ENJOY THE WORLD

You never enjoy the world aright—
   till your spirit filleth the whole
earth,
   till the sea itself floweth in your
veins,
   till you are clothed with the heavens
and crowned with the stars,
   till you perceive yourself to be the
sole heir of the whole world, and more
than so, because men are in it who are
everyone sole heirs as well as you.

You never enjoy the world aright—
   till your spirit filleth the whole
earth,
   till you are as familiar with the ways
of God in all ages as with your own
walk and table.

You never enjoy the world aright—
   till your spirit filleth the whole
earth,
   till you love men so as to desire their
happiness with a thirst equal to the zeal
for your own happiness.

You never enjoy the world aright—
   till your spirit filleth the whole
earth,
   till you can sing and rejoice and delight in God, as misers do in gold and
kings in sceptres.

You never enjoy the world aright—
   till your spirit filleth the whole
earth,
   till the stars are your jewels,
   till you are intimately acquainted
with that out of which the world was
made.

You never enjoy the world aright—
   till your spirit filleth the whole
earth,
   till you remember how lately you
were made and how wonderful it was
when you came into it, and more rejoice in the palace of your glory than if
it had been made but in the morning
of this day.

You never enjoy the world aright—
   till your spirit filleth the whole
earth,
   till you delight in God's goodness to
all men everywhere.

THOMAS TRAHERNE, 1637–1674

RELIANCE

There is the strange kind of reliance
on the grace of God which one calls
humor.

ISAK DINESEN, 1885–1962

SUFFICIENCY

To whom little is not enough, nothing
is enough.
   Give me a barley cake and a glass of
water, and I am ready to rival Zeus for
happiness.

EPICURUS, 341–270 B.C.

TRUE RELIGION

No religion is a true religion which
does not make men tingle to their fin-
gertips with a sense of infinite hazard.

WILLIAM HAZLITT, 1778–1830

From PARACELSUS

            For every joy is gain,
And gain is gain, however small.

ROBERT BROWNING, 1812–1889

From ENDYMION

A thing of beauty is a joy for ever:
Its loveliness increases; it will never
Pass into nothingness; but still will
    keep
A bower for us, and a sleep
Full of sweet dreams, and health, and
    quiet breathing.
Therefore, on every morrow, are we
    wreathing
A flowery band to bind us to the earth,
Spite of despondence, of the inhuman
    dearth
Of noble natures, of the gloomy days,
Of all the unhealthy and o'er-darken'd
    ways
Made for our searching: yes, in spite
    of all,
Some shape of beauty moves away the
    pall
From our dark spirits. Such the sun,
    the moon,
Trees old and young, sprouting a shady
    boon
For simple sheep; and such are daffo-
    dils
With the green world they live in; and
    clear rills
That for themselves a cooling covert
    make
'Gainst the hot season; the mid-forest
    brake,
Rich with a sprinkling of fair musk-
    rose blooms:
And such too is the grandeur of the
    dooms
We have imagined for the mighty
    dead;
All lovely tales that we have heard
    or read:
An endless fountain of immortal drink,
Pouring unto us from the heaven's
    brink.

Nor do we merely feel these essences

For one short hour; no, even as the
    trees
That whisper round a temple become
    soon
Dear as the temple's self, so does the
    moon,
The passion poesy, glories infinite,
Haunt us till they become a cheering
    light
Unto our souls, and bound to us so
    fast,
That, whether there be shine, or gloom
    o'ercast,
They always must be with us, or we
    die.

JOHN KEATS, 1795–1821

INEVITABLE

Always the inmost becomes the out-
most.

RALPH WALDO EMERSON,
1803–1882

The children of men that are wander-
    ing by,
Each with his packet of dreams and
    sandals of pain,
Each with a soul as vast as God's
    dreams are—
Little and lonely under the evening
    star.

AUTHOR UNKNOWN

UNFORGIVABLE SIN

Perhaps the unforgivable sin is to have
lived with something beautiful and not
have recognized it.

AUTHOR UNKNOWN

PATTERNS OF DELIGHT

Even with little else to see
Of the world's bewildering array
Of form and color, one might be
Well occupied, day after day,
Observing clouds. Enormous black
And silver clouds, ballooning by,
And gray outrider clouds that crack
Explosive whips across the sky,
And chubby little puffs of white
And pink, and massive piles of gold—
So many patterns of delight,
So various, the sky can hold,
Our eyes would have enough to do
Without this earth to notice too!

JANE MERCHANT

JOY OF LIFE

This is the true joy of life, the being used for a purpose recognized by yourself as a mighty one; the being thoroughly worn out before you are thrown on the scrapheap; the being a force of Nature instead of a feverish, selfish little clod of ailments and grievances, complaining that the world will not devote itself to making you happy.

GEORGE BERNARD SHAW, 1856–1950

THE SOUL'S DUTY

We should tell ourselves once and for all that it is the first duty of the soul to become as happy, complete, independent, and great as lies in its power.

To this end we may sacrifice even the passion for sacrifice, for sacrifice never should be the means of ennoblement, but only the sign of being ennobled.

MAURICE MAETERLINCK, 1862–1949

THE BONUS OF LAUGHTER

Life pays a bonus to those who learn that laughter is a vital part of living. It is one of God's richest gifts. The Lord loves a cheerful giver, but he also loves the cheerful. And so does everyone else.

EDWIN DAVIS

Joy is the flag flying over the citadel of the soul indicating that the King is in residence.

AUTHOR UNKNOWN

THE DUTY OF DELIGHT

God's world is one world. If happiness is the reward of righteousness there, it should bless the children of rectitude here.

The life is of more importance than the life work. Therefore, happiness is a pursuit to be followed as tirelessly as the pursuit of wisdom or of wealth.

He who seeks to do God's will first, who puts duty before pleasure, and ranks others before himself, cannot escape the glow of happiness that comes from the sense of God's approval.

The art of living justly and kindly with one's fellows—then is not more important than the art of maintaining for oneself the sense of joy and victory over life's troubles. The duty of self-denial is not more imperative than the duty of delight.

What ripeness is to the orange, what sweet song is to the lark, what culture and refinement are to the intellect, that happiness is to man.

NEWELL DWIGHT HILLIS

WHAT IS YOUR AIM

Whose aim is his own happiness is bad,
Whose aim is the good opinion of others is weak,
Whose aim is the happiness of others is virtuous,
Whose aim is God is great.

LEO TOLSTOY, 1828–1910

BORN A TWIN

All who would win joy, must share it; happiness was born a twin.

GEORGE GORDON BYRON, 1788–1824

HIS MIRTH

Joy is the gigantic secret of the Christian.

The tremendous Figure which fills the Gospels towers in this respect, as in every other, above all the thinkers who ever thought themselves tall.

His pathos was natural, almost casual. The Stoics, ancient and modern, were proud of concealing their tears. He showed them plainly on His open face at any daily sight, such as the far sight of His native city.

Yet He concealed something. There was something that He hid from all men when He went up into a mountain to pray. There was something that He covered constantly by abrupt silence or impetuous isolation. There was some one thing that was too great for God to show men when He walked upon our earth; and I have sometimes fancied that it was His mirth.

GILBERT KEITH CHESTERTON,
1874–1936

INSTANTS OF HAPPINESS

You know the thrill of a letter or parcel that comes from someone you are fond of, far away. As you undo the string, you say, foolishly, but with a genuine quaver of sentiment, "When that was tied up, So-and-so handled it!"

Well, there are instants of preposterous happiness, clear insight, that are just like that—little packages of reality, tied up in the twine of our time sense, that come to us direct, intact, from the eternity and infinity we call God.

It matters little how you explain that great word to yourself. Perhaps you mean by it the sum total of all human awareness of beauty.

In that sense of prevailing loveliness we are all obscurely united. In those moments, moments of heavenly force and unredeemable tragedy, we can forgive ourselves for being only human.

But in these matters silence is the final eloquence. One does not argue with moonlight.

Men talk of "finding God," but no wonder it is difficult. He is hidden in that darkest of hiding places, your own heart. You yourself are a part of Him.

CHRISTOPHER MORLEY, 1890–1957

Sow the living part of yourselves in the furrow of life.

MIGUEL DE UNAMUNO, 1864–1936

YOUR NURSERY

Change is the nursery of music, joy, life, and Eternity.

JOHN DONNE, 1572–1631

HESITANCY

It is the heart that is not yet sure of its
God that is afraid to laugh in His presence.

GEORGE MACDONALD, 1824–1905

❧

DESIDERATA

Go placidly amid the noise and the
haste, and remember what peace there
may be in silence.

As far as possible without surrender
be on good terms with all persons.

Speak your truth quietly and clearly;
and listen to others, even the dull and
ignorant; they too have their story.

Avoid loud and aggressive persons.
They are vexations to the spirit.

If you compare yourself with others,
you may become vain and bitter. Always there will be greater and lesser
persons than yourself.

Enjoy your achievements as well as
your plans. Keep interested in your
own career, however humble. It is a
real possession in the changing for-
tunes of time.

Exercise caution in your business
affairs, for the world is full of trickery.
But let this not blind you to what virtue there is. Many persons strive for
high ideals. Everywhere life is full of
heroism.

Be yourself. Especially do not feign
affection.

Neither be cynical about love; for
in the face of all aridity and disen-
chantment, it is as perennial as the
grass.

Take kindly the counsel of the years,
gracefully surrendering the things of
youth.

Nurture strength of spirit to shield
you in sudden misfortune. But do not
distress yourself with imaginings.
Many fears are born of fatigue and
loneliness.

Beyond a wholesome discipline, be
gentle with yourself. You are a child
of the universe no less than the trees
and the stars. You have a right to be
here. And whether or not it is clear to
you, no doubt the universe is unfolding
as it should.

Therefore, be at peace with God,
whatever your labors and aspirations,
in the noisy confusion of life keep
peace with your soul. With all its
sham, drudgery, and broken dreams, it
is still a beautiful world.

Be careful.

Strive to be happy.

FROM SEVENTEENTH-CENTURY
MANUSCRIPT FOUND IN A BAL-
TIMORE CHURCH

DON'T

Don't be a cloud
because you can't
be a star.

TONIC

The finding of a better method, the
better understanding that insures the
better performance is hat and coat, is
food and wine, is fire and horse and
health and holiday. At least, I find
that any success in my work has the
effect on my spirits of all these.

RALPH WALDO EMERSON,
1803–1882

JOY AND PRAISE

To see what the doctrine really means, we must suppose ourselves to be in perfect love with God—drunk with, drowned in, dissolved by, that delight which, far from remaining pent up within ourselves as incommunicable, hence hardly tolerable, bliss, flows out from us incessantly again in effortless and perfect expression, our joy no more separable from the praise in which it liberates and utters itself than the brightness a mirror receives is separable from the brightness it sheds. The Scotch catechism says that man's chief end is "to glorify God and enjoy Him forever." But we shall then know that these are the same thing. Fully to enjoy is to glorify. In commanding us to glorify Him, God is inviting us to enjoy Him.

C. S. LEWIS, 1898–1963

TRUE HAPPINESS

Some have much, and some have more,
Some are rich, and some are poor,
Some have little, some have less,
Some have not a cent to bless
Their empty pockets, yet possess
True riches in true happiness.

JOHN OXENHAM, 1852–1941

VESPER THOUGHT

The reflection on a day well spent furnishes us with joys more pleasing than ten thousand triumphs.

THOMAS A KEMPIS, 1379–1471

TAKE JOY HOME

Let thy day be to thy night
A teller of good tidings. Let thy praise
Go up as birds go up that, when they wake,
Shake off the dew and soar.
So take joy home.
And make a place in thy great heart for her;
There will she come, and oft will sing to thee,
When thou art working in the furrows; ay,
Or weeding in the sacred hour of dawn.
It is a comely fashion to be glad—
Joy is the grace we say to God.
Art tired?
There is a rest remaining. Hast thou sinned?
There is a Sacrifice. Lift up thy head.
The lovely world, and the over-world alike,
Ring with a song eternal, a happy rede,
"Thy Father loves thee."

JEAN INGELOW, 1820–1897

THE MIND TO SEE

I pray not for the joy that knows
No saving benison of tears;
The placid life of ease that flows
Untroubled through the changing years.

Grant me, O God, the mind to see
The blessings which my sorrows bring;
And give me, in adversity,
The heart that still can trust and sing.

MARION FRANKLIN HAM,
1867–1956

ENTHUSIASM

*Nothing great was ever achieved
without enthusiasm. The way of life
is wonderful; it is by abandonment.*

RALPH WALDO EMERSON, 1803–1882

THE MAGIC TOUCH

There are some who possess the magic touch, the infectious spirit of enthusiasm; who have the same effect as a beautiful morning which never reaches noon. Under this spell one's mind is braced, one's spirit recreated; one is ready for any adventure, even if it only be the doing of the next disagreeable task lightheartedly.

KATE DOUGLAS WIGGIN, 1856–1923

GENIUS OF SINCERITY

Enthusiasm is the genius of sincerity, and truth accomplishes no victories without it.

EDWARD BULWER-LYTTON,
1803–1873

HEROES

They dared beyond their strength, hazarded beyond their judgment, and in extremities were of excellent hope.

THUCYDIDES, C. 460–400 B.C.

WHAT RELIGION MEANS

The submergence of self in the pursuit of an idea, the readiness to spend oneself without measure prodigally, almost ecstatically, for something great and noble, to spend oneself one knows not why—some of us like to believe that this is what religion means.

BENJAMIN NATHAN CARDOZO,
1870–1938

From ASOLANDO

One who never turned his back but
   marched breast forward,
Never doubted clouds would break,
Never dreamed, though right were
   worsted, wrong would triumph,
Held we fall to rise, are baffled to fight
   better,
Sleep to wake.

ROBERT BROWNING, 1812–1889

In things pertaining to enthusiasm, no man is sane who does not know how to be insane on proper occasions.

HENRY WARD BEECHER, 1813–1887

If a man would move the world,
he must first move himself.

SOCRATES, 469–399 B.C.

TOUCH OF IMMORTALITY

The supreme art, to which all the arts
rightly understood and used minister,
is the art of living.

The material out of which art is
made is everywhere; but the artist appears only at intervals.

The great majority use life as the
artisan uses his material; a very small
minority use it in the spirit and with
the power of the artist.

The artisan is often sincere, dili-
gent, and fairly skilful, but he is imita-
tive, conventional, and devoid of creative power.

The artist, on the other hand, is
free, individual, constructive; he sees
the higher possibilities of the material
which he commands and gives to the
familiar and commonplace a touch of
immortality.

HAMILTON WRIGHT MABIE,
1845–1917

Ten Christians who became notably
different and far better Christians
would produce a greater effect in the
world than a hundred who were in-
duced to enter the Christian life for the
first time.

The world will begin to wonder at
the Church far more through something that happens to the Christian
people themselves than it will through
some showy and dramatic increase of
its members.

HENRY DRUMMOND, 1851–1897

From A SLEEP FOR PRISONERS

Thank God our time is now when
    wrong
Comes up to face us everywhere,
Never to leave us till we take
The longest stride of soul men ever
    took.
Affairs are now soul size.
The enterprise
Is exploration into God,
Where no nation's foot has ever trod-
    den yet.

CHRISTOPHER FRY

WHAT CAN ONE DO?

You ask what you can do? You can
furnish one Christian life.

PHILLIPS BROOKS, 1835–1893

ABOUT PLYMOUTH COLONY

All great and honorable actions are
accompanied with great difficulties,
and must be both enterprised and overcome with answerable courages.

WILLIAM BRADFORD, 1590–1657

You can put two men to sleep in the
same bed, but you can't make them
dream the same dream.

CHINESE PROVERB

YOUR MARK

You cannot meet a man upon the street
without leaving your mark upon him.

RALPH WALDO EMERSON,
1803–1882

TAKING OUR BEARINGS

Where am I, astronomically speaking?
Where am I, geographically speaking?
Where am I, temporally speaking?
The only time I have is this fleeting,
significant now.
Where am I, circumstantially speaking?
Real life is lived within circum-
stances. It is master of them.
Where am I, relationally speaking?
I am a husband or wife, a son or
daughter, sister or brother, friend,
neighbor, employer or employee,
child of God. In each relationship
there is an ideal to be achieved.
Where am I, eternally speaking?
What hope is molding my life?
What vision gleams in my eyes?
What character is it toward which
I grow?

M. K. W. HEICHER, 1882–1967

TWO CREATURES

The most radical division that it is
possible to make of humanity is that
which splits it into two classes of creatures: those who make great demands
on themselves, piling up difficulties
and duties; and those who demand
nothing special of themselves, but for
whom to live is to be every moment
what they already are, without imposing on themselves any effort toward
perfection; mere buoys that float on
the water.

JOSÉ ORTEGA Y GASSET,
1883–1955

Let us walk joyfully over this earth
answering to that of God in every man.

GEORGE FOX, 1624–1691

MENTAL NEUTERS

While I am not in favor of maladjust-
ment, I view this cultivation of neutral-
ity, this breeding of mental neuters,
this hostility to eccentricity and con-
troversy, with grave misgivings. One
looks back with dismay at the possibil-
ity of a Shakespeare perfectly adjusted
to bourgeois life in Stratford, a Wesley
contentedly administrating a country
parish, George Washington going to
London to receive a barony from
George III, or Abraham Lincoln pros-
pering in Springfield with nary a concern for the preservation of the
crumbling Union.

ADLAI E. STEVENSON, 1900–1965

THE IRRESISTIBLE INTENTION

Spring shows
what God can do
with a drab and dirty world.
Deep in the heart of all things good
is the urge to grow and blossom.
One might as well order back the buds
as to defy the irresistible intention of
man
to be better!

VIRGIL A. KRAFT

ABIDING ENTHUSIASM

Happiness is the sense that one mat-
ters.
Happiness is an abiding enthusiasm.
Happiness is single-mindedness.
Happiness is whole-heartedness.
Happiness is a by-product.
Happiness is faith.

SAMUEL M. SHOEMAKER, 1893–1963

CATEGORICAL IMPERATIVE

There is but one categorical imperative: "Act only on that maxim whereby thou canst at the same time will that it should become a universal law."

IMMANUEL KANT, 1724–1804

BLIND

"Show me your God!" the doubter cries.
I point him to the smiling skies;
I show him all the woodland greens;
I show him peaceful sylvan scenes;
I show him winter snows and frost;
I show him waters tempest-tossed;
I show him hills rock-ribbed and strong;
I bid him hear the thrush's song;
I show him flowers in the close—
The lily, violet, and rose;
I show him rivers, babbling streams;
I show him youthful hopes and dreams;
I show him maids with eager hearts;
I show him toilers in the marts;
I show him stars, the moon, the sun;
I show him deeds of kindness done;
I show him joy; I show him care;
And still he holds his doubting air,
And faithless goes his way, for he
Is blind of soul, and cannot see!

JOHN KENDRICK BANGS, 1862–1922

CHALLENGE

Above the upturned faces of the brokenhearted men and women rose the calm, set features of Garibaldi, lit up with that serene and simple regard of fortitude and faith which gave him power to lead the feeble multitudes of mortal men. The sonorous, thrilling voice was heard almost to the outskirts of the vast crowd:

"I offer neither pay, nor quarters, nor provisions; I offer hunger, thirst, forced marches, battles and death. Let him who loves his country in his heart and not with his lips only, follow me."

GEORGE TREVELYAN, 1888–1928

If men revere them, they rejoice not.

If men insult them, they are not angered.

But only those are capable of this who have passed into the eternal harmony of God.

By the warmth of affection they sought the harmony of joy, to blend together all within the four seas as brothers.

And their wish was to plant this everywhere as the chief thing to be pursued.

CONFUCIUS, 500 B.C.

Every great and commanding moment in the annals of the world is the triumph of some enthusiasm.

RALPH WALDO EMERSON, 1803–1882

There are only three kinds of persons in the world: the immovable, the movable and those that move.

ARABIAN PROVERB

Years wrinkle the skin, but to give up enthusiasm wrinkles the soul.

SAMUEL ULLMAN

THE ART OF ADVENTURE

A man practices the art of adventure when he heroically faces up to life. . . . When he says, like Frank Crane: "My soul is a Columbus; and not watery wastes, nor glooming mysteries . . . shall send me back, nor make me cry 'Enough!' "

When he has the daring to open doors to new experiences and to step boldly forth to explore strange horizons.

When he is unafraid of new ideas, new theories, and new philosophies.

When he has the curiosity to experiment . . . to test and try new ways of living and thinking.

When he has the flexibility to adjust and adapt himself to the changing patterns of life.

When he refuses to seek safe places and easy tasks and has, instead, the courage to wrestle with the toughest problems and difficulties.

When he valiantly accepts the challenge of mountain-top tasks and glories in a job well done.

When he has the moral stamina to be steady in the support of those men in whom he has faith and those causes in which he believes.

When he breaks the chain of routine and renews his life through reading new books, traveling to new places, making new friends, taking up new hobbies, and adopting new viewpoints.

When he considers life a constant quest for the noblest and best.

When he has the nerve to move out of life's shallows and venture forth into the deep.

When he recognizes that the only ceiling life has is the one he gives it and comes to realize that he is surrounded by infinite possibilities for growth and achievement.

When he keeps his heart young and his expectations high and never allows his dreams to die.

When he concludes that a rut is only another name for a grave and that the only way to stay out of ruts is by living adventurously and staying vitally alive every day of his life.

WILFERD A. PETERSON

FACING THE INEVITABLE

I like the man who faces what he
    must,
    With step triumphant and a heart of
    cheer;
    Who fights the daily battle without
    fear;
Sees his hopes fail, yet keeps unfaltering trust
That God is God—that somehow, true
    and just,
    His plans work out for mortals; not
    a tear
    Is shed when fortune, which the
    world holds dear,
Falls from his grasp—better, with love,
    a crust
    Than living in dishonor: envies not,
Nor loses faith in man; but does his
    best,
    Nor ever murmurs at his humbler
    lot;
But, with a smile and words of hope,
    gives rest
    To every toiler: he alone is great
    Who by a life heroic conquers fate.

SARAH KNOWLES BOLTON,
1841–1916

FLOWERS

*If I give you a rose, you will not
doubt of God.*

CLEMENT OF ALEXANDER,
150?–220?

DIVINE AUTOGRAPH

Every rose is an autograph from the
hand of God on His world about us.
He has inscribed His thoughts in these
marvelous hieroglyphics which sense
and science have, these many thousand
years, been seeking to understand.

THEODORE PARKER, 1810–1860

From TO A YOUNG LADY

Won't you come into my garden?
I would like my roses to see you.

RICHARD BRINSLEY SHERIDAN,
1751–1816

WHAT IS CHAFF?

The sepal holds the rosebud while it
is trying to be a bud, and protects it.
Yet, when the time comes for the rose
to blossom, if that sepal is glued together, and sticks, the rose cannot blossom.

"Chaff," we say. What is chaff?
It is that which is wrapped around
the grain, and which, while it is nas-
cent, in milk, as we say, nourishes and
supplies it with the juice by which it
becomes wheat; but after it has become
wheat, shall the chaff yet stick?

HENRY WARD BEECHER, 1813–1887

From CONSIDER THE LILIES
OF THE FIELD

Flowers preach to us if we will hear:
The rose saith in the dewy morn:
"I am most fair;
Yet all my loveliness is born
Upon a thorn."
The lilies say: "Behold how we
Preach without words of purity."
But not alone the fairest flowers:
The merest grass
Along the roadside where we pass,
Lichen and moss and sturdy weed,
Tell of His love who sends the dew,
The rain and sunshine too,
To nourish one small seed.

CHRISTINA GEORGINA ROSSETTI,
1830–1894

DWELLING WITH A ROSE

A Persian fable says: One day
A wanderer found a piece of clay
So redolent of sweet perfume
Its odor scented all the room.
"What art thou?" was the quick de-
    mand,
"Art thou some gem from Samarcand?
Or spikenard rare in rich disguise?
Or other costly merchandise?"
"Nay, I am but a piece of clay."
"Then whence this wondrous sweet-
    ness, pray?"
"Friend, if the secret I disclose,
I have been dwelling with a rose."
                        AUTHOR UNKNOWN

Evening after evening in the summer,
I have gone to see the white clover fall
asleep in the meadow.

Kneeling and looking very closely,
one sees the two lower leaves on each
stalk gently approach one another like
little hands that were going to clap but
thought better of it, and at last lie
folded quietly as though for prayer.

Then the upper leaf droops, as a
child's face might, until it rests on the
others.

Everywhere in the dusk the white
clover leaves are sleeping in an attitude
of worship.

                        MARY WEBB, 1881–1927

From AUGURIES OF INNOCENCE

To see a World in a grain of sand
And a Heaven in a wild flower,
Hold Infinity in the palm of your hand
An Eternity in an hour.

                        WILLIAM BLAKE, 1757–1827

THE MOST UNFORGETTABLE FLOWER IN CHRISTENDOM

When Clovis, "Master of all Frankish
men," was on his way to be baptized
in the Cathedral at Rheims—back in
the year 496—an ancient chronicle tells
us that an angel flew down to place
three golden lilies in the hands of
Queen Clotilda.

Those three lilies are now our priceless heirloom, for a three-petalled
fleur-de-lis is the most unforgettable
flower in Christendom.

Since that time, in unbroken se-
quence, the fleur-de-lis has not only
been embroidered on the state robes
of all the royal families of France, but
also has been carved into French cathedrals and engraved on the gates of old
French cities.

Much later, when Queen Clotilda's
great-granddaughter, Bertha, was sent
across to Britain to marry King Ethel-
bert of Canterbury, the royal fleur-de-
lis went with her to become an English
emblem also; since then, to this very
day, it appears in the royal crown of
England.

Through all these long centuries the
fleur-de-lis has also always stood in
ecclesiastical usage as the symbol for
the Holy Spirit, although nobody explained exactly why or how, until half
a century ago, when scholars noticed
that the pattern of the fleur-de-lis was
undoubtedly a conventionalized dove:
the central portion bulging upward, his
body; the two out-sweeping side
flanges, his wings; the two shorter side
hooks, below, his claws; and the down-
ward plunging point, his beak—the
descent of the Dove, therefore, at
Christ's baptism.

Flowers may beckon toward us, but they speak toward heaven and God.

HENRY WARD BEECHER, 1813–1887

CLIENTS OF THE SUN

Around the year 1600, when flowers were in bloom in the Cathedral Close, the Bishop of Exeter and Norwich said:

"These flowers are true clients of the sun. How observant they are of his motion and influence.

"At even they shut up, as mourning over his departure; without whom they neither can nor would flourish in the morning. They welcome his rising with cheerful openness, and at noon are fully displayed in a free acknowledgement of his bounty.

"Thus doth the good heart unto God. When thou turnest away thy face I was troubled, saith the man after God's own heart; but in thy presence is life.

"Thus doth the carnal heart to the world. When that withdraws his favor, he is dejected; and revives with a smile.

"All is in our choice. Whatsoever is our sun will thus carry us.

"O God, be Thou to me such as Thou art in Thyself; Thou shalt be merciful in drawing me; I shall be happy in following Thee."

The famous Carl Linnaeus said almost the same thing when he carved over the lintel of his plant laboratory:

LIVE BLAMELESS

GOD IS NEAR

He also wrote in his notebook, after examining plants: "I saw God in His glory passing near me and bowed my head in worship."

From AURORA LEIGH

There are nettles everywhere,
But smooth green grasses are more common still;
The blue of heaven is larger than the cloud.

ELIZABETH BARRETT BROWNING,
1806–1861

WEEDS

All sorts of famous men have found kind words to say about weeds:

A flower is an educated weed.

LUTHER BURBANK, 1849–1926

And what is a weed? A plant whose virtues have not yet been discovered.

RALPH WALDO EMERSON,
1803–1882

A weed is no more than a flower in disguise,
Which is seen through at once, if love give a man eyes.

JAMES RUSSELL LOWELL,
1819–1891
From A FABLE FOR CRITICS

The only way to enjoy a weed is to feel unworthy of a weed . . . the strange and staggering heresy that a human being has a right to dandelions; that in some extraordinary fashion we can demand the pick of all dandelions in the garden of Paradise; that we owe no thanks for them at all and feel no wonder at them at all; and above all no wonder at being thought worthy to receive them.

GILBERT KEITH CHESTERTON,
1874–1936

From SHE DWELT AMONG
THE UNTRODDEN WAYS

A violet, by a mossy stone
  Half hidden from the eye!
Fair as a star, when only one
  Is shining in the sky.
        WILLIAM WORDSWORTH, 1770–1850

GARDEN

Who rears four walls around a little
    plot—
Some still, secluded spot—
And digs and sows therein, has done
    a thing
Beyond his reckoning.
In a small, fended space,
Beauty and deep untellable content
Make their abiding place.
And measureless peace is pent.
There time takes note of tender hap-
    penings,
The shimmer of a butterfly's blue
    wings—
Above the clustered phlox;
A spider's will to work a miracle
Between two hollyhocks;
The twilight cricket's humble prophe-
    cies;
A brown bird by a pole; and all that
    goes
Into the lovely life-time of a rose;
A pansy's lore; and little questing bees'
Strange sweet biographies.

Who makes a garden plans beyond his
    knowing,
Old roads are lost; old dwellings have
    their day;
And he himself, far summoned, passes
    hence
An unfamiliar way.
But lo, he has not perished with his
    going,

For year by year as April's heart is
    stirred,
Spring after punctual Spring,
Across the little acre's wintry gray
Comes, slowly traced, an old authentic
    word
In radiant lettering:
A shining script of tendril, vine, and
    whorl,
New green, faint rose, clear lavender,
    and pearl.
Petal by delicate petal, leaf by leaf . . .
As though his own hand from the
    Mystery
Wrote, for all earth to see upon
A fadeless, beauteous scroll, his brief
For immortality.
                    NANCY BYRD TURNER

SWEET PEAS

Here are sweet peas, on tiptoe for a
    flight:
With wings of gentle flush o'er deli-
    cate white,
And taper fingers catching at all things,
To bind them all about with tiny rings.
Linger awhile upon some bending
    planks
That lean against a streamlet's rushy
    banks,
And watch intently Nature's gentle
    doings:
They will be found softer than ring-
    dove's cooings.
How silent comes the water round the
    bend!
Not the minutest whisper does it send
To the o'erhanging sallows: blades of
    grass
Slowly across the chequer'd shadows
    pass.
                    JOHN KEATS, 1795–1821

PRAYER RUG

Here by me is a prayer-rug, just wide enough to kneel on, of the richest gold interwoven with crimson. All the Sultans of the East never had such beauty as that to kneel on.

It is, indeed, too beautiful to kneel on, for the life in these golden flowers must not be broken down even for that purpose. They must not be defaced, not a stem bent; it is more reverent not to kneel on them, for this carpet prays itself. I will sit by it and let it pray for me.

It is so common, the bird's foot lotus, it grows everywhere; yet if I purposely searched for days I should not have found a plot like this, so rich, so golden, so glowing with sunshine.

You might pass by it in one stride, yet it is worthy to be thought of for a week and remembered for a year.

RICHARD JEFFERIES, 1848–1887

TEMPLE FLOWER

And the chapiters that were upon the top of the pillars were of lily work in the porch. . . . And upon the top of the pillars was lily work. 1 Kings 7:19, 22. Hiram of Tyre directed the interior decoration and the utensils of Solomon's Temple. The lily mentioned here is the one that floats on the surfaces of lakes and pools in the Holy Land. It is a rich powder blue, with anthers of clear yellow. Fleshy stems grow up from a root not far below the bottom of the pool, and leaves that lie horizontally on the water help to support the flowers. The scent of the flowers is odd and heavy. Because of its beauty, the plant is a great favorite in the gardens of the wealthy. The rootstocks contain an abundance of nutritious starchy mucilage and sugary matter, while the seeds are filled with floury albumen and are edible. In Nubia the natives use the seeds as a grain to make bread, and in Egypt the people eat both seeds and root stocks.

WINIFRED WALKER

GOD IS HERE

God is here! I hear His voice
While thrushes make the woods rejoice.

I touch His robe each time I place
My hand against a pansy's face.

I breathe His breath if I but pass
Verbenas trailing through the grass.

God is here! From every tree
His leafy fingers beckon me.

MADELEINE AARON

SCENT OF FLOWERS

The origin of flower scents is full of mystery. Sometimes they seem to run through the minute veins like an ichor, as in wallflowers, with their scented petals; sometimes they are locked in the pollen casket or brim the nectarcups; sometimes they come from the leaf-pores, as in balm, and sometimes from the roots in addition, as in primroses and lilies. The essence lies in the arms of that small creature, the seed, who seldom tells her secret.

MARY WEBB, 1881–1927

A GARDEN CLUB LESSON

Garden club members will be richer for remembering that back in the days when the Conquistadores returned to Spain from Peru and Mexico they brought home gifts, even as good husbands always do.

And what was more portable than seeds? Especially with such surprising stories to share.

For instance, sunflower seeds. Over in Peru, the men would say, in all religious processionals the sun-worshiping Inca priestesses would carry tall yellow sunflowers as ceremoniously as Catholic priests carry crucifixes. All because this particular flower kept its face turned toward the sun when he rose and turned toward the sun when he set.

Therefore, the Inca priestesses ate the sunflower seeds. Curious? Well, yes, of course; but it may have seemed as much of a Eucharist rite for an Inca as the Loaf and the Cup seemed to a Christian.

The husbands also brought back to Spain all sorts of other seeds from flowers which were sun-turning: morning glories, four o'clocks, heliotrope, marigolds, cosmos, zinnias, and nasturtiums.

There must have been considerable suspense in many an old Spanish garden, waiting for these strange seeds to bloom in a new climate and in unknown soil. Would the flowers ever come? When they did, spectacular and vivid, all was well.

Spanish bees enjoyed their flavor, and helped to spread the species. And many Spanish fathers also helped, by going over the Pyrenees to France, carrying gifts in their pockets for French hosts and hostesses.

Again, what more portable or unusual than seeds from the New World? When the flowers bloomed in France, and the French bees improved each shining hour, then once more there were lands tied together so delightfully that when Frenchmen crossed the English Channel into Britain it seemed to be a pleasant piece of courtesy to take along some seeds.

By the time the Pilgrims began crossing the Atlantic toward our bleak and rock-bound coast, practically every trunk had seeds from some old English garden to keep the Colonists from feeling homesick. This meant that, moment by moment, ever since leaving Peru, flowers had been tying the two Americas together the long way around.

⚜

FAMILIARITY

Carl Linnaeus, the famous Swedish naturalist, found it unfortunate that, in every foreign soil, each flower was given a different name. Therefore, he gave them Latin names, which need not be changed from place to place, no matter what other names people called them.

All very universal and scientific, of course. But just as a "forget-me-not" sounds more unforgettably blue and familiar in English than the formidable Latin "myosotis" ever could, so a similar thing was happening to the Bible in Latin. It fell on deaf unloving ears, until John Wyclif gave men "God in English." Then devotion quickened until that seed, too, tied lands together into one common cause called Christendom.

FLOWERS

For the Flowers are great blessings.

For the Flowers have their Angels, even the words of God's creation.

For the Flower glorifies God and the root parries the adventure.

For there is a language of flowers.

For Flowers are peculiarly the poetry of Christ.

For I am under the same accusation with my Saviour—for they said, He is beside Himself.

For the officers of the peace are at variance with me and the watchman smites me with his staff.

For Silly Fellow! is against me and belongeth neither to me nor to my family.

For I am in twelve hardships, but He that was born of a virgin shall deliver me out of all.

For He is a Spirit, and therefore He is God.

For He is King, and therefore He is God.

For Love is love, and therefore He is God.

For Musick is Musick, and therefore He is God. . . .

Hallelujah from the heart of God, and from the hand of the Artist inimitable, and from the echo of the heavenly harp—in sweetness magnifical and mighty. Hallelujah.

CHRISTOPHER SMART, 1722–1771

ASSURANCE

When that persevering traveller, Mungo Park, was at one period of his course fainting in the vast wilderness of an Africa desert, naked and alone, considering his days as numbered and nothing appearing to remain for him to do but to lie down and die, a small moss-flower of extraordinary beauty caught his eye.

"Though the whole plant," says he, "was no larger than one of my fingers, I could not contemplate the delicate conformation of its roots, leaves, and capsules without admiration.

"Can that Being who planted, watered, and brought to perfection, in this obscure part of the world, a thing which appears of so small importance, look with unconcern upon the situation and suffering of creatures formed after His own image?

"Surely not.

"Reflections like these would not allow me to despair; I started up and, disregarding both hunger and fatigue, travelled forward, assured that relief was at hand; and I was not disappointed."

ERNEST HEMINGWAY, 1899–1961

From NO TIME LIKE THE OLD TIME

Fame is the scentless sunflower, with gaudy crown of gold;
But friendship is the breathing rose, with sweets in every fold.

OLIVER WENDELL HOLMES, 1809–1894

IMMINENCE

His tenderness in the springing grass,
His beauty in the flowers,
His living love in the sun above—
All here, and near, and ours.

CHARLOTTE PERKINS GILMAN, 1860–1935

HEIRLOOMS

Every man of us has all the centuries
in him.

JOHN MORLEY, 1888–1923

NOTHING IS EVER COMPLETED

What the father has made, the son can make and enjoy, but he has also work of his own appointed to him. Thus all things wax and roll onwards—arts, establishments, opinions; nothing is ever completed, but completing.

THOMAS CARLYLE, 1795–1881

HERITAGE

Heritage is an omnibus in which all our ancestors ride, and every once in a while one of them puts his head out the window and embarrasses all the rest of us.

OLIVER WENDELL HOLMES,
1809–1894

When ancient opinions and rules of life are taken away, the loss cannot possibly be estimated. From that moment we have no compass to govern us, nor can we know to what port to steer.

EDMUND BURKE, 1729–1797

OUR GREATEST DEBT

Notwithstanding the revolt of the new generation, human experience cannot be annihilated, nor can the traits it has produced in us be obliterated or ignored. The human past shines upon us like a great light.

There is one supreme human relationship, that which has created the home and made the family fireside the source out of which man's highest qualities have grown up to transform the world. As historical fact, it is to family life that we owe the greatest debt which the mind of man can conceive.

The echoes of our own past from immemorial ages bid us unmistakably to venerate, to cherish, and to preserve a relationship to which the life of man owes this supreme debt.

JAMES H. BREASTED, 1863–1935

THE NEXT GENERATION SPEAKS

"You know, Dad, that vase which has been in our family for generations? Well, this generation has broken it!"

PROPER RESPECT

It is one proof of a good education, and of a true refinement of feeling, to respect antiquity.

LYDIA H. SIGOURNEY, 1791–1865

PETER'S LITTLE BOAT

How astonished the Apostle Peter would have been if he could have known that the very shape of his old fishing craft would actually govern church architecture down to this mid-century moment in Christian history.

The word "navy" comes from the Latin word "navis," meaning ship. "Nave" comes from this same word "navis."

This ship is Peter's little boat, in which the disciples were always safe when their Lord was on board; for the nave is, of course, the place where the people sit. In an early church document, *Apostolic Constitutions,* dating from the third century the specific directions read:

"When thou callest an assembly of the church as one that is the commander of a great ship, appoint the assemblies to be made with all possible skill, charging the deacons as mariners to prepare places for the brethren as for passengers, with all due care and decency.

"But first let the building be oblong, with its head towards the east, with its vestries on both sides at the east end, so that it will be like a ship. In the middle let the bishop's throne be placed, and on each side of him let the presbytery sit down; and let the deacons stand near at hand, in close and small girt garments, for they are like

the mariners and managers of the ship: with regard to these, let the laity sit on the other side, with all quietness and good order."

Memory is a capricious and arbitrary creature.

You never can tell what pebble she will pick up from the shore of life to keep among her treasures, or what inconspicuous flower of the field she will preserve as the symbol of thoughts that do often "lie too deep for tears."

And yet I do not doubt that the most important things are always the best remembered.

HENRY VAN DYKE, 1852–1933

SIXTEENTH-CENTURY HEIRLOOM

God be in myn hede
And in myn understandynge.

God be in myn eyen
And in myn lokynge.

God be in myn mouth
And in myn spekynge.

God be in myn herte
And in myn thynkynge.

God be at myn ende
And at myn departynge.

SARUM PRIMER, 1529

Let men know by your deeds who your ancestors were.

JAPANESE PROVERB

RAISED AND BORNE ALOFT

We are like dwarfs seated on the shoulders of giants. We see more things than the ancients and things more distant, but this is due neither to the sharpness of our own sight, nor to the greatness of our own stature, but because we are raised and borne aloft on that giant mass.

ST. BERNARD OF CLAIRVAUX
1091–1153

IN STAR, STONE, FLESH AND SOUL

I have gone the whole round of creation: I saw and I spoke:
I, a work of God's hand for that purpose, received in my brain
And pronounced on the rest of His handwork—returned Him again
His creation's approval or censure: I spoke as I saw. . . .
Do I task any faculty highest, to image success?
I but open my eyes—and perfection, no more and no less,
In the kind I imagined, full-fronts me, and God is seen God
In the star, in the stone, in the flesh, in the soul and the clod.
And thus looking within and around me, I ever renew
(With that stoop of the soul which in bending upraises it too)
The submission's of man's nothing-perfect to God's all complete,
As by each new obeisance in spirit, I climb to His feet.

ROBERT BROWNING, 1812–1889
From SAUL

NOSTALGIA

It has been felt that to respect tradition is to extend the vote to our ancestors. But think how ancestors themselves have kept changing—from civilized cities in England to pioneer wildernesses in Virginia and Massachusetts to Levittowns and skyscrapers; from candles to fluorescent lights; from warming pans to central-heating; from two-hour sermons on hard benches to Dial-a-Prayer at home for half a minute. Yet tradition is nostalgia; tenderness toward something basic now missing; and when such hunger controls a home, something noble could begin Christianizing the nervous systems of an entire household.

INHERITANCE

It is one thing for the Constitution to assure us of our priceless heirloom in being "created free and equal." But just how free and equal can a child be? During his first ten years—

he has inherited his parents,
he has inherited his nationality,
he has inherited his race,
he has inherited his language,
he has inherited his home,
he has inherited his neighborhood,
he has inherited his diet,
he has inherited his family customs,
he has inherited his relatives,
he has inherited his school,
he has inherited his teachers.

Moreover, in just a few square inches of his face he gives away many of the secrets of this heritage and some twist in his speech may identify others.

NOBLY REMEMBERED

Consider whether we ought not to be more in the habit of seeking honor from our descendants than from our ancestors; thinking it better to be nobly remembered than nobly born; and striving so to live, that our sons, and son's sons, for ages to come, might still lead their children reverently to the doors out of which we had been carried to the grave, saying: "Look, this was his house, this was his chamber."

JOHN RUSKIN, 1819–1900

HEIRS

We are living in a world of beauty, but few of us open our eyes to see it!

What a different place this world would be if our senses were trained to see and to hear!

We are the heirs of wonderful treasures from the past: treasures of literature and of the arts. They are ours for the asking—all our own to have and to enjoy, if only we desire them enough.

LORADO TAFT, 1860–1936

From ULYSSES

I am a part of all that I have met;
Yet all experience is an arch wherethro'
Gleams that untravell'd world whose
   margin fades
For ever and for ever when I move.
How dull it is to pause, to make an
   end,
To rush unburnish'd, not to shine in
   use!

ALFRED TENNYSON, 1809–1892

From VOICES OF THE PAST

O there are Voices of the Past,
   Links of a broken chain,
Wings that can bear me back to Times
   Which cannot come again;
Yet God forbid that I should lose
   The echoes that remain!

ADELAIDE ANN PROCTER, 1825–1864

OLD AND NEW

Old and new put their stamp on everything in nature. The snowflake that is now falling is marked by both; the present gives the motion and color to the flakes; antiquity its form and properties. All things wear a luster which is the gift of the present and a tarnish of time.

RALPH WALDO EMERSON, 1803–1882

PEDIGREES OF NATIONS

I am always sorry when any language is lost, because languages are the pedigrees of nations.

SAMUEL JOHNSON, 1709–1784

YOUR STIPEND

Jesus Christ is your inheritance,
O ye ministers of the Lord:
Jesus Christ is your sole domain:
   His name is your wealth:
   His name is your inheritance:
   His name is your stipend:
A stipend not of money but of grace,
Your inheritance is not dried up by
   heat,
Not devastated by storms.

ST. AMBROSE, 339?–397

CANNIBAL ANCESTORS

An English-speaking Christian may be tempted to look down upon a cannibal as a hopeless specimen of a degenerate race. Why spend strength upon such a wretch?

Condescension might be chastened by these words of Jerome, the Christian scholar of the fourth century:

"When I was a boy living in Gaul, I saw the Scottish people in Britain eating human flesh and though they had plenty of cattle and sheep at their disposal, yet they would prefer the ham of the herdsman or a slice of the female breast as a luxury."

Is it any special merit of ours that we, whose ancestors were also cannibals, have now a little ahead of our brethren climbed out of that horrible morass?

HARRY EMERSON FOSDICK

FINEST HOPE IS
FINEST MEMORY

The faith that life on earth is being
    shaped
To glorious ends, that order, justice,
    love,
Means man's completeness, means
    effect as sure
As roundness in the dew-drop—that
    great faith
Is but the rushing and expanding
    stream
Of thought, of feeling, fed by all the
    past.
Our finest hope is finest memory.

GEORGE ELIOT, 1819–1880
From A MINOR PROPHET

INFINITE IDEAS

For your life and mine, today and tomorrow, if we wish to maintain a republic, we must keep in mind our own part in living up to the ideas of the fathers.

This is not because they were the ideas of the fathers, but because they are infinite ideas.

They represent the eternities which are but three.

They represent faith, hope, and love.

If you please to put it so, they rest on absolute religion, the religion in which all men are of one blood.

EDWARD EVERETT HALE, 1822–1909

HERITAGE

"The lines have fallen unto me in
    pleasant places,
Yea, I have a goodly heritage."
Not stocks and bonds,
Nor broad ancestral acres
Compose this heritage of ours.
But rather, the intangibles,
Bequeathed to us by those who
Walked this way before:
The dauntless courage that led them to
    cross dark valleys;
The faith in God that never wavered
Through all the ills to which mankind
    is heir;
Unselfish love, which bound them to
    each other,
Enabling the strong to aid the weak;
Integrity that lifted high the Christian
    virtues;
For such a heritage, we thank thee,
    Lord.

NELLIE HINDS HAMMER

THE VOICE

Atoms as old as stars,
Mutation on mutation,
Millions and millions of cells
Dividing yet still the same,
From air and changing earth,
From ancient Eastern rivers,
From turquoise tropic seas,
Unto myself I came.

My spirit like my flesh
Sprang from a thousand sources,
From cave-man, hunter, and shepherd,
From Karnak, Cyprus, Rome;
The living thoughts in me
Spring from dead men and women,
Forgotten time out of mind
And many as bubbles of foam.

Here for a moment's space
Into the light out of darkness,
I come and they come with me
Finding words for my breath;
From the wisdom of many lifetimes
I hear them cry: "Forever
Seek for Beauty, she only
Fights with man against Death!"

SARA TEASDALE, 1884–1933

JOY OF WORKMANSHIP

Note the all-round excellency and fit-
ness of old home-fittings.

Every article in the house, farm out-
building, church, market-stall, articles
of personal attire—or what not—bears
the stamp of delight in the making of
it, and a certain deftness of shape and
play of fancy about it, which denote
that beauty as well as use was considered in its manufacture—beauty that
was there as an indispensable quality,
an integral part of the thing, not something to be charged three pence-half
penny extra for—beauty that the poor
would share equally with the rich.

And every man who did a piece of
conscious decoration to sheep-pen,
plough-harness, yeoman's stout table,
or the watch which he lugs from some
deep-down pocket—as you would draw
a bucket from a well—or the knight's
sword-sheath, the lady's work-box, the
mayor's mace, the bishop's staff, the
baby's spoon was an artist in this way.

The tithe-barn, the monastery, the
castle, and the manor-house had the
same kind of windows and doors,
roofs and buttresses; the same device is
in the bosses of roofs, the same orna-
ment in the panels, the same grotesques
to the parapets, the same vein of hu-
mour is tapped for secular or religious
structure.

The only difference in their treatment is that the place which enshrines
the presence of the Most High God is
made more glorious that the other,
more instinct with the spirit of sacrifice and adoration.

JOHN D. SEDDING

A GOODLY HERITAGE

The Lord is the portion of mine inheritance and of my cup: thou main-
tainest my lot.
The lines are fallen unto me in pleasant places; yea, I have a goodly
heritage.
Thou wilt show me the path of life:
in thy presence is fulness of joy; at
thy right hand there are pleasures
for evermore.

PSALM 16:5–6, 11

THE LIVING DREAM

You may bury the bones of men and later dig them up to find they have moldered into a white ash that crumbles in your fingers. But their ideas won. Their wisdom came through.

Men and women who gave all they had and wished they had more to give—how can we say they are sunk and buried?

They live in the sense that their dream is on the faces of living men and women today.

In a rather real sense the pioneers, old settlers, First Comers as some call themselves—they go on, their faces here now, their lessons worth our seeing.

They ought not to be forgotten—the dead who held in their clenched hands that which became the heritage of us, the living.

CARL SANDBURG
In REMEMBRANCE ROCK

PRAISE FOR FAMOUS MEN

Let us now praise famous men,
and our fathers in their generations.
The Lord apportioned to them great glory,
his majesty from the beginning.
These were those who ruled in their kingdoms,
and were men renowned for their power,
giving counsel by their understanding,
and proclaiming prophecies;
leaders of the people in their deliberations
and in understanding of learning for the people,
wise in their words of instruction;
those who composed musical tunes,
and set forth verses in writing;
rich men furnished with resources,
living peaceably in their habitations—
all these were honored in their generations,
and were the glory of their times.
ECCLESIASTICUS 44:1–7

We live in time, and the past
must always be the most momentous
part of it.
LIONEL JOHNSON, 1867–1902

What riches have you that you deem me poor,
Or what large comfort that you call me sad?
Tell me what make you so exceeding glad:
Is your earth happy or your heaven sure?
I hope for heaven, since the stars endure
And bring such tidings as our fathers had.
I know no deeper doubt to make me mad,
I need no brighter love to keep me pure.
To me the faiths of old are daily bread;
I bless their hope, I bless their will to save,
And my deep heart still meaneth what they said.
It makes me happy that the soul is brave,
And, being so much kinsman to the dead,
I walk contented to the peopled grave.
GEORGE SANTAYANA, 1863–1952

HISTORY

*A person's spiritual life is always
dwarfed when cut apart from history.*

RUFUS M. JONES, 1863–1948

There is one mind common to all individuals. Of the works of this mind history is the record. There is a relation between the hours of our life and the centuries of time.

We, as we read, must become Greeks, Romans, Turks, priest and king, martyr and executioner, must fasten these images to some reality in our secret experience, or we shall see nothing, learn nothing, keep nothing.

We must attain and maintain that lofty sight where facts yield their secret sense, and poetry and annals are alike.

Every history should be written with a wisdom which divined the range of our affinities and looked at facts as symbols.

RALPH WALDO EMERSON, 1803–1882

From LOCKSLEY HALL

Yet I doubt not thro' the ages one
  increasing purpose runs,
And the thoughts of men are widen'd
  with the process of the suns.

ALFRED TENNYSON, 1809–1892

THE ETERNAL DRAMA

Out in front of us is the drama of men and nations, seeking, struggling, laboring, dying. Upon this tragic drama in these days our eyes are all set in an anxious watchfulness and in prayer.

But within the silences of the souls of men an eternal drama is ever being enacted, in these days as well as in others. And on the outcome of the inner drama rests, ultimately, the outer pageant of history.

It is the drama of the Hound of Heaven baying relentlessly upon the track of man. It is the drama of the lost sheep wandering in the wilderness, restless and lonely, feebly searching, while over the hills comes the wiser Shepherd. For his is the shepherd's heart, and he is restless until he holds his sheep in his arms.

It is the drama of the Eternal Father drawing the prodigal home unto himself, where there is bread enough and to spare. It is the drama of the Double Search, as Rufus M. Jones calls it. And always its chief actor is the Eternal God of Love.

THOMAS KELLY, 1893–1941

From IO VICTIS

      They only the victory win,
Who have fought a good fight, and
  have vanquished the demon that
  tempts us within;
Who have held to their faith unse-
  duced by the prize that the world
  holds high;
Who have dared for a high cause to
  suffer, resist, fight—if need be, to
  die.
Speak, History! Who are Life's victors? Unroll thy long annals and say:
Are they those whom the world called
  the victors, who won the success of a
  day?
The martyrs, or Nero? The Spartans
  who fell at Thermopylae's trust,
Or the Persians and Xerxes? His
  judges or Socrates, Pilate or Christ?
        WILLIAM WETMORE STORY,
              1819–1895

THE SAVIOUR'S LOVING POWER

No wonder if the Christians made an
impression out of all proportions to
their numbers. Conviction in the midst
of waverers, fiery energy in a world of
disillusion, purity in an age of easy
morals, firm brotherhood in a loose
society, heroic courage in time of persecution, formed a problem that could
not be set aside, however polite society
might affect to ignore it; and the religion of the future turned on the answer
to it. Would the world be able to explain it better than the Christians, who
said it was the loving power of the
risen Saviour.

        HENRY MELVILL GWATKIN,
              1844–1916

OUR DEBT

The growing good of the world is
partly dependent on unhistoric acts.
That things are not so ill with you and
me as they might have been is half ow-
ing to those that lived faithfully a hidden life, and now rest in unvisited
tombs.

        GEORGE ELIOT, 1819–1880

MEANING OF HISTORY

The world struggles ignorantly and
desperately towards Christ. This to me
is the meaning of history.

        JOHN MIDDLETON MURRY,
              1889–1957

DEEP FURROW

Jesus, whose name is not so much written as ploughed into the history of this
world.

        RALPH WALDO EMERSON,
              1803–1882

INSCRIPTION

In the year 1653,
when all things sacred
were throughout the nation
either demolished or profaned,
Sir Robert Shirley, Baronet,
founded this church,
whose singular praise
it is to have done
the best things
in the worst times
and hoped them
in the most calamitous.

        IN AN ENGLISH CHURCH

JOYOUS CREATIVITY

Faith is something given, not won, and no man can claim to be educated without inquiring into what it is, without studying its manifestations in human history, not least in the literature of religion, and without trying to find a way into its life-giving influence.

Back of the methodical thinker is the man, and in him, rightly oriented, must be found an incentive to joyous creativity.

This latter, in my judgment, strikes deeper than intellect to become, in whatever language or tradition it be clothed, a religious attitude.

NATHAN M. PUSEY

HOUSEHOLDS

The history of humanity is not the history of its wars, but the history of its households.

JOHN RUSKIN, 1819–1900

The entire history of Christianity may be explained in nine imperishable words: "The Word of the Lord has come unto me." Afterwards nothing could ever be quite the same to any man or woman. Strickland Gillilan once said: "God kept right on talking when His Book had gone to press."

OUR CALL

Christian history
is the written story of
"Here am I. Send me."

RICH PARABLE

Not a blessing does the Anglo-Saxon race enjoy today that has not been baptized with blood and tears.

How easily do we take for granted the innumerable blessings that have permeated our lives because the Christian Gospel has been for sixty generations among us.

In the English Book of Common Prayer, Dean Stanley calls our attention to the strange tautologies which the book contains: "assemble and meet together," "acknowledge and confess," "humble and lowly," "goodness and mercy."

Why this curious reduplication of ideas? Because "assemble," "confess," "humble," and "mercy" are Norman French, and "meet together," "acknowledge," "lowly," and "goodness" are Anglo-Saxon.

Imbedded in the very structure of the book are the relics of an old struggle, where with blood and strife two races were trying to live together on the Isle of Britain and one Church was striving to put her arms around both.

Here is a true parable of every Christian blessing that Christendom enjoys.

They have been bought and paid for with other blood than ours, and with sacrificial toil that we can never repay.

HARRY EMERSON FOSDICK

THREAD OF LIFE

Language is the memory of the human race. It is as a thread or nerve of life running through all the ages, connecting them into one common, prolonged, and advancing existence.

WILLIAM HENRY SMITH, 1808–1872

LEGACY

Church history has no braver story than that of a little Scotch girl in the dark century when the powers-that-be in Scotland had forbidden all going to church by Protestants on Sunday. Yet in the gloaming this "wee bit lassie" was crossing the heath toward a kirk when up rose a soldier from behind a large rock, stopping her at the point of his sword and asking her destination.

With complete truthfulness the little girl said, "And if it please ye, kind sir, my Elder Brither has dee-ed; and I wad gang to my Faither's hoose for to see what He has left me in His last Wull and Testament!"

This fell with a thrifty tune on his Scotch ears, and he gave her a blessing: "Aye, aye, lassie! Gang yere gait!"

But as the little girl walked away she must have known that on the way home there could easily be other soldiers, behind other rocks, also lying in wait to pounce on churchgoers. And not only on this Sunday, but on next Sunday also, and on all the Sundays next month and next year and down through a lifetime of Sundays, always there was the likelihood of this five minutes of panic while approaching that drawn sword and answering that hard question convincingly.

For you realize how convincing she was. She wanted to learn what her Elder Brither had left her in "His last Wull and Testament." She knew He had left her His world!

Liberty has still a continent to live in.
HORACE WALPOLE, 1718–1797

GOING TO THE DOGS

My granddad, viewing earth's worn cogs,
Said, "Things are going to the dogs."
His granddad, in a house of logs,
Said, "Things are going to the dogs."
His granddad, from the Irish bogs,
Said, "Things are going to the dogs."
His granddad, in rough jungle yogs,
Said, "Things are going to the dogs."
Well, here's one thing I'd like to state:
The dogs have had a good long wait.
AUTHOR UNKNOWN

STATUE OF LIBERTY

Not like the brazen giant of Greek fame,
With conquering limbs astride from land to land;
Here at our sea-washed, sunset gates shall stand
A mighty woman with a torch, whose flame
Is the imprisoned lightning, and her name
Mother of Exiles. From her beacon-hand
Glows world-wide welcome; her mild eyes command
The air-bridged harbor that twin cities frame.
"Keep, ancient lands, your storied pomp!" cries she
With silent lips. "Give me your tired, your poor,
Your huddled masses yearning to breathe free,
The wretched refuse of your teeming shore,
Send these, the homeless, tempest-tost to me,
I lift my lamp beside the golden door."
EMMA LAZARUS, 1849–1887
From THE NEW COLOSSUS

TO LIVE IN PEACE

William Penn thought that the Indians should be paid for the land on which they had lived from time out of mind. He used various quaint and honest devices for measuring every acre bought.

In one case, he agreed to pay the Indians "30 match coats, 20 hunting guns, 30 kettles, 1 great kettle, 30 pairs of hose, 30 petticoats, 70 knives" and other articles.

Another time, Penn measured the land by laying breeches end to end along the earth, at so much a pair.

Again, he promised to pay for as much as a man could walk over in three days. Several Quakers and several Indians covered the route, and it did not escape the Indians' notice that these amazing people walked at a very natural pace, even counting in the time for food and rest and sleep.

When Penn summoned the Indians for his famous pact with them, he said: "The Great Spirit rules in the heavens and the earth. He knows that we have come here with a hearty desire to live with you in peace.

"We use no hostile weapons against our enemies. Good faith and good will toward men are our defenses. We believe you will also deal kindly and justly by us. I will not call you children, for parents sometimes chide their children severely; nor brothers only, for brothers differ.

"The friendship between me and you I will not compare to a chain, for that the rains might rust, or the falling tree might break.

"We are the same as if one man's body were to be divided into two parts. We are all of one flesh and one blood.

"We will transmit this league between us to our children. It shall be made stronger and stronger, and be kept bright and clean, without rust or spot, between our children and our children's children, while the creeks and rivers run, and while the sun, moon, and stars endure."

At every sentence, all the Indians shouted a response in their own language. At the end, the Chief himself replied for all his people, "We will live in love with William Penn and his children as long as the sun and moon shall shine!"

Whereupon Penn gave a wampum belt to every Indian present.

FROM THE CHINESE

An old man lived with his son in a fort. One day the son lost his horse. The neighbors rushed into the house to express their sympathy, but the old man said: "How do you know that this is bad luck?"

A few days later, the horse came back with a number of wild horses. So the neighbors flocked indoors to congratulate him, but the old man said: "How do you know this is good luck?"

Now that he had so many horses to ride, the son one day rode away on one of the wild horses. He fell off, breaking his leg. Again the neighbors knocked at the door to say: "Alas! Alas!" but the old man said: "Tut! Tut! How do you know this is bad luck?"

Sure enough, before many weeks had passed, there was a great war in the Middle Flowery Kingdom, but because the old man's son was crippled, he did not have to go off to fight.

ROOTAGE

No human soul lives deeply and fruitfully in and by the present, except it be profoundly and affectionately rooted in the past.

FRIEDRICH VON HÜGEL, 1852–1925

AS WE WOULD HAVE DONE

All that Shakespeare says of the king, yonder slip of a boy that reads in the corner feels to be true of himself.

We sympathize in the great moments of history, in the great discoveries, the great resistances, the great prosperities of men; because there law was enacted, the sea was searched, the land was found, or the blow was struck, for us, as we ourselves in that place would have done or applauded.

RALPH WALDO EMERSON, 1803–1882

From CENTENNIAL ODE

Long as thine art shall love true love,
Long as thy science truth shall know,
Long as thine eagle harms no dove,
Long as thy law by law shall grow,
Long as thy God is God above,
Thy brother every man below,
So long, dear land of all my love,
Thy name shall shine, thy fame shall glow.

SIDNEY LANIER, 1842–1881

Not that which men do worthily, but that which they do successfully, is what history makes haste to record.

HENRY WARD BEECHER, 1813–1887

HISTORY'S LESSON

The march of Providence is so slow
and our desires so impatient;
the work of progress is so immense
and our means of aiding it so feeble;
the life of humanity is so long, that of
the individual so brief,
that we often see only the ebb of the
advancing ways, and are thus discouraged.
It is history that teaches us to hope.

ROBERT E. LEE, 1807–1870

INSIGHT

We can know nothing of the history of our nation unless we know something of all nations.

AGNES REPPLIER,
1855–1950

From THE MORAL WARFARE

Our fathers to their graves have gone;
Their strife is past,—their triumph
won;
But sterner trials wait the race
Which rises in their honored place,—
A moral warfare with the crime
And folly of an evil time.

So let it be. In God's own might
We gird us for the coming fight,
And, strong in Him whose cause is
ours
In conflict with unholy powers,
We grasp the weapons He has given,—
The Light, the Truth, and Love of
Heaven.

JOHN GREENLEAF WHITTIER,
1807–1892

THE CROSS IN HISTORY

A few years ago *Time* printed the results of an enquiry directed to thirty prominent people in America. They were given a hundred famous events in history and asked to list them in order of significance for mankind.

The result of the poll was interesting. Top place was given to Columbus' discovery of America. In the fourteenth place three events were placed equal: the discovery of x-rays; the Wright brothers' first plane flight; and the Crucifixion of Jesus Christ.

Among those making this judgment there must have been various members and adherents of the Christian Church —that is to say, men and women who have countless times confessed in worship their belief that the crucified and risen Christ is the Saviour of the world; heard the declaration of pardon in the name of Jesus Christ who died for our sins; received the Holy Communion of the body and blood of the Lord; and joined in singing such hymns as "In the cross of Christ I glory, towering o'er the wrecks of time." How do they reconcile the tremendous affirmations they make in church with the sober judgment, made when their religious guard is down, that the Cross of Christ shares fourteenth place in order of importance for mankind?

If any professing Christian who took part in that questionnaire had been challenged about the rating, he might well have answered: "Of course, this was just a secular judgment. I wasn't thinking of religion."

What possible right have we to make such a decision?

DAVID H. C. READ

PREPARATION

Before every great opportunity God gave me a great trial.

MARTIN LUTHER, 1483–1546

The restoration of man to his original relation to God is the supreme purpose of history. This is Christ's revelation of the meaning of history.

"According to thy promise declared unto man in Christ Jesus, our Lord," is in essence, in very concentrated essence, the Christian philosophy of history. It is the "bovrilisation" of history.

To bring men and women into repentance, to initiate them into a new life, to start them on a new career in which altruism displaces egoism as the natural tendency is the end to which history is working. This is what Christ means to history, and what history means for the Christian.

The ultimately significant thing in history is the repentance of individual men and women. "There is more joy in heaven over one sinner that repenteth than over ninety-nine just men."

The things that impress the world, the great events, the movements, the cataclysms, the revolutions, the pomps and panoplies, are important only in their relation to the experience of personal repentance. And this never strikes the headlines.

When John Smith, one of the world's great "unknowns," repents in dust and ashes, more has been done for the world, for historic development than when dictators or presidents and prime ministers meet.

D. R. DAVIS

HOME

*The dear things of home
have eternal life.*

MOTTO ON A SUNDIAL

HE WAS DESPISED AND REJECTED

Homeless!
The Living Bread
Hungered
Where all beside were fed.
To their warm holes the foxes ran,
Birds flew to nest when the west was
    red,
But the Son of Man
Had not where to lay His head.

Open Door
Henceforth for all
Hungers,
Hearth and Banquet Hall
For hurt and loneliness is He
Thrust from Nazareth to roam
Vagabond of Galilee,
Who is every outcast's Home.

KATHARINE LEE BATES,
1859–1929

THE VIEW FROM HERE

I live in a very small house, but my
windows look out on a very large
world.

CONFUCIUS, 500 B.C.

THE HOUSE YOU ARE BUILDING

Every spirit builds itself a house, and
beyond its house a world, and beyond
its world a heaven. Know then that the
world exists for you. For you is the
phenomenon perfect.

What we are, that only can we see.

All that Adam had, all that Caesar
could, you have and can do. Adam
called his house, heaven and earth.
Caesar called his house, Rome.

You perhaps call yours a cobbler's
trade; a scholar's garret. Yet line for
line and point for point, your dominion is as great as theirs, though without fine names.

Build therefore your own world. As
fast as you conform your life to the
pure idea in your mind, that will unfold into great proportions.

RALPH WALDO EMERSON, 1803–1882

When fighting lion at front door don't
forget tiger at back door.

CHINESE PROVERB

TO THE LITTLE HOUSE

Dear little house, dear shabby street,
Dear books and beds and food to eat!
How feeble words are to express
the facets of your tenderness.

How white the sun comes through the
    panes!
In tinkling music drips the rain!
How burning bright the furnace
    glows!
What paths to shovel when it snows!

O dearly loved Long Island trains!
O well remembered joys and pains!
How near the housetops Beauty leans
Along that little street in Queens!

Let these poor rhymes abide for proof
Joy dwells beneath a humble roof;
Heaven is not built of country seats
But little queer suburban streets!

CHRISTOPHER MORLEY, 1890–1957

REQUISITES

Six things are requisite to create a
"happy home." Integrity must be the
architect, and tidiness the upholsterer.
It must be warmed by affection, lighted
up with cheerfulness; and industry
must be the ventilator renewing the
atmosphere and bringing in fresh salu-
brity day by day; while over all, as a
protecting canopy and glory, nothing
will suffice except the blessing of God.

JAMES HAMILTON

SON OF MAN

He often spoke of things of home,
Of linen white as snow,
Of platters cleansed inside and out,
Of leaven hid in dough,

And lost coin sought with broom and
    lamp.
Was He wishful, He
Who walked alone the road toward
    death,
Homeless in Galilee?

LESLIE SAVAGE CLARK

WHEN WILL THE KINGDOM COME?

When each home is a temple,
Its every room a shrine,
Its heart a sacred altar,
Inscribed to things divine;
When each eye in the circle
Reflects the altar flame,
Each mealtime sacramental
Unto the wondrous Name.

AUTHOR UNKNOWN

SERVICE

There are strange ways of serving God;
You sweep a room or turn a sod,
And suddenly, to your surprise,
You hear the whirr of seraphim,
And find you're under God's own eyes
And building palaces for him.

HERMANN HAGEDORN

RESPONSIBILITY

I find the gayest castles in the air that
were ever piled far better for comfort
and for use than the dungeons in the
air that are daily dug and caverned out
by grumbling, discontented people. A
man should make life and nature happier to us, or he had better never been
born.

RALPH WALDO EMERSON, 1803–1882

From A SEVENTEENTH-CENTURY MANUSCRIPT

Yet if his majesty, our sovereign lord,
  Should of his own accord
  Friendly himself invite,
And say, "I'll be your guest to-morrow
    night,"
How should we stir ourselves, call and
    command
All hands to work! "Let no man idle
    stand!

"Set me fine Spanish tables in the hall,
  See they be fitted all;
  Let there be room to eat,
And order taken that there want no
    meat.
See every sconce and candlestick made
    bright,
That without tapers they may give a
    light.

"Look to the presence: are the carpets
    spread,
  The dazie o'er the head,
  The cushions in the chairs,
And all the candles lighted on the
    stairs?
Perfume the chambers, and in any case
Let each man give attendance to his
    place."

Thus if the king were coming would
    we do,
  And 'twere good reason too;
  For 'tis a duteous thing
To show all honor to an earthly king,
And after all our travail and our cost,
So he be pleased, to think no labor
    lost.

But at the coming of the King of
    Heaven
  All's set at six and seven:
  We wallow in our sin,
Christ cannot find a chamber in the
    inn.

We entertain Him always like a
    stranger,
And, as at first, still lodge Him in the
    manger.

The sweetest type of heaven is home.
          JOSIAH GILBERT HOLLAND,
                     1819–1881

Not a change for the better in our
housekeeping has ever taken place that
wise and good men have not opposed it
and have not prophesied that the world
would wake up to find its throat cut
in consequence.
    JAMES RUSSELL LOWELL, 1819–1891

APPROACHES

When thou turn'st away from ill,
Christ is this side of thy hill.

When thou turn'st toward good,
Christ is walking in thy wood.

When thy heart says: "Father, par-
    don!"
Then the Lord is in thy garden.

When stern Duty wakes to watch,
Then His hand is on the latch.

But when Hope thy song doth rouse,
Then the Lord is in thy house.

When to love is all thy wit,
Christ doth at thy table sit.

When God's will is thy heart's pole,
Then is Christ thy very soul.
    GEORGE MACDONALD, 1824–1905

BIBLE MEALS

Certain Bible meals might well haunt a modern hostess. Not rich repasts like Belshazzar's feast or Queen Esther's banquet, or even supermarket gifts of food such as Abigail and the Queen of Sheba brought David and Solomon. Yet each more modest meal had its own haunting handwriting on the wall, which has never been forgotten. For even after several thousand years of translation, food still seems sacramental, wrapping up bread, beauty, and brotherhood.

I

Consider the first meal. Why on earth did that little old first grandmother of our race ever offer Adam the forbidden fruit? Don't tell me we haven't inherited her curiosity, her disobedience of Divine orders, her willingness to try anything once! Every Eve among us still sampling some better-not-touch-apple-a-day to keep some doctors away, with disaster on descendants.

II

When the widow of Sarepta was down to her last drop of oil, her final fistful of flour, why bake Elijah the cake he wanted? To hand down to us the Bible's stewardship of supply. Our God is inexhaustible plenteousness, honoring each shared crumb. Always. Anywhere.

III

Imagine that picnic lunch of five loaves and two small fishes. Picture that boy dashing home to boast: "Wait till you hear what I and Jesus did today!" Surely the mother surmised the kind of man Jesus must be if a hungry boy gave away all his food.

IV

Martha, getting a meal, then letting the meal get her, grumbled at Mary for listening to their Guest instead of scurrying around with pots and pans. How humiliating now for Martha to notice that wherever the Gospel is preached, all 2,000-plus languages echo her grumble around the globe, just as Jesus had foreseen that Mary's spikenard would also spread.

V

The smallest Supper of all is laid on the table. A mere morsel of bread and a mere sip from a cup become the drama of our redemption. His body broken to nourish our famine. His blood spilt as the greatest transfusion in history. So that we belong to a new Ancestor now. The Bread of Life and the Wine assures us: "Apart from me ye can do nothing." Every church in every land regularly says "Thank You" in the Eucharist in grateful remembrance.

VI

After that Last Breakfast—the one on the sea-shore at daybreak, our Lord Himself cooking fish over the coals—would Peter ever forget the question asked three times, "Lovest thou Me more than these?"; or his heartfelt answer, "Yea, Lord, thou knowest I love Thee"; or the lifelong errand requested, "Feed my sheep"? Peter's three denials were canceled out by his three promises, each reader being one of his lasting results!

I DREAM'D IN A DREAM

I dream'd in a dream I saw a city
invincible to the attacks of the whole
of the rest of the earth,
I dream'd that was the new city of
Friends,
Nothing was greater there than the
quality of robust love, it led the
rest.
It was seen every hour in the actions
of the men of that city,
And in all their looks and words.

WALT WHITMAN, 1819–1892

SMALL-TOWN SYMPATHY

I cannot hope that Sorrow's feet forever and a day
Will pass my little House of Love
where latticed sunbeams stray,
But when she lays her hand at last
upon the swinging latch,
And steps where happy years have
smiled beneath our spring-sweet
thatch,
Grant me, ah God, this heartfelt
prayer, that somewhere it may be
Where little small-town sympathy may
fold and comfort me.

The little small-town sympathy that
runs across the fields
In blue-checked gingham aprons, and
with flour upon its hands.
That bakes and brews, and sweeps and
dusts, that wakeful serves and
shields—
The little small-town sympathy that
knows and understands.
Thy cities, God, are builded high with
carven stone on stone,
But hearts may ache, and lives may
droop unheeded and alone,
And souls may dwell unknown, un-
loved, a single wall between.
Not so the quiet, home-sweet lives
that fringe the village green.
Let others reap the splendors, Lord,
but give instead to me.
The homely round of living blent with
small-town sympathy.

The little small-town sympathy that
steals on neighbor feet
From tiny lamp-lit houses down a
maple-shaded street;
That lends its strength on tear-dimmed
ways its own bruised feet have trod,
The little small-town sympathy—the
very soul of God.

MARTHA HASKELL CLARK

FURNITURE

Henry David Thoreau put only three
chairs in his lonely cabin at Walden
Pond. One was for solitude, the second
for friendship, and the third for visi-
tors.

When Ludwig Bemelmans was a
poor young artist in a Greenwich Village apartment, he went one better
than Thoreau. The place was so bare
that he furnished it by painting chairs,
tables, and lamps on the walls. The
idea amused everybody so much that he
copied this gaiety in a restaurant he
opened.

Emily Dickinson felt an even richer
insight: God's residence was next to
hers, His furniture, love!

The grandest of heroic deeds are those
which are performed within four walls
and in domestic privacy.

JEAN PAUL RICHTER, 1763–1825

TO BE AT HOME

God's thoughts, His will, and His love are a man's home. To think God's thoughts, to choose His will, to love His love, to judge His judgment, and thus to know that He is in us is to be at home and brings us into the presence of One who is dear and awful and strangely near.

AUTHOR UNKNOWN

We need to think of the home as the cradle into which the future is born.

We need to think of the family as the nursery in which the new social order is being reared.

The family is a covenant with posterity.

SIDNEY GOLDSTEIN

YOUR HOME

I am your home.
I am a bundle of bricks or stone and some wood, I can be sold or bought in the market for a few thousand dollars in money.
But I am more than these. I am—
Thousands of years of human history with the long struggle of mankind for love and protection;
Dreams and visions and aspirations;
Tears and struggles and disappointments that rend the soul apart;
A lull and breathing space in the hot hard struggle of life;
Horny hands and self-discipline and laughter.
They say that I am held together by nails and cement and mortar. But I am held together by—

Forgiveness that even forgets;
Love that fails not;
Trust and confidence that laugh at mistakes;
    goes deep and reaches far and lasts
And understanding of each other that forever.

PERCY R. HAYWARD

Half the cruelty in the world comes from our inability to put ourselves in the place of others.

JOHN FISKE, 1842–1901

From EAST LONDON

O human soul! as long as thou canst so
Set up a mark of everlasting light,
Above the howling senses' ebb and flow,
To cheer thee, and to right thee if thou roam—
Not with lost toil thou laborest through the night!
Thou mak'st the heaven thou hop'st indeed thy home.

MATTHEW ARNOLD, 1822–1888

FROM THE CHINESE

If there is righteousness in the heart,
There will be beauty in the character.

If there is beauty in the character.
There will be harmony in the home.

If there is harmony in the home,
There will be order in the nation.

If there is order in the nation,
There will be peace in the world.

From SNOW-BOUND

Shut in from all the world without,
We sat the clean-winged hearth about,
Content to let the north-wind roar
In baffled rage at pane and door.
What matter how the night behaved?
What matter how the north-wind
 raved?
Blow high, blow low, not all its show
Could quench our hearth-fire's ruddy
 glow.
And while, with care, our mother laid
The work aside, her steps she stayed
One moment, seeking to express
Her grateful sense of happiness
For food and shelter, warmth and
 health,
And love's contentment more than
 wealth,
With simple wishes (not the weak,
Vain prayers which no fulfillment seek,
But such as warm the generous heart,
O'er-prompt to do with Heaven its
 part)
That none might lack, that bitter
 night,
For bread and clothing, warmth and
 light.

JOHN GREENLEAF WHITTIER,
1807–1892

❧

Come, O Lord, in much mercy down
into my soul, and take possession and
dwell there. A homely mansion, I confess, for so glorious a majesty, but
such as Thou art fitting up for the
reception of Thee, by holy and fervent desires of Thine own inspiring.
Enter then, and adorn, and make it
such as Thou canst inhabit, since it
is the work of Thy hands.

ST. AUGUSTINE, 354–430

Where is the true man's fatherland?
 Is it where he by chance is born?
 Doth not the yearning spirit scorn
In such scant borders to be spanned?
Oh, yes! his fatherland must be
As the blue heaven wide and free!

Is it alone where freedom is,
 Where God is God and man is man?
 Doth he not claim a broader span
For the soul's love of home than this?
Oh, yes! his fatherland must be
As the blue heaven wide and free!

Where'er a human heart doth wear
 Joy's myrtle-wreath or sorrow's
  gyves,
 Where'er a human spirit strives
After a life more true and fair,
There is the true man's birthplace
 grand,
His is a world-wide fatherland!

JAMES RUSSELL LOWELL, 1819–1891

❧

From THE GREAT LOVER

These have I loved:
White plates and cups, clean-gleaming,
Ringed with blue lines; and feathery,
 faëry dust;
Wet roofs, beneath the lamp-light; the
 strong crust
Of friendly bread; and many-tasting
 food;
Rainbows; and the blue bitter smoke of
 wood.

RUPERT BROOKE, 1887–1915

❧

A comfortable house is a great source
of happiness. It ranks immediately after health and a good conscience.

SYDNEY SMITH, 1771–1845

EVERY THING

Since man has been articulate,
Mechanical, improvidently wise,
(Servant of Fate,)
He has not understood the little cries
And foreign conversations of the small
Delightful creatures that have followed
    him
Not far behind;
Has failed to hear the sympathetic call
Of Crockery and Cutlery, those kind
Reposeful Teraphim
Of his domestic happiness; the Stool
He sat on, or the door he entered
    through;
He has not thanked them, overbearing
    fool!
What is he coming to?

But you should listen to the talk of
    these.
Honest they are, and patient they have
    kept,
Served him without his *Thank-you* or
    his *Please* . . .
I often heard
The gentle Bed, a sigh between each
    word,
Murmuring, before I slept.
The Candle, as I blew it out, cried
    aloud,
Then bowed,
And in a smoky argument
Into the darkness went.

The Kettle puffed a tentacle of
    breath;—
"Pooh! I have boiled his water, I don't
    know
Why; and he always says I boil too
    slow.
He never calls me 'Sukie dear,' and oh,
I wonder why I squander my desire
Sitting submissive on his kitchen fire."

Now the old Copper Basin suddenly

Rattled and tumbled from the shelf,
Bumping and calling: "I can fall by
    myself;
Without a woman's hand
To patronize and coax and flatter me,
I understand
The lean and poise of gravitable land."
It gave a raucous and tumultuous shout,
Twisted itself convulsively about,
Rested upon the floor, and, while I
    stare
It stares and grins at me.

The old impetuous Gas above my head
Begins irascibly to flare and fret,
Wheezing into its epileptic jet,
Reminding me I ought to go to bed.

The Rafters creak; an Empty-Cupboard
    door
Swings open; now a wild Plank of the
    floor
Breaks from its joist, and leaps behind
    my foot.
Down from the chimney half a pound
    of Soot
Tumbles, and lies, and shakes itself
    again.
The Putty cracks against the window
    pane,
A piece of Paper in the basket shoves
Another piece, and toward the bottom
    moves.
My independent Pencil, while I write,
Breaks at the point; the ruminating
    clock
Stirs all its body and begins to rock,
Warning the waiting presence of the
    Night,
Strikes the dead hour, and tumbles to
    plain
Ticking of ordinary work again.

You do well to remind me, and I praise

Your strangely individual foreign
  ways.
You call me from myself to recognize
Companionship in your unselfish Eyes.
I want your dear acquaintances,
  although
I pass you arrogantly over, throw
Your lovely sounds, and squander them
  along
My busy days. I'll do you no more
  wrong. . . .

HAROLD MONRO

A RIVER OF GRACE

Make of my heart an upper room, I
  pray,
  Swept clean of pride, let self be but
  a door
Through which young lives may come
  to Thee this day
  To know Thee as they have not
  known before.

Speak through my voice that they may
  hear Thine own.
  Shine through my life in beauty and
  in truth
That they may see the Comrade Christ
  alone
  And in the glad impulsiveness of
  youth

Rise up as did those fisher lads of
  Thine
  Who left their boats and nets to
  follow Thee,
So may they walk beside Thee, these
  of mine
  Whom out of all the world "Thou
  gavest me."

MOLLY ANDERSON HALEY

From THE MONK
IN THE KITCHEN

Brazen pan and iron pot,
Yellow brick and gray flag-stone
That my feet have trod upon—
Ye seem to me
Vessels of bright mystery.
For ye do bear a shape, and so
Though you were made by man, I
  know
An inner Spirit also made,
And ye his breathings have obeyed.

Shape, the strong and awful Spirit,
Laid his ancient hand on you.
He waste chaos doth inherit;
He can alter and subdue:
Verily, he doth lift up
Matter like a sacred cup.
Into deep substance he reached, and lo
Where ye were not, ye were; and so
Out of useless nothing, ye
Groaned and laughed and came to be.
And I used you, as I can,
Wonderful uses, made for man,
Iron pot and brazen pan. . . .

ANNA HEMPSTEAD BRANCH,
1875?–1937

DIVINE THOUGHT

When God thought of mother, He
must have laughed with satisfaction,
and framed it quickly—so rich, so
deep, so divine, so full of soul, power,
and beauty was the conception.

HENRY WARD BEECHER, 1813–1887

All the mischief in the world is done
by one thing: the inability to remain
at rest within one's own room.

BLAISE PASCAL, 1623–1662

HOUSE AND HOME

Anyone can build an altar; it requires God to provide the flame.

Anyone can build a house; we need the Lord for the creation of a home.

A house is an agglomeration of brick and stones, with an assorted collection of manufactured goods; a home is the abiding-place of ardent affection, of fervent hope, of genial trust.

There is many a homeless man who lives in a richly furnished house. There is many a fifteen-pound house in the crowded street which is an illuminated and beautiful home.

The sumptuously furnished house may only be an exquisitely sculptured tomb; the scantily furnished house may be the very hearthstone of the eternal God.

JOHN HENRY JOWETT,
1863–1923

WHAT MAKES A HOME?

Love and sympathy and confidence,
The memories of childhood,
The kindness of parents,
The bright hopes of youth.
The sisters' pride,
The brothers' sympathy and help,
The mutual confidence,
The common hopes and interests and
    sorrows—
These create and sanctify the home.
JOHN LUBBOCK, 1834–1913

MIGRATIONS

They have no home on the earth,
the unhomed,
the movers, the hungry,
they have no roots in the rich earth,
they have no home but a word,
but hope:
the word and the hope build no walls.
They have no home, they are homeless
    as water.
They rise as a wave,
they break on the earth,
take no root.
They have no home, they build home
of a word,
of a little love:
the love has no walls.

On all the shores of the world they
    have broken,
tide on tide, and the safe men trem-
    bling,
wave on wave, the meek, the menacing,
rootless as water, the unhomed;
with the feel of walls around them
and no walls,
with the feel of meat in the jaws
and meat rarely,
on all the shores of the world;
now this shore,
America
(and the safe men trembling)
tide on tide,
the unhomed,
the hungry men, the meek, the movers.
They broke like a flood on the Eastern
    shore,
(a few remained, joined the safe
    men);
the tide
moved, moves with the sun
Westward,
over California,
over the valleys,
the unhomed with the feel of walls
    around them,
no home but a word.

ELSA GIDLOW

From THE CITY OF GOD

O thou not made with hands,
Not throned above the skies,
Nor wall'd with shining walls,
Nor framed with stones of price,
　More bright than gold or gem,
　God's own Jerusalem.

Where'er the gentle heart
Finds courage from above;
Where'er the heart forsook
Warms with the breath of love;
　Where faith bids fear depart,
　City of God! thou art.

Thou art where'er the proud
In humbleness melts down;
Where self itself yields up;
Where martyrs win their crown;
　Where faithful souls possess
　Themselves in perfect peace.

Where in life's common ways
With cheerful feet we go;
When in His steps we tread
Who trod the way of woe;
　Where He is in the heart,
　City of God! thou art.

FRANCIS TURNER PALGRAVE,
1824–1897

CHINESE PHILOSOPHY

The ancients who wished to illustrate the highest virtue throughout the empire first ordered well their own states.

Wishing to order well their states, they first regulated their families.

Wishing to regulate their families, they first cultivated their own selves.

Wishing to cultivate their own selves, they first rectified their hearts.

Wishing to rectify their hearts, they first sought to be sincere in their thoughts.

Wishing to be sincere in their thoughts, they first extended to the utmost their knowledge.

Such extension of knowledge lay in the investigation of things.

Things being investigated, knowledge became complete.

Their knowledge being complete, their thoughts were sincere.

Their thoughts being sincere, their hearts were then rectified.

Their hearts being rectified, their own selves were cultivated.

Their own selves being cultivated, their families were regulated.

Their families being regulated, their states were rightly governed.

Their states being rightly governed, the whole empire was made tranquil and happy.

CONFUCIUS, 500 B.C.

The house that I am living in
Is not the home I planned;
I built it of little things
That came into my hand;
Of loneliness and memories
You wouldn't understand.

The house that I am living in
A fragile haven seems;
Uncertain its foundations,
Unsure its joists and beams;
I wish I had been strong enough
To build my home of dreams.

WINIFRED THORN BAILEY

All happy families resemble one another; every unhappy family is unhappy in its own way.

LEO TOLSTOY, 1828–1910

IMAGINATION

Imagination is more important than knowledge.

ALBERT EINSTEIN, 1879–1955

PECULIAR EXCELLENCE

Imagination plays a distinct role in that it belongs both to the realm of reason and the realm of sense perception.

Its peculiar excellence consists in its capacity of making visible what is invisible and of detecting the invisible element in the visible situation.

Our real life is an affair not of the senses nor of the intellect; we live within the medium of imagination.

RICHARD KRONER

THE WONDER THAT WOULD BE

For I dipt into the future, far as human eye can see,
Saw the Vision of the world, and all the wonder that would be;

Saw the heavens fill with commerce, argosies of magic sails,
Pilots of the purple twilight, dropping down with costly bales;

Heard the heavens fill with shouting, and there rain'd a ghastly dew
From the nation's airy navies grappling in the central blue;

Far along the world-wide whisper of the south-wind rushing warm,
With the standards of the peoples plunging thro' the thunder-storm;

Till the war-drum throbb'd no longer, and the battle-flags were furl'd
In the Parliament of man, the Federation of the world.

ALFRED TENNYSON, 1809–1892
From LOCKSLEY HALL

From A MIDSUMMER NIGHT'S DREAM

And as imagination bodies forth
The forms of things unknown, the poet's pen
Turns them to shapes and gives to airy nothing
A local habitation and a name.

WILLIAM SHAKESPEARE,
1564–1616

LEVELS OF INTELLECT

There are one-story intellects, two-story intellects, three-story intellects with skylights.

All fact collectors who have no aim beyond their facts are one-story intellects.

Two-story men compare, reason, generalize, using the labors of the fact collectors as well as their own.

Three-story men idealize, imagine, predict. Their best illumination comes from above through the skylight.

OLIVER WENDELL HOLMES,
1809–1894

The poor man is not he who is without a cent, but he who is without a dream.

HARRY KEMP

Imagination, the real and eternal World of which this Vegetable Universe is but a faint shadow. What is the life of Man but Art and Science?

WILLIAM BLAKE, 1757–1827

From SAUL

Have I knowledge? confounded it
  shrivels at Wisdom laid bare.
Have I forethought? how purblind,
  how blank, to the Infinite Care!
Do I task any faculty highest, to
  image success?
I but open my eyes, and perfection, no
  more and no less,
In the kind I imagined, full-fronts me,
  and God is seen God

In the star, in the stone, in the flesh,
  in the soul, in the clod.
And thus looking within and around
  me, I ever renew
With that steep of the soul which in
  bending up raises it too,
The submission of man's nothing-perfect to God's all-complete,
As by each new obeisance of spirit, I
  climb to His feet.

ROBERT BROWNING, 1812–1889

CREATIVE IMAGINATION

It was in West Africa in 1927 that a blood specimen was taken from a black native named Asibi who was sick with yellow fever. This specimen was inoculated into a rhesus monkey which had just been received from India. Asibi recovered but the monkey died of the disease. All the vaccine manufactured since 1927, both by the Rockefeller Foundation and other agencies as well, derives from the original strain of virus obtained from this humble native. Carried down from the present day from one laboratory and by enormous multiplication, it has offered immunity to yellow fever to millions of people in many countries. Through the creative imagination of science, the blood of one man in West Africa has been made to serve the whole human race.

ROCKEFELLER FOUNDATION REPORT

From ECCLESIASTICAL SONNETS

                    The mightiest lever
Known to the moral world, Imagination.

WILLIAM WORDSWORTH, 1770–1850

FROM AN OLD ENGLISH DOCUMENT

A Gentilmanne, having led a Companie of children beyond their usual Journeye, they beganne to wearie & Joyntly cryed unto him to carrie them, which because of their Multitude he cd. not do, but told them he wd. provide them horses to ride on. Then, cutting lyttel wands out of ye hedge as nagges for them, & a great stake as a gelding for himselve, thus mounted, *Phancie put Metall into their Legges,* & they rode cheerfullie Home.

RECONCILING IMAGE

We need a reconciling image—huge enough to hold all things, passionate enough to burn through all
    contradictions to an underlying peace, powerful enough to thrust beyond all the
    petty separations to the magnitude of unity underneath them,
compassionate enough to leave nothing in man outside its mercy or insight,
holy enough to bring God's blessing,
hopeful enough to revive man's trust in life,
humble enough to force him to kneel,
rich enough in joy to celebrate in praise, honest enough to reach to the lowest level of earth,
sublime enough to climb toward the light that rests on the highest summits,
touched with shame enough not to equivocate,
and faithful enough to labor tirelessly at the endless shaping of the world to fit God's dream.

SAMUEL H. MILLER

Those who feel the gale
of the Holy Spirit go forward
even in sleep.

THOMAS A KEMPIS, 1379–1471

HEAVENWARD VISION

An ideal which a man can achieve in his lifetime is unworthy of the reach of his imagination, the chivalry of his spirit, the hardihood of his faith.

Only such tasks and ambitions are worthy of us which lay bare the finitude of our bodies and the infinitude of our souls, the impotence of flesh and the omnipotence of spirit, the brevity of our days and the eternity of our dreams.

Blessed is the man whose dream outlives him! The flame of life may burn low, but from the undefiled altars of his ageless soul the holy incense of his vision will rise heavenward.

ABBA HILLEL SILVER, 1893–1963

The most beautiful thing we can experience is the mysterious. It is the source of all true art and science. He to whom this emotion is a stranger, who can no longer pause to wonder and stand in awe, is as good as dead; his eyes are closed.

ALBERT EINSTEIN, 1879–1955

POSSIBILITIES

The world is full of hopeful analogies and handsome dubious eggs called possibilities.

GEORGE ELIOT, 1819–1880

PARTAKER OF THY GLORY

Lord, turn my necessities into virtue,
the works of nature into marks of
    grace,
by making them orderly, regular, and
    temperate;
and let no pride or self-seeking,
no covetousness or revenge,
no little ends and low imaginations
pollute my spirit and unhallow
any of my words and actions;
but let my body be a servant of Jesus;
that, doing all things for Thy glory
    here,
I may be a partaker of Thy glory here-
    after.

                JEREMY TAYLOR, 1619–1667

Greater than an army with banners is
an idea whose time has come.

                VICTOR HUGO, 1802–1885

EVER INSURGENT

God, though this life is but a wraith,
    Although we know not what we use,
Although we grope with little faith,
    Give me the heart to fight—and
        lose.

Ever insurgent let me be,
    Make me more daring than devout;
From sleek contentment make me free,
    And fill me with a buoyant doubt.

Open my eyes to visions girt
    With beauty, and with wonder lit—
But let me always see the dirt,
    And all that spawn and die in it.

Open my ears to music; let
    Me thrill with Spring's first flutes
        and drums—

But never let me dare forget
    The bitter ballads of the slums.

From compromise and things half-
    done
    Keep me, with stern and stubborn
        pride;
And when, at last, the fight is won,
    God, keep me still unsatisfied.

                LOUIS UNTERMEYER

Man's spiritual nature, the vital force
which dwells in him, is essentially one
and indivisible. That which we call
imagination, fancy, understanding, and
so forth, are but different figures of the
same power of insight, all indissolubly
connected with each other; so that if
we knew one of them, we might know
all of them.

Morality itself, what we call the
moral quality of a man, what is this
but another side of the one vital force
whereby he is and works?

All that a man does is typical of him.
You may see how a man would fight by
the way in which he sings. His courage,
or want of courage, is visible in the
word he utters, in the opinion he has
formed, no less than in the stroke he
strikes.

He is one, and preaches the same
self abroad in all these ways.

                THOMAS CARLYLE, 1795–1881

Far away there in the sunshine are my
highest aspirations. I may not reach
them, but I can look up and see their
beauty, believe in them, and try to follow where they lead.

                LOUISA MAY ALCOTT, 1832–1888

SHALL WE PSYCHOANALYZE?

Shall we psychoanalyze the rose,
Tell why its color comes and where it
    goes;
Learnedly seek to say how dew reclines
On honeysuckle vines?

Shall we psychoanalyze the dawn?
Show how silver and purple, rose and
    fawn
Never bestowed the ecstasy we
    caught—
Dupes of our own intoxicated thought?

Come, O moderns! Shall we analyze
Thrusts of the living soul that ever tries
Over and over again to strike her spark
Here in the muddled depths of human
    dark?

Search as you may, ponder and prove
    and plan—
Never yet have you compassed the
    range of man,
Never yet have you touched the mys-
    terious rim—
Blazing border of light that circles him.

Shatter the rose, sunder the roots of
    trees,
Find if you can the soul of the singing
    breeze,
Show the lover his vision, part by
    part—
You cannot kill, thank God, his dream-
    ing heart.

ANGELA MORGAN, 1874–1957

WONDER

The great problem of literature
is to invent a probability
and make it wonderful.

JOHN DRYDEN, 1631–1700

From CYRANO DE BERGERAC

Has your imagination the gout, that it
limps so?

EDMOND ROSTAND, 1868–1918

FACULTY OF IMAGINATION

When Paul says, "I know whom I
have believed," his certainty is based
on what he had seen plus what he had
interpreted plus what he had reason to
believe—all of which were derived
from capacities that are integral to personality.

In this act of knowing, the faculty of
imagination plays a role which deserves
more intellectual respect than is commonly accorded it.

Furthermore, the imagination becomes creative and with a leap of intuition outruns the leaden feet of logic.
The poet's insight and the artist's
vision are roads to reality, even though
they cannot be surveyed with the measuring rods of science. "Poetry," said
Shelley, "redeems from decay the visi-
tations of divinity in man."

Moreover, there is much resem-
blance between the scientist's flash of
discovery and the intuitive insight of
the artist, the poet, or the religious seer.

When asked how he had discovered
the law of gravity, Sir Isaac Newton
replied: "By thinking about it constantly. I keep the object of my research constantly before me, waiting
until the first light begins to dawn,
little by little. Finally this changes and
at last the light is complete."

In our respect for science let us not
overlook its debt to imagination and
intuition.

RALPH W. SOCKMAN

LABOR

Usefulness is the rent we pay for room on earth.

GRACE HOADLEY DODGE, 1856–1914

I hold that if the Almighty had ever made a set of men that should do all the eating and none of the work, he would have made them with mouths only and no hands; and if he had ever made another class that he intended to do all the work and no eating, he would have made them with hands and no mouths.

ABRAHAM LINCOLN, 1809–1865

From A GLANCE BEHIND THE CURTAIN

No man is born into the world whose work
Is not born with him; there is always work,
And tools to work withal, for those who will;
And blessed are the horny hands of toil!

JAMES RUSSELL LOWELL, 1819–1891

God gives no linen, but flax to spin.

GERMAN PROVERB

It is the art of mankind to polish the world, and everyone who works is scrubbing in some part.

HENRY DAVID THOREAU, 1817–1862

From ANDREW RYKMAN'S PRAYER

Make my mortal dreams come true
With the work I fain would do;
Clothe with life the weak intent,
Let me be the thing I meant;
Let me find in Thy employ
Peace that dearer is than joy;
Out of self to love be led
And to heaven acclimated,
Until all things sweet and good
Seem my natural habitude.

JOHN GREENLEAF WHITTIER,
1819–1892

The Moravians had a wonderful symbol—a bull, standing between an altar on one side and a plow on the other, below which were the words: "Ready for either."

Success in your work, the finding of a better method, the better understanding that insures the better performance is hat and coat, is food and wine, is fire and horse and health and holiday. At least, I find that any success in my work has the effect on my spirits of all these.

RALPH WALDO EMERSON, 1803–1882

O Lord, let me not live to be useless; for Christ's sake. Amen.

JOHN WESLEY, 1703–1791

THE RIGHT ANGLE

The philosophy behind daily witnessing cannot be better put than by Martin Buber, when he speaks of "Enoch . . . a cobbler, and with each stitch of his bodkin as it sewed the upper leather and the sole together, he joined together God and his Shekinah."

There is something unforgettable about that parallel, of God and the "upper leather," and his Shekinah and "the sole."

It reminds us that religion is not idealism, but realism plus faith; that if we let the horizontal line represent life and facts, and the vertical line represent God and faith, religion goes into effect just at the right angle where faith meets fact.

SAMUEL M. SHOEMAKER, 1893–1963

Work is love made visible. If you bake bread with indifference, you bake a bitter bread that feeds but half man's hunger.

KAHLIL GIBRAN, 1883–1931

ALTARS

A man I know has made an altar of his
  factory bench,
And one has turned the counter of his
  store
Into a place of sacrifice and holy
  ministry.
Another still has changed his office-
  desk
Into a pulpit-desk, from which to
  speak and write,
Transforming commonplace affairs
Into the business of the King.
A Martha in our midst has made
Her kitchen-table a communion-table.
A postman makes his daily round
A walk in the temple of God. . . .

To all of these each daily happening
Has come to be a whisper from the
  lips of God,
Each separate task a listening-post,
And every common circumstance
A wayside shrine.

EDGAR FRANK

When gas first lighted the streets of Boston, a certain clergyman preached against it, saying that if God had wanted a brighter night He could have made a bigger moon and larger stars. Another clergyman preached against anesthetics used in childbirth, quoting chapter and verse to prove that pain was in the divine plan.

They that sit at rest while others work are tender turtles and earn their quiet with disgrace.

ST. AUGUSTINE, 354–430

INVENTIONS

In 1853, a clerk resigned from the Patent Office in Washington saying that it seemed wise to get a better job while it was still available, since everything possible had been invented that the mind of man could think of.

Yet there followed in quick succession the steam engine, the telegraph, the telephone, the steam boat, the automobile, the submarine, the airplane, the radio, the television, the bomb.

When someone asked Henry Thoreau if he did not consider the railroad a great improvement over the stagecoach he said dryly: "Provided it carries better people. Otherwise it's only meanness going faster!"

LONDON CALLING

Clever men
Like Christopher Wren
Only occur just now and then;
Never a cleverer dipped his pen
Than clever Sir Christopher—
Christopher Wren.

With his chaste designs
On classical lines
His elegant curves and neat inclines
And never an hour went by but when
London needed Sir Christopher Wren.
  "Salisbury Square
  Decidedly bare,
  Can you put one of your churches
    there?"

  "London calling
  From ten to ten
  London calling
  Christopher Wren."

HUGH CHESTERMAN

OUR ONLY EMPLOYER

It comes like a nudge to be reminded that no matter for whom we may work, actually God is our only employer. And to be worth our salt has Biblical significance, since "salary" originated in the Latin *sal,* meaning salt.

A CRAFTSMAN'S CREED

I hold with none who think not work
  a boon,
Vouchsafed to man that he may aid his
  kind
With offerings from his chisel, wheel,
  or loom.

Fashioned with loving heart and loving mind,
All of the fine traditions and the skill
Come from my elders through the long
  line down,
Are mine to use to raise our craft's re-
  nown,
And mine to teach again with reverent
  will.

Thus do I live to serve, though least for
  pay,
With fingers which are master of the
  tool,
And eyes which light to see the patterns play
As it unfolds, obedient to each rule of
  our dear art.

So all my craft is praise to God—
At once part homage and part song;
My works, my prayer, I sing the whole
  day long,
As Faith and Beauty shape the forms I
  raise.

AUTHOR UNKNOWN

EARTH IS ENOUGH

We men of Earth have here the stuff
Of Paradise—we have enough!
We need no other stones to build
The Temple of the Unfulfilled—
No other ivory for the doors—
No other marble for the floors—
No other cedar for the beam
And dome of man's immortal dream.

Here on the paths of every-day—
Here on the common human way
Is all the stuff the gods would take
To build a Heaven, to mold and make
New Edens. Ours the stuff sublime
To build Eternity in time.

EDWIN MARKHAM, 1852–1940

PRAYER OF A RENT-PAYER TO THE LORD

Father in heaven, I would like all the
holy company of angels to be here;
I would like abundance of peace on
this earth;
I would like full baskets to give to the
poor;
I would like rich treasures of mercy;
I would like Jesus to be here;
I would like the three Marys from the
gospels to be present here;
I would like all the friends of Heaven
to be gathered around us from all
parts of the earth;
And I would like to be a rent-payer to
the Lord.

ST. BRIGID, 453?–523?

RESIDENCE

Though my head and my hand be at
labor, yet doth my heart dwell in God.

JACOB BOEHME, 1575–1624

From KINSHIP

As I go commonly sweeping the stair,
Doing my part of the everyday care,
Human and simple my lot and my
share,
I am aware of a marvelous thing:
Voices that call me—voices that ring
From far lands of ocean on heavenly
wing.
Here in my hand their hands seem to
meet;
I hear in my heart the melodious beat
Of the nations that circle Divinity's
feet,
As I go commonly sweeping the stair.

ANGELA MORGAN, 1874–1957

MAKE ME A SAINT

Lord of all pots and pans and tins,
since I've no time to be
A saint by doing lovely things, or
watching late with Thee,
Or dreaming in the twilight, or storm-
ing heaven's gates,
Make me a saint by getting meals and
washing up the plates.

Although I must have Martha's hands,
I have a Mary mind;
And when I black the boots and shoes,
Thy sandals, Lord, I find;
I think of how they trod the earth, each
time I move.

Warm all the kitchen with Thy love
and light it with Thy peace;
Forgive me all my worrying and make
all grumbling cease;
Thou who didst love to give men food
—in room or by the sea—
Accept this service that I do, I do it
unto Thee.

AUTHOR UNKNOWN

George Washington Carver put over the door of his laboratory at Tuskegee a sign suitable for every factory, office, or toolshed:

GOD'S LITTLE WORKSHOP

Everybody prizes the story of the day this superb Negro genius held a peanut in the palm of his hand and asked God to tell him its secret.

God seemed to suggest that he should go back into his workshop and simply use the three laws God had already given him—temperature, pressure, and compatibility—and put together the different parts hidden in the peanut.

Dr. Carver, taking God at His word, found a wealth of revelation no other scientist had ever discovered: proteins, carbohydrates, oils, pigments, and cellulose. From these he made more than three hundred products from the peanut alone: rubber, shoe polishes, mock soups, dyes, stains, synthetic leathers, soaps, explosives, beverages, and milk.

This former slave boy who had once been exchanged for a race horse, became one of the world's greatest scientists. And Dothan, Alabama, inaugurated a national festival honoring Dr. Carver's peanut which had brought prosperity to the farmers at a time when bankruptcy faced them as a result of the boll weevil. And Enterprise, Alabama, erected a statue to the boll weevil whose havoc had ruined their fields but turned them, with gratitude, to the raising of peanuts and a multi-million-dollar business!

Their real debt, however, was to "God's Little Workshop" and to God's little black saint who handled water and light and earth as sacred discoveries for the help of all mankind.

When you are laboring for others, let it be with the same zeal as if it were for yourself.

CONFUCIUS, 500 B.C.

JOY OF CREATION

In the museums and monastic libraries of Europe there are volume after volume of illuminated manuscripts of the Middle Ages.

This is indeed art for art's sake, pure clean passion for beauty—inspired by the mind's constant occupation with the loveliness of God, who has created us in His image so that we also can realize the joy of creation.

Year in and year out the craftsman sat and painted borders with flowers shining like jewels, with playful birds and clinging vines on the smooth, yellowish-white parchment.

The frames which the capital letters required, he filled out with a polished gold ground and with delightful small pictures, the faces of saints, not so big as wood-anemones, drawn with lines as fine as the veins of anemone petals.

Each little flower was painted in order that it should be perfect in itself, without thought whether anyone was ever going to study it carefully.

Perhaps this maker of pictures can help us, not to understand but to get a glimmering of God's great love for His creation, which caused Him to come to His own as a little child in a crib and to die upon the cross to save each soul He had created in His image —to perfect one tiny little forget-me-not in the Eternal manuscript of the universe.

SIGRID UNDSET, 1882–1949

LEISURE

How do you suppose some people will spend Eternity when they don't know how to spend the next half hour?

RALPH WALDO EMERSON,
1803–1882

THE INNER MAN

We do not know a nation until we know its pleasures of life, just as we do not know a man until we know how he spends his leisure.

It is when a man ceases to do the things he has to do, and does the things he likes to do, that the character is revealed.

It is when the repressions of society and business are gone and when the goads of money and fame and ambition are lifted, and man's spirit wanders where it listeth, that we see the inner man, the real self.

LIN YUTANG

NATURAL PICTURE GALLERY

To a person uninstructed in natural history, his country or seaside stroll is a walk through a gallery filled with wonderful works of art, nine-tenths of which have their faces turned to the wall.

THOMAS H. HUXLEY, 1825–1885

From LEISURELY LANE

Is there no road now to Leisurely Lane?
    We traveled it long ago!
A place for the lagging of leisurely
    steps, sweet and shady and slow.

VIRGINIA WOODWARD CLOUD

PLAY

The real joy of life is in its play. Play is anything we do for the joy and love of doing it, apart from any profit, compulsion, or sense of duty. It is the real living of life with the feeling of freedom and self-expression. Play is the business of childhood, and its continuation in later years is the prolongation of youth.

WALTER RAUSCHENBUSCH,
1861–1918

To be entirely at leisure for one day is to be an immortal.

CHINESE PROVERB

TIME TO SPARE FOR GOD

Blessed is the man who is glad to have time to spare for God.

Blessed is the soul which heareth the Lord speaking within her, and receiveth from His mouth the word of consolation.

Blessed are the ears that catch the pulses of the Divine whisper, and give no heed to the whisperings of this world.

Blessed are they that enter far into things within, and endeavor to prepare themselves more and more, by daily exercises, for the receiving of heavenly secrets.

Blessed are they who are glad to have time to spare for God.

THOMAS A KEMPIS, 1379–1471

From AS YOU LIKE IT

And this our life, exempt from public haunt,
Finds tongues in trees, books in the running brooks,
Sermons in stones and good in every thing.

WILLIAM SHAKESPEARE, 1564–1616

EMBROIDERY

"Never less idle than when idle" was the motto which the admirable Vittoria Colonna wrought upon her husband's dressing-gown. And may we not justly regard our appreciation of leisure as a test of improved character and growing resources?

HENRY THEODORE TUCKERMAN,
1818–1871

CHORE WORK

The monotony that bores us is the fact that "chore work is never done." The same dishes have to be washed yesterday, today, and tomorrow. The same route to the same office. The same faces in the same places. The dullness of routines. But if, as Marcus Aurelius said so many centuries ago, "The soul is dyed the color of its leisure thoughts," then the solution to boredom lies in what we are thinking about all day.

ESCAPE INTO TRUE KINGDOMS

All real and wholesome enjoyments possible to men have been just as possible to him since he was made of the earth as they are now, and they are possible to him chiefly in peace.

To watch the corn grow and the blossoms set; to draw hard breath over plough-share or spade; to read, to think, to love, to hope, to pray—these are the things that make men happy.

Now and then a wearied king, or a tormented slave, found out where the true kingdoms of the world were, and possessed himself in a furrow or two of garden ground, of a truly infinite dominion.

JOHN RUSKIN, 1819–1900

MOTTO IN COVENTRY CATHEDRAL

God be in my limbs
and in my leisure.

WARREN OST REPORT

Try calling any smallest spot of leisure "The Blink" to discover what glee and brio this spicy, fresh word can inject into humdrum ordeals. Perhaps by always carrying in pocket or purse some intriguing tidbit ready to read, or some card to write to a favorite shut-in, or even only the humming of some beloved tune. Anything, really, so that a Blink can prove instantly restoring, reviving, releasing, and redemptive.

In Greek, the term for leisure is *shole,* and in Latin *scola,* from which we derive our word "school." Leisure thus conceived is an aspect of the educational or learning process. The spirit of leisure is the spirit of learning, of self-cultivation, the time for discovery, the freeing of the mind from immediate concerns to a consideration of ultimate concerns, rediscovering the meaning and purpose of life.

ROBERT LEE

A normal man who never rests gets taut, overwrought, strained, and ultimately breaks down. Leisure has its place in life. There is a rhythmic law underlying all existence, an ebb and flow, a movement of periodicity. And in that ebb and flow, work and leisure both have a place.

W. E. SANGSTER

It's the leisure hours, happily used, that have opened up a new world to many a person.

GEORGE M. ADAMS

RELIGION AND LEISURE

It has frequently been argued that religion is the mother of leisure pursuits in view of the inspiration it gave to the arts, drama, dance, music, and literature in the Middle Ages.

Indeed the influence of religion on leisure is clearly discernible in the life of primitive man, whose ritualistic festivities aimed at propitiating the gods through dance and music, contest and combat.

Moreover, holidays, nearly all of which originated as "holy days" in the ancient world, were a chief source of leisure during the pre-industrial period.

In medieval times holy days consisted of the five major feasts of Mary, the days of all the Apostles, and a great number of saints' days, such as the feasts of St. Michael, St. Stephen, and St. John the Baptist.

Another group of holy days was made up of the feasts of special patron saints, of which there were hundreds.

Still a third group of saints' days were observed as holy days within families and among friends and neighbors. It was the general custom to celebrate the feast of the saint whose name was received at baptism. For the one whose feast day it is, the rest of the day is free from regular chores and duties in household or farming, and is spent in the manner and mood of the true holiday.

Today when we think of a festivity like New Year's Eve, seldom do we have in mind an occasion for celebrating the fullness of shared joy in God's work.

ROBERT LEE

Leisure is gone; gone where the spin-ning-wheels are gone, and the pack-horses, and the slow wagons, and the peddlers who brought bargains to the door on sunny afternoons.

GEORGE ELIOT, 1819–1880

LATIN WISDOM

The bow that's always bent will quickly break;
  But if unstrung will serve you at your need.
So let the mind some relaxation take
  To come back to its task with fresher heed.

PHAEDRUS, FIRST CENTURY A.D.

UNCONSECRATED LEISURE

As the demands of life have been lifted, and as we have been given more leisure and spare time, we have discovered a dark center in ourselves which we hate to look at, fear to admit, long to be rid of.

It is the dark center of the meaningless, the alone, the absence of a call within man to a higher, more nourishing and sustaining life than can be known in the world of weekends, television, automation, and accumulated things.

Unconsecrated leisure is little more satisfactory than exploited overwork. Too little inwardness with which to meet so much confused outwardness leaves us possessors of a kingdom of noise, much traffic, great comings and goings, but little sensitivity to the meaning of it all.

MATTHEW WARREN

VACATION PRAYER

God of the Hills, grant me Thy strength to go back to cities without faltering,
Strength to go back to my daily task without tiring, and with enthusiasm;
Strength to help my neighbor who has no hills to remember.

God of the Lake, grant me Thy peace and Thy restfulness;
Peace to bring into the world of hurry and confusion,
Restfulness to carry to the tired ones whom I shall meet every day,
Content to do small things with a freedom from littleness,
Self-control for the unexpected emergency and patience for the wearisome task;
Deep depths within my soul to bear with me through the crowded places;
The hush of the night-time where the pine trees are dark against the sky line;
The humbleness of the hills which in their mightiness know not their strength;
And the laughter of the sunny days to brighten the cheerless spots of a long winter.

God of the Stars, may I take back the gift of friendship, of love for all.
Fill me with a great tenderness for the needy person at every turning.

IRENE MOTT

BOON

What the banker sighs for, the meanest clown may have—leisure and a quiet mind.

HENRY DAVID THOREAU, 1817–1862

BRIEF INTERLUDES

Ludus in Latin means to play, and *Homo Ludens* is the man who knows how to enjoy himself.

Even the person who is quite sure he has no leisure whatever, always has brief interludes for wonder, love, and praise, if only he trains himself to recognize them. For instance, while dressing and undressing; while walking to or from work; when solitary at meals; between dates; while waiting for a telephone call to come through.

Even if he carried only a poem in his pocket to be pulled out and merely glanced at, he could have a brief escape into a beloved haven of beauty and peace.

QUESTION

It used to be that when a woman needed a new dress she had to raise the sheep, shear the fleece, card the wool, spin the thread, weave the cloth, and of course, cut out the material and sew the seams together by hand.

Nowadays, although she seems to have saved an endless amount of time, she wonders where on earth all this leisure goes?

CRITERION

The best test of the quality of a civilization is the quality of its leisure. Not what the citizens do when they are obliged to do, but what they do when they can do anything by choice is the criterion of a people's life.

IRWIN EDMAN, 1896–1954

There is a world within that is spacious, and awesome, and of ineffable beauty. Its entrance is smaller than a needle's eye, and busy, hustling men, rushing to and fro, with no leisure for God, have not the time nor the vision to discover it.

SHERWOOD EDDY, 1871–1963

UNDREAMED OF ENERGY

There is all about us a knowable and discoverable spiritual world surcharged with undreamed of energy, which may be tapped and utilized when the right contact is made. This experience is available for all men.

There is a world within that is spacious, and awesome, and of ineffable beauty. But it is a world of singleness and simplicity. Prodigals may enter freely, but righteous Pharisees never find it.

SHERWOOD EDDY, 1871–1963

AN ARTIST IN OUR PLAY

A man's chosen work is ideally meant to provide him a daily avenue of self-expression; the kind of play which he freely selects reveals the range and tone of his personality.

The best kinds of play are those which engage the free exercise of our higher faculties and so include the higher enjoyments.

Be it aesthetic or athletic, it is the higher and better the more it engages our skill and subtlety and the more creative it is.

That is what we mean when we say of a man admiringly that he is an artist in his play.

RADOSLOV A. TSANOFF

LETTERS

As long as there are postmen,
life will have zest.

WILLIAM JAMES, 1842–1910

INSCRIPTION ON THE WASHINGTON POST OFFICE

Messenger of sympathy and love,
Servant of parted friends,
Consoler of the lonely,
Bond of the scattered family,
Enlarger of the common life,
Carrier of news and knowledge,
Instrument of trade and industry,
Promoter of mutual acquaintance,
Of peace and good-will
Among men and nations.

CHARLES W. ELIOT, 1834–1926

FORM OF PRAYER

Writing a letter is a form of prayer, for words are the one fundamental sacrament, the outward and visible-audible sign of an inward and spiritual grace. See how contagious and disturbing and exciting you can be. Pray before you write, and while you write, and after you write, so that the recipient may take that letter out of its pigeonhole in the desk to read and reread and reread. And even if it gets torn up, it may still haunt.

We had letters to send; couriers could not go fast enough nor far enough; but we found out that the air and earth were full of electricity; and always going our way!

Now that is the wisdom of a man, in every instance of his labor, to hitch his wagon to a star, and see his chore done by God Himself.

We cannot bring the heavenly powers to us, but if we will only choose our jobs in the direction in which they travel, they will undertake them with the greatest pleasure.

RALPH WALDO EMERSON, 1803–1882

SYMPATHY

Ask God to give thee skill
    In comfort's art,
That thou may'st consecrated be
    And set apart
Upon a life of sympathy
For heavy is the weight of ill
    In every heart;
And comforters are needed much
    Of Christlike touch.

ANNA E. HAMILTON, 1846?–1876

INVOCATION

Just as the devout when they pray enter into the presence of God, so does the spirit, in beginning a letter, place itself in the presence of the absent friend. Every letter is an invocation, and the truest memory of a friend lies in what we have written to him.

ELLEN GLASGOW, 1874–1945

LETTERS FROM GOD

Science books are letters from God, telling how He runs His universe.

TOYOHIKO KAGAWA, 1888–1960

THIS IS MY LETTER

This is my letter to the world,
    That never wrote to me,—
The simple news that Nature told,
    With tender majesty.

Her message is committed
    To hands I cannot see;
For love of her, sweet countrymen,
    Judge tenderly of me.

EMILY DICKINSON, 1830–1886

LETTER TO THOMAS WENTWORTH HIGGINSON

If I read a book and it makes my whole body so cold no fire can ever warm me, I know that is poetry. If I feel physically as if the top of my head were taken off, I know that is poetry. These are the only ways I know it. Is there any other way?

EMILY DICKINSON, 1830–1886

From SONG OF MYSELF

Why should I wish to see God better than this day?
I see something of God each hour of the twenty-four, and each moment then,
In the faces of men and women I see God, and in my own face in the glass,
I find letters from God dropt in the street, and every one is sign'd by God's name,
And I leave them where they are, for I know that wheresoe'er I go
Others will punctually come forever and ever.

WALT WHITMAN, 1819–1892

THOSE METHODIST PREACHERS

The Duchess of Buckingham indignantly wrote to Selina Hastings, the Countess of Huntington and friend of George Whitefield:

"I thank your ladyship for the information concerning the Methodist preachers.

"Their doctrines are most repulsive and strongly tinctured with impertinence and disrespect towards their superiors in perpetually endeavoring to level all ranks and do away with all distinctions.

"It is monstrous to be told that you have a heart as sinful as the common wretches that crawl on earth.

"This is highly offensive and insulting, and I cannot but wonder that your ladyship should relish any sentiments so much at variance with high rank and good breeding."

GRANDMOTHER'S ADVICE

Her exalted rank did not give Queen Victoria immunity from the trials of a grandmother.

One of her grandsons, whose recklessness in spending money provoked her strong disapproval, wrote to the queen reminding her of his approaching birthday and delicately suggested that money would be the most acceptable gift.

In her own hand she answered, sternly reproving the youth for the sin of extravagance and urging upon him the practice of economy.

His reply staggered her: "Dear Grandma, thank you for your kind letter of advice. I have sold the same for five pounds."

HERBERT V. PROCHNOW

IN RESPONSE TO A LETTER

In December 1850, Harriet Beecher Stowe, with a meager income and a struggle to make both ends meet, described herself as follows: "Forty years old, a little woman just as thin and dry as a pinch of snuff, never much to look at in my best days, and looking like a used-up article now." (And wanting more than anything else a new silk dress to improve her looks, but never able to afford it on a minister's salary.)

Her sister had just written her about the attempted enforcement of the Fugitive Slave Law: "Now, Hattie, if I could use a pen as you can, I would write something that would make this whole nation feel what an accursed thing slavery is!"

She cried, "God helping me I will write something if I live."

And after communion at church one Sunday, she rushed home, frantic, to write her inspiration on brown wrapping paper: "It seemed to me that there was no hope, that nobody would read, nobody would pity, that this system would pursue its victims into free states, and might at least threaten them even in Canada. I put my life blood, my prayers, my tears into the book. Yet I didn't do it! I didn't write it! God wrote *Uncle Tom's Cabin*. I merely did His dictation."

Three thousand copies were sold the first day; 10,000 in ten days; 300,000 the first year. Three paper mills vainly tried to supply the necessary paper. Three printing presses ran twenty-four hours a day.

She earned $10,000 in four months. She became by far the most prominent woman in the world as her book was translated into Armenian, Bohemian, Danish, Dutch, Finnish, French, German, Hungarian, Greek, Russian, Servian, Spanish, and Swedish.

When she was introduced to Abraham Lincoln in Washington, he said: "What! are you the little woman that caused this great war?"

THE BEST WORDS

Letters,
such as written
by wise men,
are, of all
the words of men,
in my judgment,
the best.

FRANCIS BACON, 1561–1626

TO PETER ABELARD

What cannot letters inspire?
They have souls;
they can speak;
they have in them all that force which
    expresses the transports of the heart;
they have all the fire of our passions;
they can raise them as much as if the
    persons themselves were present;
they have all the tenderness and the
    delicacy of speech, and sometimes
    even a boldness of expression be-
    yond it.

                    HÉLOÏSE, DIED 1164

TO HIS SMALL SON

To my dear son, Hans Luther:

Grace and peace in Christ, my dar-
ling son. I am very glad to hear that
you are studying well and praying dili-
gently. Go on doing so, my little son,
and when I come home I will bring you
a beautiful present.

I know a lovely, pretty garden,
where there are many children. They
wear golden coats, and pick up fine
apples, pears, cherries, and plums under the trees. They sing and jump and
are very merry. They also have beautiful little horses with bridles of gold
and saddles of silver.

I asked the man who owned the
garden who the children were. He answered, "These are the children who
gladly pray and study and are good."

Then I said, "Dear man, I also have
a son named Hans Luther. Wouldn't
he like to come into the garden and eat
such beautiful apples and pears and
ride such fine horses and play with
these children?"

Then the man said, "If he prays and
studies gladly, and is good, he too
shall come into the garden, and Lippus
and Jost with him. And when they are
all here, they shall have whistles and
drums and lutes, and all sorts of things
to make music with, and they shall
dance and shoot with little crossbows."

And he showed me a beautiful
meadow in the garden fixed for dancing. Gold whistles were hung there,
and drums and silver crossbows.

But it was early and the children had
not yet eaten, so I couldn't wait for
the dance, and I said to the man: "Dear
sir, I will go fast as I can and write it
all to my dear son Hans, that he may
study and pray well and be good and so
come into this garden. But he has an
Aunt Lena whom he will have to bring
with him."

Therefore, dear little son Hans,
study and pray bravely, and tell Lippus and Jost to do so too, and you shall
come into the garden with each other.

The dear God take care of you.
Greet Aunty Lena and give her a kiss
for me.

                    Your loving father,
                    Martin Luther

BELSHAZZAR

Belshazzar had a letter,—
He never had but one;
Belshazzar's correspondent
Concluded and begun
In that immortal copy
The conscience of us all
Can read without its glasses
On revelation's wall.

                    EMILY DICKINSON, 1830–1886

Words are wind in empty space,
Writing leaves a lasting trace.
FROM THE CHINESE

⚜

"MAGNIFICENT OBSESSION"

Dear————:

You have asked me to do a good deed to help you and I will.

In return, I ask you to prove your gratitude by keeping alive my good deed. Pledge me you will not let it die.

When the "other fellow" needs help, think of this day and help him if you can. So will my good deed continue to live on in yours.

And if you bind him to help others, too, and he binds them, and so on, then, if they keep their pledge, neither my good deed, nor yours, nor his, nor theirs will ever die.

Then thousand years hereafter, perhaps, our simple deed of kindness still will be active in the earth, passing from heart to heart of men and women who will never have heard of us but who, nevertheless, will be heartened and comforted because today I tried to help you and you, in return, pledged me truly to keep my good deed alive.
ARCHER C. JONES

⚜

LETTER TO A NIECE

I condole with you. We have lost a most dear and valuable relation. But it is the will of God and nature that these mortal bodies be laid aside, when the soul is to enter into real life. This is rather an embryo state, a preparation for living.

A man is not completely born until he is dead. Why then should we grieve that a new child is born among the immortals, a new member added to their happy society?

We are spirits. That bodies should be lent us while they afford us pleasure, assist us in acquiring knowledge, or in doing good to our fellow creatures, is a kind and benevolent act of God.

When they become unfit for these purposes and afford us pain instead of pleasure, instead of an aid become an incumbrance, and answer none of the intentions for which they were given, it is equally kind and benevolent that a way is provided by which we can get rid of them. Death is that way.

We ourselves, in some cases, prudently choose a partial death. A mangled painful limb, which cannot be restored, we willingly cut off. He who plucks out a tooth, parts at once with all pains and possibilities of pains and diseases which it is liable to.

Our friend and we are invited abroad on a party of pleasure, which is to last forever. His chair was ready first, and he is gone before us. We could not conveniently all start together, and why should you and I be grieved at this, since we are soon to follow, and know where to find him?

Adieu,
Benjamin Franklin

Neither snow, nor rain,
nor heat, nor night
stays these couriers
from the swift completion
of their appointed rounds.
HERODOTUS, 484?–425? B.C.

A DAY IN SPRING

ACT I

In a Radcliffe College classroom, Professor William James is conducting a semi-final examination in Philosophy.

Outdoors, a charming breeze with the radiance of Spring. Enter Gertrude Stein.

She has attended the opera in Boston every night that week.

What with weather so lovely outdoors and music still sounding in her ears, it is hard for her to settle down.

But she sits. She glances briefly at the examination paper. She feels an immense boredom sweep over her. Thereupon she writes: "Dear Professor James, I am so sorry, but I simply do not feel a bit like an examination paper on Philosophy today."

Exit Gertrude Stein.

Curtain.

ACT II

The next morning she receives a post card bearing the following message: "Dear Miss Stein, I understand perfectly how you feel. I often feel like that myself."

Underneath Professor James recorded Miss Stein's grade—the highest mark in all that class.

A TEACHER RECEIVES AN AZALEA PLANT FROM HIS STUDENTS

Dear Young Ladies,

I am deeply touched by your remembrance.

It is the first time anyone ever treated me so kindly, so you may well believe that the impression on the heart of the lonely sufferer will be even more durable than the impression on your mind of all the teachings of Philosophy 2A.

I now perceive one immense omission in my Psychology,—the deepest principle of human nature is the craving to be appreciated, and I left it out altogether from the book, because I had never had it gratified till now.

I fear you have let loose a demon in me, and that all my actions will now be for the sake of such rewards.

However, I will try to be faithful to this one unique and beautiful azalea tree, the pride of my life and delight of my existence.

Winter and summer will I tend and water it—even with my tears. Mrs. James shall never go near it or touch it.

If it dies, I will die too, and if I die, it shall be planted on my grave.

Don't take all this too jocosely, but believe in the extreme pleasure you have caused me, and in the affectionate feelings with which I am and shall always be faithfully your friend,

William James

A pleasant letter I hold to be the pleasantest thing that this world has to give.

ANTHONY TROLLOPE, 1815–1882

TO A FRIEND

There is nothing to write about, you say. Well, then, write and let me know just this—that there is nothing to write about.

PLINY THE YOUNGER,
A.D. 62?–C. 113

LETTER TO THE EDITOR

Some years ago a little girl in Rockville, Maryland, wrote the following letter to *The Washington Post:*

"We are studying the world. We would like to have some information on these topics:

"How the world started.

"How the world changed.

"How the world actually is now.

"Our relation to the world.

"How we can best leave this world for others who follow us."

The editor replied in the paper in these words:

"We can answer just one point: how the world is now. The answer is, terrible."

But when the editor saw his reply in print, he reconsidered and in the second edition on the same day he offered a totally different response:

"All the answers are in the Bible, particularly in the story of Jesus. We do know one thing: the world is a beautiful place."

TO A GRIEVING HUSBAND

My dear friend,

I have thought much about our meeting last Sunday, and the few words we had together.

May I try to tell you again where your comfort lies? It is not in forgetting the happy past. People bring us well-meant but miserable consolation when they tell us what time will do to our grief. We do not want to lose our grief, because our grief is bound up with our love and we could not cease to mourn without being robbed of our affection.

But if you know, as you do know, that the great and awful change, which has come into your life and brought you such distress, has brought your dear wife the joy of heaven, can you not, in the midst of all your suffering, rejoice for her?

And if knowing she is with God, you can be with God, too, and every day claim His protection and try to do His will, may you not still in spirit be very near to her?

She is not dead, but living, and if you are sure what care is holding her, and educating her, you can be very contentedly with her in spirit, and look forward confidently to the day when you shall also go to God and be with her.

I know that this does not take away your pain. No one can do that. You do not want any one to do that, not even God. But it can help you to bear it, to be brave and cheerful, to do your duty, and to live the pure, earnest, spiritual life which she, in heaven, wishes you to live.

My dear friend, she is yours forever. God never takes away what He has once given. May He make you worthy of her! May He comfort you and make you strong!

> Your friend, sincerely,
> Phillips Brooks

CHARM

Our thoughts, as expressed in our respective letters, are very much alike, but comparison will prove what has been so often remarked, that female correspondence has a charm in it of which that of my sex is always devoid.

JOHN SCOTT

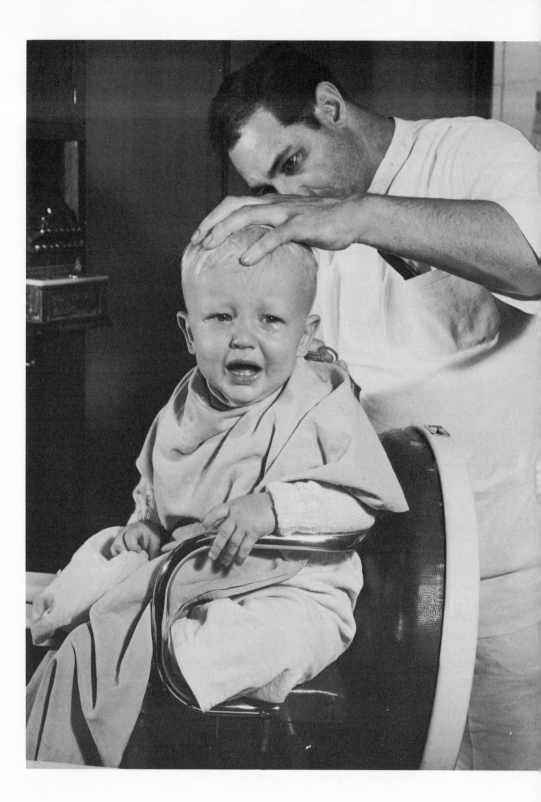

LIFE

*There is surely a piece of Divinity
in us, something that was before the
Elements, and owes no Homage to
the Sun.*

SIR THOMAS BROWNE, 1605–1682

FIREPROOF UNIVERSE

I take great comfort in God. I think
He is sometimes much amused at the
human race, but on the whole He loves
us. He would never have let us get at
the match-box if He had not known
that the frame-work of the universe
is fireproof.

JAMES RUSSELL LOWELL, 1819–1891

Never point a finger of scorn at another, for in so doing you are pointing
three fingers of scorn at your own self.

BURMESE PROVERB

TO MOVE THE MASSES

It takes a soul
To move a body; it takes a high-
    minded man
To move the masses, even to a cleaner
    style;
It takes the ideal, to blow a hair's
    breadth off
The dust of the actual—Ah, your
    couriers failed
Because not poet enough to under-
    stand
That life develops from within.

ELIZABETH BARRETT BROWNING,
1806–1861

MAN IS A REED
THAT THINKS

Man is but a reed, the feeblest thing
in nature. But he is a reed that thinks.

An exhalation, a drop of water,
suffices to destroy him; but were the
universe to crush man, man is yet
nobler than the universe, for he knows
that he dies, and the universe, even in
prevailing against him, knows not its
power.

BLAISE PASCAL, 1623–1662

Burn up, like thorns, all my transgressions.
Purge Thou my soul, and hallow my
imagination.
Knit firm my bones and joints withal.
Shine into all the five senses of my
body.

Fasten me wholly in the fear of Thee.
Guard, shield, and shelter me evermore from every deed and word
which stains the soul.
Cleanse, wash, adorn me. Set me right.
Give me understanding. Enlighten me.
Prove me the habitation of Thy Spirit
and in no wise the dwelling-place
of sin.

From DIVINE LITURGY
(Greek Orthodox)

✧

INHERITANCE
I am the owner of the sphere,
Of the seven stars and the solar year,
Of Caesar's hand, and Plato's brain,
Of Lord Christ's heart, and Shake-
speare's strain.

RALPH WALDO EMERSON,
1803–1882

✧

SKY-WOVEN
To the eye of vulgar logic, what is
man? An omnivorous biped that wears
breeches.

To the eye of pure reason, what is
he? A soul, a spirit, a divine apparition.

Round his mysterious me, there lies,
under all these woolrags, a garment of
flesh, contextured in the loom of
heaven; whereby he is revealed to his
like, and dwells with them in union

and division; and sees and fashions
for himself a universe of years.

Deep-hidden is he under that
strange garment; amid sounds and
colors and forms, as it were, swathed
in, and inextricably overshadowed. Yet
it is sky-woven, and worthy of a God.

THOMAS CARLYLE, 1795–1881

✧

YOURS ARE THE HANDS
Christ has no body now on earth but
yours,
Yours are the eyes through which
Christ looks out upon the world,
Yours are the feet with which He is
to go about doing good,
Yours are the hands with which He is
to bless us now.

ST. TERESA, 1515–1582

✧

From STRADIVARIUS
God be praised,
Antonio Stradivari has an eye
That winces at false work and loves
the true.

*

And for my fame—when any master
holds
'Twixt chin and hand a violin of mine,
He will be glad that Stradivari lived,
Made violins, and made them of the
best.

*

I say not God Himself can make man's
best
Without best men to help Him.

*

'Tis God gives skill,
But not without men's hands: He could
not make
Antonio Stradivari's violins
Without Antonio.

GEORGE ELIOT, 1819–1880

Every man is the builder of a temple called his body. We are all sculptors and painters, and our material is our own flesh and blood and bones. Any nobleness begins at once to refine a man's features, any meanness or sensuality to imbrute them.

HENRY DAVID THOREAU, 1817–1862

MOMENTOUS MOMENT

Here you sit, held together by a fabulous interweaving of flexible muscles and tendons and cartilages, all comfortably tucked inside an enormous envelope called skin, which in turn is made up of literally billions of cells, each busy every blessed second wearing out, eliminating, and then building up.

Yet you take your incredible body for granted, unless something goes wrong.

Even the Psalmist centuries ago noticed. "I am fearfully and wonderfully made."

Part of the wonder is that you have so little fear. Rarely do you remind your pulse: "For heaven's sake, beat!" Or your heart: "Did you pump? Did you count it? How often per minute? Five quarts a moment, I hope. Seventy-five an hour, remember!" Or to each little drop of blood: "Are you taking your exciting excursion trip through 169 miles of my canalways and blood vessels in three minutes?" Or to your eyelids: "Did you blink? And are my tear ducts sluicing off the dust from my eye-balls regularly?"

Best of all, how blest you should feel that instead of making you embarrassingly tall to contain the thirty-five to forty feet of tubes inside your intestinal and kidney tracts, your Creator cleverly looped them into a neat little twenty cubic inches.

It might be well, therefore, to say to your brain, "Ponder!" For your body is a temple made for worship and thanksgiving, and you have much for which to be profoundly grateful every moment of every day that you dare live so carefree of all these details.

THE BODY IS A JEWEL

What diamonds are equal to my eyes?
What labyrinths to my ears?
What gates of ivory or ruby leaves to
    the double portal of my lips and
    teeth?
Is not sight a jewel?
Is not hearing a treasure?
Is not speech a glory?

O my Lord, pardon my ingratitude,
    and pity my dullness who am not
    sensible of these gifts.
The freedom of Thy bounty hath deceived me
These things were too near to be considered.
Thou presenteth me with Thy blessings, and I was not aware.
But now I give thanks and adore and
    praise Thee for Thine inestimable
    favors.

THOMAS TRAHERNE, 1637–1674

A man finds room in a few square inches of the face for the traits of all his ancestors, the expression of all his story, and his wants.

RALPH WALDO EMERSON, 1803–1882

OUR COMMON SPIRIT

I am sure that there is a common Spirit that plays within us.

This is that gentle heat that broodeth on the waters and in six days hatched the world.

This is that irradiation that dispels the mists of hell, the clouds of horror, fear, sorrow, despair, and preserves the region of the mind in serenity.

Whosoever feels not the warm gale and ventilation of the Spirit (though I feel his pulse) I dare not say he lives; for truly without this, there is no heat under the tropick; nor any light, though I dwell in the body of the sun.

SIR THOMAS BROWNE, 1605–1682

LIFE

Forenoon and afternoon and night,—
    Forenoon,
And afternoon, and night,—Forenoon,
    and—what!
The empty song repeats itself. No
    more?
Yea, that is Life: make this forenoon
    sublime,
This afternoon a psalm, this night a
    prayer,
And Time is conquered, and thy crown
    is noon.

EDWARD ROWLAND SILL, 1841–1887

MAKE A CIRCUIT
AROUND YOURSELF

Imitate, if you can, the hexagons of the bees, the barns of the ants, the webs of the spiders, the threads of the silkworm.

Endure, if you can, those mean crea-tures of your bed and of your roof, the venom of the mosquito, the beetle's poison, the spear and trumpet of the gnat.

Of what kind will the greater creatures be, when you are helped or harmed by such small things, that you may not even in small things despise the Creator?

Make a circuit around yourself. Survey man within and without. Even this work of God will please you, because the Lord, the greater God, loved it so well, and for the sake of the human body toiled to descend from Heaven among these poverty-stricken elements, for the sake of which, even in this little cell of the Creator, He was crucified.

But see—up to this moment He has not disdained the water with which He washes His own people, nor the oil wherewith He anoints them, nor the mingled milk and honey wherewith He feeds His children, nor the bread which is the representation of His own body.

TERTULLIAN, C. 150–C. 230

O Lord, we have a busy world around us. Eye, ear, and thoughts will be needed for all our work to be done in the world. Ere we enter upon that work we would commit eye, ear, and thought to Thee. Do Thou bless them, and keep their work Thine, that, as through Thy natural laws our hearts beat and our blood flows without any thought of ours for them, so our spiritual life may hold course at those times when our minds cannot consciously turn to Thee.

THOMAS ARNOLD, 1795–1842

YOUR ATTITUDE TOWARD YOUR BODY

Do not pay too much attention to the stupid old body. When you have trained it, made it healthy, beautiful, and your willing servant, why, then do not reverse the order and become its slave and attendant. (The dog must follow the master, not the master the dog.)

Remember that if you walk away from it and leave it behind, it will have to follow you. It will grow by following, by continually reaching up to you. Incredibly beautiful it will become, and suffused by a kind of intelligence.

But if you turn and wait upon it— and its mouth and its belly and its sex-wants and all its little ape-tricks, preparing and dishing up pleasures and satisfactions for these,—why, then, instead of the body becoming like you, you will become like the body, incredibly stupid and unformed— going back in the path of evolution—you too with fishmouth and toad belly, and imprisoned in your own members, as it were an Ariel in a blundering Caliban.

Therefore, quite lightly and decisively at each turning-point in the path, leave your body a little behind.

With its hungers and sleeps, and funny little needs and vanities. Pay no attention to them.

Slipping out at last a few steps in advance, till it catch you up again.

Absolutely determined not to be finally bound and weighted down by it.

Or fossilized into one set form.

Which alone, after all, is death.

EDWARD CARPENTER

WHAT IS THE WORTH OF A MAN?

In two worlds we live, with one of which visibility, time, and death have everything to do, but in the other of which there is a sense of timelessness, as though truth and love and beauty and character might go on expanding forever.

An average man contains enough fat to make seven bars of soap, enough iron to make a medium-sized nail, enough sugar to fill a shaker, enough lime to whitewash a chicken-coop, enough phosphorus to make twenty-two hundred match tips, enough magnesium for a dose of magnesia, enough potassium to explode a toy cannon, together with a little sulphur. And the chemists figured that at market rates then current these chemical elements could be obtained for about ninety-eight cents.

That's what we are made of. That's what all our seers and prophets, the great musicians, the great poets, the great leaders of the race, have been made of, about ninety-eight cents' worth of chemical materials.

And if death ends everything, they were made of nothing else, merely these fugitive, transient elements, and all that seemed eternal in them of our glory and our hope, was but an accidental by-product of ninety-eight cents' worth of chemicals.

Man, if you can believe that, you can believe anything. No, it is the eternal in us that even here is the realest part of us.

HARRY EMERSON FOSDICK

THE MAKING OF MAN

The One bethought him to make man
Of many-colored dust,
And mixed the Holy Spirit in
In portions right and just;

Each had a part of mind and heart
From One Himself in trust;
Thus came the brown and yellow man,
And black and white and red.

So different in their outer look,
Alike in heart and head—
The selfsame dust before their birth,
The selfsame dust when dead.

                              PAI TA-SHUN

From SONG OF MYSELF

I have said that the soul is not more
    than the body,
And I have said that the body is not
    more than the soul,
And nothing, not God, is greater to
    one than one's self is,
And whoever walks a furlong without
    sympathy walks to his own funeral
    drest in his shroud.

        WALT WHITMAN, 1819–1892

FILLED WITH LIGHT

The one who has seen his foot in an
x-ray machine, such as are kept in the
corrective shoe-fitting departments of
many stores, has seen his foot in a different light. It is seen not as a solid and
impenetrable thing covered with skin
but as a shape made up of light, the
bones being merely a shadow in that
light.

    "But that is not the reality," we may
say.

Why not? We are seeing the foot illuminated by a greater light. Why may
not that more intense light-vibration
show as true a reality as the naked eye
can see?

Science tells us that it does, for the
body is made not of matter but of
energy, open and penetrable to the
various forces in the air. Sunlight penetrates the open spaces of the body. The
vibrations of electric shock treatments
can be sent through apparently solid
flesh. The light of x-ray and radium
shines through the body as easily as if
it were made of light itself, as indeed
it is.

And above and beyond all these, a
spiritual light vibration penetrates and
fills every cell of the body. In other
words, we are porous like a sponge
and filled with God.

                          AGNES SANFORD

PROVERBIAL LORE

You can't dance at two weddings with
    one pair of feet.

                          HEBREW PROVERB

The heart carries the feet.

                          HEBREW PROVERB

Compromise is one pair of feet trying
    to go two different directions at
    once.

                          AFRICAN PROVERB

Move hand and foot, so help you God.

                          DANISH PROVERB

I complained because I had no shoes
    until I met a man who had no feet.

                          ARABIAN PROVERB

Life is a succession of lessons which must be lived to be understood.

RALPH WALDO EMERSON,
1803–1882

✠

BEHOLD THE MICROBE!

We're not so much after all, we human beings, compared with a microbe.

They are so small we can't see them, but they can knock us galley-west in a few hours these Spring days.

Dr. Slosson tells of a scientist who has conceived of a way to tell us just about how big a microbe is compared with a man.

The plan is to imagine a bacterium enlarged to the size of a sphere one inch in diameter. If the average man were enlarged in like proportions, he would be thirty miles tall.

Dr. Slosson also tells us that this rascal of a bacterium has a wicked way about him of reproducing himself every twenty minutes. At this rate at the end of twenty minutes more each will be adult size and will have reproduced again. Within eight hours the one bacterium will have become 16,000,000 in number.

Can you get that? If not, let this gentle thought sink into your reader mind; at the end of twenty-four hours—just one day—if nothing happened to kill those nice little bacteria, there would be just 500 tons of them by weight.

WILLIAM L. STIDGER, 1885–1949

✠

I wonder if heaven will not be a long gazing on a face ye canna tire of, but must ever have one more glimpse.

MARY WEBB, 1881–1927

RENEWAL

Everything in our physical bodies is renewed completely every seven years —everything but the enamel on our teeth.

Dare we say that if skin and bone and tissue and hair and nails are renewable automatically, that there is not enough life also to renew our spirits more abundantly?

The Apostle Paul in his famous letter to the Corinthians about victorious living and dying, gives us an epitaph to live with: "I die daily." Christ must increase; I must decrease. It has been done, impossible as that seems.

John the Baptist did it.

Peter did it.

David Livingstone did it.

Robert Moffat did it.

Growth is a constant rehearsal of death and resurrection. Sleep is a constant rehearsal of death and awakening. Winter is a constant rehearsal of summer. Low tide is a constant rehearsal of high tide.

And some of us are far higher than we think. For instance, in Bunhill Fields Cemetery, London, there is an epitaph reading:

BORN A MAN
DIED A GROCER.

Most of us live above that low level.

✠

You must learn, you must let God teach you, that the only way to get rid of your past is to make a future out of it. God will waste nothing.

PHILLIPS BROOKS, 1835–1893

A LIVING SACRIFICE

With eyes wide open to the mercies of God, I beg you, my brothers, as an act of intelligent worship, to give him your bodies, as a living sacrifice, consecrated to him and acceptable by him. Don't let the world around you squeeze you into its own mold, but let God remold your minds from within, so that you may prove in practice that the plan of God for you is good, meets all his demands and moves toward the goal of true maturity.

ROMANS 12:1—2
Tr. J. B. PHILLIPS

INDIRECTION

Fair are the flowers and the children,
    but their subtle suggestion is fairer;
Rare is the roseburst of dawn, but the
    secret that clasps it is rarer;
Sweet the exultance of song, but the
    strain that precedes it is sweeter;
And never was poem yet writ, but the
    meaning outmastered the meter.

Never a daisy that grows, but a mystery
    guideth the growing;
Never a river that flows, but a majesty
    scepters the flowing;
Never a Shakespeare that soared, but a
    stronger than he did enfold him,
Nor ever a prophet foretells, but a
    mightier seer has foretold him.

Back of the canvas that throbs, the
    painter is hinted and hidden;
Into the statue that breathes, the soul
    of the sculptor is hidden;
Under the joy that is felt, lie the infinite issues of feeling;
Crowning the glory revealed is the
    glory that crowns the revealing.

Great are the symbols of being, but
    that which is symboled is greater;
Vast the created and beheld, but vaster
    the inward creator;
Back of the sound broods the silence,
    back of the gift stands the giving;
Back of the hand that received, thrill
    the sensitive nerves of receiving.

Space is as nothing to spirit, the deed is
    outdone by the doing;
The heart of the wooer is warm, but
    warmer the heart of the wooing;
And up from the pits where these
    shiver, and up from the heights
    where those shine,
Twin voices and shadows swim starward, and the essence of life is
    divine.

RICHARD REALF, 1834—1878

PAUL SPEAKS ON MARS' HILL

God that made the world and all things therein, seeing that he is Lord of heaven and earth, dwelleth not in temples made with hands;

Neither is worshipped with men's hands, as though he needed anything, seeing he giveth to all life, and breath, and all things;

And hath made of one blood all nations of men for to dwell on all the face of the earth, and both determined the times before appointed, and the bounds of their habitation;

That they should seek the Lord, if haply they feel after him, and find him, though he be not far from every one of us:

For in him we live, and move, and have our being.

ACTS 17:24—28

ON HIS NINETIETH BIRTHDAY

You need not end by shrinking,
Use all the little you have still,
With all the power you have still,
For all the people you still know.
Keep thinking.
And so praise God and grow.

JOHN R. MOTT, 1865–1955

A PRAYER FOR OLD AGE

Lord, thou knowest better than I know myself that I am old and growing older.

Keep me from the fatal habit of thinking that I must say something on every subject and on every occasion.

Release me from craving to straighten out everybody's affairs.

Make me thoughtful but not moody; helpful but not bossy. With my store of wisdom it seems a pity not to use it all, but Thou knowest that I want a few friends at the end.

Keep me free from the recital of endless details; give me wings to get to the point.

Seal my lips on my aches and pains. They are increasing, and love for rehearsing them is becoming sweeter as the years go by.

I dare not ask for grace enough to enjoy the details of others' aches and pains, but help me to endure them with patience.

I dare not ask for improved memory, but rather I ask for a growing humility and a lessening cocksureness when my memory seems to clash with the memory of others.

Teach me the gracious lesson that occasionally I may be mistaken.

Keep me reasonably sweet. I do not want to be a saint—some of them are so hard to live with—but a sour old person is one of the crowning works of the devil.

Give me the ability to see good things in unexpected places and talents in unexpected people. Give me the grace to tell them so.

AUTHOR UNKNOWN

ROADMAKERS

We are multiplied by our proxies. How easily we adopt their labors!

Every ship that comes to America got its chart from Columbus.

Every novel is a debtor to Homer.

Every carpenter who shaves with a foreplane borrows the genius of a forgotten inventor.

Life is girt all around with a zodiac of sciences, the contributions of men who have perished to add their point of light to our sky.

Engineer, broker, jurist, physician, moralist, theologian, and every man, in as much as he has any science, is a definer and mapmaker of the latitudes and longitudes of our conditions. These roadmakers on every hand enrich us.

We must extend the area of life and multiply our relations. We are as much gainers by finding a new property in the old earth as by acquiring a new planet.

We are too passive in the reception of these material and semi-material aids. We must not be sacks and stomachs.

RALPH WALDO EMERSON, 1803–1882

LOVE

From A DEATH IN
THE DESERT

*For life, with all its yields of joy and
 woe,
And hope and fear,—believe the aged
 friend,—
Is just our chance o' the prize of learning love,
How love might be, hath been indeed,
 and is.*

ROBERT BROWNING, 1812–1889

HIDDENNESS

Up then, noble soul! Put on thy jump-
ing boots which are Intellect and Love,
and overleap thy mental powers, overleap thine understanding, and spring
into the heart of God, into the hidden-
ness where thou art hidden from all
creatures.

MEISTER ECKHART, 1260–1328

BEST PORTION

That best portion of a good man's life,
His little, nameless, unremembered
 acts
Of kindness and of love.

WILLIAM WORDSWORTH, 1770–1850
From TINTERN ABBEY

TO LIVE IS TO LOVE

To love abundantly is to live forever.
Hence, eternal life is inextricably
bound up with love.

We want to live forever for the same
reason that we want to live tomorrow.

Why do you want to live tomorrow?
It is because there is someone who
loves you, and whom you want to see
tomorrow, and be with, and love back.

There is no other reason why we
should live on than that we love and
are beloved.

It is when a man has no one to love
him that he commits suicide.

So long as he has friends, those who
love him and whom he loves, he will
live, because to live is to love.

HENRY DRUMMOND, 1851–1897

CLASSROOM OF LOVE

I am the man who, when Love lectures
in the heart, takes notes, and then re-
tells the lessons to the rest of men.

DANTE ALIGHIERI, 1265–1321

Love makes its record in deeper colors
as we grow out of childhood into man-
hood: as the emperors signed their
names in green ink when under age,
but when of age, in purple.

HENRY WADSWORTH LONGFELLOW,
1807–1882

OUR HARDEST LESSON

Love is the hardest lesson in Christianity; but, for that reason, it should be
most our care to learn it.

WILLIAM PENN, 1621–1670

AUGMENTED LOVE

We cannot know whether we love
God, although there may be strong reasons for thinking so, but there can be
no doubt about whether we love our
neighbor or no.

Be sure that in proportion as you advance in fraternal charity, you are increasing in your love of God, for His
Majesty bears so tender an affection for
us, that I cannot doubt He will repay
our love for others by augmenting, in
a thousand different ways, that which
we bear for Him.

ST. TERESA, 1515–1582

ALL-EMBRACING LOVE

And let not man's sin dishearten thee.
Love a man even in his sin, for that
love is a likeness of the divine love,
and is the summit of love on earth.

Love all God's creation, both the
whole and every grain of sand. Love
every leaf, every ray of light. Love the
animals, love the plants, love each
separate thing.

If thou love each thing, thou wilt
perceive the mystery of God in all; and
when thou perceive this, thou wilt
thenceforward grow every day to a
fuller understanding of it, until thou
come at last to love the whole world
with a love that will then be all-embracing and universal.

FEODOR DOSTOEVSKI, 1821–1881

IN PRAYER

I: I want to be alone with you, Lord.
    Who is he standing there?
LORD: Your needy brother.
I: But I want to be alone with you
    when I commune with you.
LORD: He is always with me.

ARTHUR B. RHINOW

WE EXIST TO LOVE

Who can doubt that we exist only to
love? Disguise it, in fact, as we will,
we love without intermission. Where
we seem most effectually to shut out
love, it lies covert and concealed; we
live not a moment exempt from its influence.

BLAISE PASCAL, 1623–1662

REVERENCE FOR LIFE

Albert Schweitzer took Americans by storm when he lectured across this country. He was wise and gentle and simple and gay.

People were stirred by his greatness which he never seemed to know he possessed. Everyone turned to books about him, new and old, to discover his secret. Three words summarized the man and his mind. They were: "Reverence for Life."

When he was only a boy he used to pass a statue in Alsace-Lorraine of some magnificent French general, home from Africa, and a Negro slave, stooped over, at his feet.

One day Schweitzer thought that somebody ought to atone for the sins of all white men against all black men. And then, quite simply, came his answer: "I, Albert Schweitzer, will atone."

Next there was his wider sense of renewal when he said that he had been swept up into a new course of life for the love of God.

When men asked him why he gave up music and theology to practice medicine, his answer was simple: "I wanted to be a doctor so that I could practice a religion of love without having to talk about it!"

Some Americans found that his life was summed up for them one day in a New York railroad station when they were waiting to say good-by to him. Schweitzer noticed an old lady struggling with two suitcases. So he went over and carried them for her, as naturally as though he and she were related. As, indeed, they were. For in Christ Jesus they were both one. Here was "reverence for life" in action.

PRAYER

Receive, O Lord, my liberty, my memory, my understanding, and all my will. Thou hast given me all that I am and possess, and I surrender all to Thy divine will that Thou mayst dispose of me. Give me only Thy love and Thy grace. With these I shall be rich enough, and I ask for nothing more.

ST. IGNATIUS OF LOYOLA, 1491–1556

The true measure of loving God is to love Him without measure.

ST. BERNARD OF CLAIRVAUX, 1090?–1153

Love is an overworked word for an unemployed emotion.

AUTHOR UNKNOWN

ACT OF LOVE

I make an act of love toward all my fellowmen. I accept them as they are, with all their sins and failures, and declare my solidarity with them.

If any have wronged or grieved me, I place my mind within the all-comprehending and all-loving mind of God, and here and now forgive.

I desire to minister God's love to men and to offer no hindrance to the free flow of His love through me.

I affirm my faith in life. I call life good and not evil.

I accept the limitations of my own life and believe it is possible for me to live a beautiful and Christ-like life within the conditions set for me.

WALTER RAUSCHENBUSCH, 1861–1918

THOSE WHO HELP

All knowledge is frivolous for the same reason that it is innocent, namely because it does not of itself move what is serious, the will. Only the will can will to make use of knowledge.

As demagogues know only too well, knowledge itself is apt, if anything, to ensnare the mind in frivolous self-reflection and paralyze the will.

How often is it true that the ignorant who do not know how to help their neighbor and the weak who lack the power to help him, nevertheless, are the ones who love him, while the learned and strong who could help him, do not because they no longer love him; on the contrary they use their knowledge and power to rob and enslave him.

W. H. AUDEN

By loving hands the cloak is shared and the loaf is shared, and the work and the penny are shared. The sorrows and the prayers and hopes are shared. By loving hearts they are shared, and by the fulfillers of the commandment. By desperate men and by the servant of Christ they are shared. To what new country do they rush forward—these two, hand in hand, with the winds of God behind them, and before them, in the dark night, the shining of a bright and morning Star?

JEAN KENYON MAC KENZIE, 1874–1936

See how these Christians love one another!

TERTULLIAN, C. 150–C. 230

We are born for love. It is the principle of existence and its only end.

BENJAMIN DISRAELI, 1804–1881

Love, then, hath every bliss in store;
'Tis friendship, and 'tis something more.
Each other wish they give;
Not to know love is not to live.

JOHN GAY, 1685–1732

THE RETURN

Instead of allowing yourself to be unhappy, just let your love grow as God wants it to grow. Seek goodness in others. Love more persons more. Love them more impersonally, more unselfishly, without thought of return. The return, never fear, will take care of itself.

HENRY DRUMMOND, 1851–1897

GROWING IN LOVE

Everything we do, if we learn to do it simply for God, is, here and now, the one means of growing in love for Him.

Today it is cooking and scrubbing; tomorrow it may be utterly different.

Let us practice a genial concentration upon just the one thing picked out for us by God. More than half our life goes into wishing for things other than those sent us.

Yet it is these things, as sent, and when willed and at last loved as sent, that train us for Home, that can form a Spiritual Home for us even here and now.

FRIEDRICH VON HÜGEL, 1852–1925

YOUR SECRET VOICE

You in whose veins runs the fire of
loving,
For people, for plants, for little animals,
For rocks and earth, stars and the elements,
You have a secret Voice, always singing.

It is never still. It runs with your haste
And idles in your silence. It is every-
where.
O you, for whom this passionate Voice
sings
And will not be silent, think now of
those
For whom no voice sounds. Of those
who toil
Without the singing voice,
And live in a world which has not yet
come through
Into your world
Oh, can you not hear that the song
your Voice is singing
Is the song which is to bring that
world of theirs
Into the light which must light all
men?

Why else do you imagine that this
Voice is singing?
Why else do you imagine that the fire
of love
Runs in your veins?
                    ZONA GALE, 1874–1938

Pursue, keep up with, circle round and
round your life, as a dog does his
master's chaise. Do what you love.
Know your own bone; gnaw at it, bury
it, unearth it, and gnaw it still.
    HENRY DAVID THOREAU, 1817–1862

MEDIEVAL PRAYER

Almighty God, Father, Son, and Spirit,
who art power, wisdom, and love,
inspire in us those same three things:
power to serve Thee,
wisdom to please Thee,
and love to accomplish Thy will;
power that I may do,
wisdom that I may know what to do,
and love that I may be moved to do all
    that is pleasing to Thee.

Enable us, O God, to rise above ourselves to Thee, and from Thee to go
below ourselves in love, and to remain
always in Thee, and in love.
            MARTIN LUTHER, 1483–1546

LOVE AND PRAYER

The germ of love is the germ of prayer.
    The development and the perfection
of love are the development and perfection of prayer.
    If you do not understand this, you
have never yet loved and never prayed.
        JEAN NICOLAS GROU, 1731–1803

I am in wretched health, but God does
so much through me that sometimes I
have to laugh at myself.
            ST. TERESA, 1515–1582

AGENT OF LOVE

He who would belong to the Kingdom of Love as a recipient must belong to it as an agent.

AUTHOR UNKNOWN

SAYING YES AND NO

We have to ask God to teach us together to say no and to say yes in truth.

No to all that flouts the love of Christ, to every system, every programme, and every person that treats any man as though he were an irresponsible thing or as a means of profit, to the defenders of injustice in the name of order, to those who sow the seeds of war or urge war as inevitable.

Yes to all that conforms to the love of Christ, to all who speak for justice, to the peacemakers, to all who hope, fight, and suffer for the cause of man, to all who—even without knowing it—look for a new earth wherein dwelleth righteousness.

WORLD COUNCIL OF CHURCHES

UNACCOUNTABLE JOY

Love is, of course, the supremely unaccountable joy, I mean the love between man and woman, and to some degree its virgin sister, friendship.

Unhug your love, if you mean to keep it as sweet as its divine beginning.

Fling out, with hopeful recklessness, all that is possessive in it.

SUSAN CLEGHORN

CONFESSION TO GOD THE FATHER

Late have I loved Thee whose fairness is so old and yet so new. Late have I loved Thee.

And behold, Thou wert within, and I without, and there I sought Thee. Unlovely, I broke upon the loveliness which Thou hast fashioned.

Thou wert with me, but I was not with Thee. Long was I held from Thee by those things which, without Thee, are nothing.

Thou didst call and cry and burst my deafness. Thou didst gleam and glow and dispel my blindness. Thou didst exhale fragrance.

I draw breath, and I pant after Thee. I have tasted, and do hunger and thirst. Thou hast touched me, and I burn for Thy peace.

ST. AUGUSTINE, 354–430

From THE DOOR

Love is a proud and gentle thing, a
    better thing to own
Than all of the wide impossible stars
    over the heavens blown,
And the little gifts her hand gives are
    careless given or taken,
And though the whole great world
    break, the heart of her is not
    shaken. . . .
Love is a viol in the wind, a viol never
    stilled,

And mine of all is the surest that ever
    time has willed. . . .
And the things that love gives after
    shall be as they were before,
For life is only a small house . . . and
    love is an open door.

ORRICK JOHNS

From MY CREED

I hold that Christian grace abounds
    Where charity is seen; that when
We climb to heaven, 'tis on the rounds
    Of love to men.

I hold all else named piety
    A selfish scheme, a vain pretense;
Where center is not—can there be
    Circumference?

This I moreover hold, and dare
    Affirm where'er my rhyme may go—
Whatever things be sweet and fair,
    Love makes them so.

        ALICE CARY, 1820–1871

In three things I was beautified, and
stood up beautiful before God and
men:
    the unity of brethren,
    the love of neighbors,
    a man and a wife that agree to-
        gether.

        ECCLESIASTICUS 25:1

NOBODY CAN BE LOST

O thou good Omnipotent, who so
carest for every one of us, as if Thou
carest for him alone, and so for all, as
if all were but one!

Blessed is the man that loveth Thee,
and his friend in Thee, and his enemy
for Thee.

For he only loseth none dear to him,
to whom all are dear in Him who cannot be lost. And who is that, but our
God, the God who made heaven and
earth, and filleth them, ever by filling
them creating them.

        ST. AUGUSTINE, 354–430

THE NATURE OF LOVE

Love is a great thing, yea, altogether
a great good.

By itself it maketh light everything
that is heavy, and it beareth evenly
everything that is uneven.

Nothing is sweeter than Love, nothing stronger, nothing higher, nothing
wider, nothing more pleasant, nothing
fuller nor better in heaven and earth.

A lover flieth, runneth, and re-
joiceth; he is free, he is not holden.

He giveth all for all and hath all
in all, because he resteth in One highest above all things.

Love is watchful, and sleeping
slumbereth not. Though wearied, is not
tired; though alarmed, is not confounded.

Love is swift, sincere, affectionate,
pleasant, and delightsome; brave; patient, prudent, long-suffering, never
seeking itself.

Love is circumspect, humble, and
upright; not yielding to softness or to
lightness, nor attending to vain things.
It is sober, chaste, firm, quiet, and without sorrow none liveth in love.

        THOMAS A KEMPIS, 1379–1471

UNIVERSALITY

True universality does not consist in
knowing much but in loving much.

        JAKOB BURCKHARDT, 1818–1897

TAPPED

There is no surprise more magical than
the surprise of being loved; it is God's
finger on a man's shoulder.

        CHARLES MORGAN, 1894–1958

THE WORK OF LOVE

It is the nature of love to work in a thousand different ways.

ST. TERESA, 1515–1582

CREATIVE LOVE

Professor Pitirim A. Sorokin during the Russian Revolution was hunted, imprisoned, and condemned to die before he was finally pardoned.

At that time he wrote in his diary: "The only way is the royal road of all-giving, creative love."

Before escaping to America he carved on a tree trunk in his native land these words:

LOVE IS THE ONLY
CREATIVE FORCE.

Later he founded the Harvard Research Center in Creative Altruism where an underlining teaching is: "Hate begets hate, violence engenders violence, hypocrisy is answered by hypocrisy. Unselfish love has enormous creative and therapeutic potentialities. A life-giving force, it is goodness and freedom at its highest."

QUEEN JADWIGA'S TESTIMONY

That marvelous little princess, sent in the fourteenth century from Hungary to Poland when she was only twelve years old to be crowned Queen Jadwiga and married to the crude Jagiello of Lithuania, became a superb Christian ruler and was responsible not only for Christianizing Lithuania but also for the famous *Acts of Horodla,* which state:

Nor can that endure which has not
  its foundation upon love;
For love alone diminishes not but
  shines with its own light,
Restores peace to the world, brings
  together the sundered,
Redresses the wrong,
  aids all and injures none;
And who invokes its aid
  will find peace and safety.

LOVE—WITH DIGNITY

Dignity is added to our idea of God when we say God is love. And if in default of this understanding of love our generation has grown cynical or despairing above the redemptive qualities of love, it is not to be wondered at.

Perhaps a simple exercise in reading our Bibles might help us recover the vigor and the uplift of the New Testament idea.

Read Paul's hymn of love. Substitute the word "romance" for love wherever it appears. Listen: "Romance suffereth long and is kind; romance envieth not, . . . doth not behave itself unseemly, seeketh not her own; is not easily provoked, thinketh no evil!" Our disillusionment is complete!

But read it again, this time inserting "creative" before love wherever it appears. Listen now: "Creative love beareth all things, hopeth all things, endureth all things. Creative love never faileth."

Out of the deeps of eternity moves a cosmic tide to flood all the shallow levels of our spirits!

EDWIN MC NEILL POTEAT,
1892–1955

From THE ROAMER

Love is the bread that feeds the multi-
tudes;
Love is the healing of the hospitals;
Love is the light that breaks through
prison doors;
Love knows not rich nor poor, nor
good nor bad,
But only the beloved, in every heart
One and the same, the incorruptible
Spirit divine, whose tabernacle is life.
Love, more than hunger, feeds the
soul's desire;
Love more the spirit than the body
heals;
Love is a star unto the darkened mind;
And they who truly are Love's servants
leal,
And follow him, undoubting, to the
end,
Beyond the bounds of human right-
eousness,
Past Justice, and past Mercy, find at
last,
Past Charity, past Pardon, Love en-
throned,
Lord of all hearts, incarnate in man's
soul.

GEORGE EDWARD WOODBERRY,
1855–1930

A STEWARD'S PRAYER

Father of all mankind,
    throughout this day help me to re-
member that a very real portion of
Thy Kingdom has been placed in my
keeping. Teach me to love Thee.
With all my heart—
    that I may love those whom Thou
lovest, giving back to the most un-
lovable and difficult Thine own everlasting mercy and compassion.

With all my soul—
    that I may seek fresh ways in which
Thy divine power may surge
through my commonplace routine
from morning till night.
With all my strength—
    that my hands may work the works
of Him who sent me, that my energy
may be poured out on the needs of
Thy family, until all I own or earn
or gain may be spent in a stewardship of loving-kindness.
With all my mind—
    that I may think Thy thoughts after
Thee from moment to moment,
making beautiful and significant
each expenditure, always placing
Thee first, that Thy Kingdom may
come through my sharing, my caring, my daring.

From FOR THE TIME BEING

Our Father, whose creative Will
    Asked Being for us all,
Confirm it that Thy Primal Love
May weave in us the freedom of
The actually deficient on
    The justly actual.

Though written by Thy children with
    A smudged and crooked line,
The Word is ever legible,
The Meaning unequivocal,
And for Thy Goodness even sin
    Is valid as a sign.

Inflict Thy promises with each
    Occasion of distress,
That from our incoherence we
May learn to put our trust in Thee,
And brutal fact persuade us to
    Adventure, Art, and Peace.

W. H. AUDEN

MUSIC

To some of us the thought of God is like a sort of quiet music playing in the background of the mind.

WILLIAM JAMES, 1842–1910

VIBRATIONS

See deep enough and you see musically, the heart of Nature being everywhere music, if you can only reach it.

THOMAS CARLYLE, 1795–1881

NURSE OF THE SOUL

In the germ, when the first trace of life begins to stir, music is the nurse of the soul. It murmurs in the ear, and the child sleeps. The tones are companions of his dreams. They are the world in which he lives.

ANTOINE BETTINA

WITH GLADNESS

I write according to the thoughts I feel. When I think upon my God, my heart is so full of joy that the notes dance and leap from my pen; and since God has given me a cheerful heart, it will be pardoned me that I serve Him with a cheerful spirit.

FRANZ JOSEPH HAYDN, 1732–1809

TRUE MUSIC

There is a true music of Nature:
the song of the birds,
the whisper of leaves,
the ripple of waters upon a sandy
    shore,
and the wail of wind or sea.

JOHN LUBBOCK, 1834–1913

From IN MEMORIAM

Let knowledge grow from more to
    more,
    But more of reverence in us dwell;
    That mind and soul, according well,
May make one music as before,

But vaster.

ALFRED TENNYSON, 1809–1892

I wanted the address of someone who could do for Christianity what Franz Liszt did for the pianoforte—exemplify a technique.

ANNE PAYSON

AN ANCIENT PRAYER

O Thou who art the loveliest melody of our choir, Thou who hast commanded that the songs of our hearts should be rendered now by wind instruments, now by strings. Grant that while we are singing with this spiritual desire, we may be admitted among the everlasting choirs and praise Thee together with Thy saints.

SURSUM CORDA

I place before my inward eyes myself with all that I am—my body, soul, and all my powers—and I gather round me all the creatures which God ever created in heaven and earth, and in all the elements, each one severally with its name, whether birds of the air, beasts of the forest, fishes of the water, leaves and grass of the earth, or the innumerable sands of the sea, and to these I add all the little specks of dust which glance in the sunbeams, with all the little drops of water which ever fell or are falling from dew, snow, or rain, and I wish that each of these had a sweetly sounding stringed instrument, fashioned from my heart's inmost blood, striking on which they might each send up to our dear and gentle God a new and lofty strain of praise for ever and ever. And then the loving arms of my soul stretch out and extend themselves toward the innumerable multitude of all creatures, and my intention is, just as a free and blithesome leader of a choir stirs up the singers of his company, even so to turn them all to offer up their hearts to God.

HEINRICH SUSO, 1300?–1366

UNIVERSAL LANGUAGE

Music is a universal language.

Children sing beautiful songs before they can read.

The music of Beethoven and César Franck is intelligible alike to men who know not each other's language and are even now trying to shoot each other from barbarian trenches. Not only is it intelligible to them, but it expresses those deeper things in life with which each is in accord.

Music is the oldest of the arts and yet the youngest.

It means nothing, and yet it means everything. A Beethoven symphony is quite untranslatable into other terms. No one can say exactly what it means, and yet to those who understand, it means more than does any other utterance of man.

It is an expression in sound of feeling guided by the mind and glorified by the imagination.

Like every other work of art, it has form, style, and substance.

Unfortunately — tragically — many people believe that performing music is the only way to understand it, whereas understanding it consists in compassing it about with your feelings, your mind, and your imagination until it becomes yours—a process with which many performers have little familiarity.

THOMAS WHITNEY SURETTE

If a man does not keep pace with his companions, perhaps it is because he hears a different drummer. Let him step to the music which he hears, however measured or far away.

HENRY DAVID THOREAU, 1817–1862

From MUSIC

God is its author, and not man; he laid
The key-note of all harmonies; he
    planned
All perfect combinations, and he made
Us so that we could hear and under-
    stand.

JOHN G. BRAINARD

WHATEVER YOU DO

If thou art singing a hymn, thou art
praising God.

Then the hymn comes to an end, and
it is time for a meal. If thou keepest
thyself from overeating, thou wilt be
praising God.

Dost thou labor as a farmer? Be sure
there are no weeds left in the ground
thou art digging. This too will be an
opportunity for praising God.

Thus by the innocency of thy labors
thou canst praise God all day long.

ST. AUGUSTINE, 354–430

TWO MUSICIANS

Which is the greater, Mozart or Beethoven?

Idle question!

The one is more perfect; the other
more colossal.

The first gives you the peace of perfect art—beauty at first sight. The second gives you sublimity, terror, pity,
and a beauty of second impression.

The one gives that for which the
other rouses a desire. Mozart has the
classic purity of light and the blue
ocean. Beethoven the romantic humor
which belongs to the storms of air and
sea.

The soul of Mozart seems to dwell
on the ethereal peaks of Olympus, and
that of Beethoven climbs shuddering
the storm-beaten sides of a Sinai.

Blessed be they both! Each represents a moment of the ideal life. Each
does us good. Our love is due to both.

HENRI FRÉDÉRIC AMIEL, 1821–1881

BREAD

When music spills from golden throat
    In wild bird reveille,
I push the drab world out in space
    And live in melody.
When color glows in countless ways
    Before my hungry eyes.
I am a gourmand at the feast
    Unmindful of how time flies,
For when this pageantry is spread
I quite forget my daily bread.

When cool waves run to greet the sands
    And whisper deep-sea lore,
I stand, at crimson close of day,
    Enchanted on the shore.
Each season wafts in new delights
    As beauty flames its way,
On rock, and earth, and sky, and sea,
    With respite for the day—
And, oh, my dear, I humbly own
I cannot live by bread alone!

CHRISTINA GEORGINA ROSSETTI,
1830–1894

When I hear music, it seems to me that
all the sins of my life pass slowly by
me with veiled faces, lay their hands
on my head, and say softly, "My
child."

SIDNEY LANIER, 1842–1881

I was filled with a kind of joy when I read of Thomas Kelly.

It was formerly the custom of the Winston-Salem Community of Moravians in North Carolina to announce the passing of a member by the playing of three chorales by the church band from the top of the church tower.

So I feel I want to sing when I hear of such men emerging.

I know it is an outward loss to us—though even directly we may gain more than we lose by their joining the more active side of the communion of saints—but I keep on feeling what it must be for a man as good as he to be able to push aside this fussy veil of the body and look unblinking at the Light, never again, maybe, to be distracted, unintentional, unaware, always concentrated.

GERALD HEARD

MUSIC AND DRUM

When men turn mob
Drums throb:
When mob turns men
Music again.

When souls become Church
Drums beat the search:
When Church becomes souls
Sweet music tolls.

When State is the master
Drums beat disaster:
When master is man
Music can.

Each to be one,
Each to be whole,
Body and soul,
Music's begun.

ARCHIBALD MACLEISH

TRUE HARMONY

You can make music of a sort with white keys only, but for true harmony you need the black keys also.

JAMES E. KIVEGYIR AGGREY,
1875–1927

LITURGY OF ST JOHN CHRYSOSTOM

Heavenly King, Paraclete, Spirit of truth, present in all places and filling all things, Treasury of God, and Choirmaster of life: come and dwell within us, cleanse us from all stains and save our souls.

From HYMN TO GOD MY GOD

Since I am coming to that holy room,
    Where with Thy choir of saints for
        evermore,
I shall be made Thy music; as I come
    I tune the instrument here at the
        door,
    And what I must do then, think here
        before.

JOHN DONNE,
1572–1631

There is no truer truth obtainable
By Man than comes of music.

ROBERT BROWNING, 1812–1889

We are all strings in the concert of His joy. The spirit from His mouth strikes the note and time of our strings.

JACOB BOEHME,
1575–1624

From ODE

We are the music-makers,
    And we are the dreamers of dreams,
Wandering by lone sea-breakers,
    And sitting by desolate streams.
With wonderful deathless ditties
We build up the world's great cities,
    And out of a fabulous story
    We fashion an empire's glory:
One man with a dream, at pleasure,
    Shall go forth and conquer a crown;
And three with a new song's measure
    Shall trample a kingdom down.
        ARTHUR WILLIAM O'SHAUGHNESSY,
                            1844–1881

MUSIC AND MEDICINE

This variable composition of man's
body hath made it as an instrument
easy to distemper. Therefore, the poets
did well to conjoin music and medicine
in Apollo, because the office of medicine is but to tune this curious harp
of man's body and to reduce it to harmony.

        FRANCIS BACON, 1561–1626

MELODY OF SPRING

Alleluia with the "a" is the song of
sweetness, the voice of joy that cannot
die, the unending music of those who
abide perpetually in the security and
peace of home. It is a wild bird-note,
full of the pleasantness of Easter
weather. It calls up the laughing sunshine and the soft warm rain, the
flowers of all the woods of April, and
the very melody of spring.

        RICHARD LAWSON GALES

YOUR CHURCH HYMNAL

Touch your church hymnal and you
touch life!

Someone somewhere was so much in
love with God that he simply had to
write a poem about it. Somebody else
was so full of the same delight in Divinity that he burst into song, making
lovely music.

The tune of "Old Hundredth," coming from sixteenth-century Geneva,
was wedded a century later to the familiar words, "Praise God from Whom
all blessings flow," by Bishop Thomas
Ken. An old Welsh melody, "Ton-Y-
Botel," is linked in singing to the
words of a poem by James Russell
Lowell. How unforgettably the various generations have been brought together!

This is as Christianity should be.
Think of the bars of music in your
hymnbook as pews, and what a mixed
congregation is held in our hands! Elbow to elbow are saints and sinners,
prophets and martyrs, heroes and theo-
logians, men and women, princes and
peasants.

Actually the hymnal is a truly ecumenical heirloom of Mother Church,
an heirloom inherited from every nation, kindred, and tribe, every denom-
ination, creed, and race.

To thumb through the pages is to be
lost in wonder, love, and praise over
dates so ancient, languages so foreign
yet perfectly translated, and spiritual
testimony so variously suited to every
human need that as William Cowper
wrote:

    Sometimes a light surprises
    The Christian while he sings;
    It is the Lord who rises
    With healing in His wings!

From IL PENSEROSO

There let the pealing organ blow,
To the full-voiced quire below,
In service high, and anthems clear,
As may with sweetness, through mine
    ear,
Dissolve me into ecstacies,
And bring all heaven before mine eyes.

JOHN MILTON, 1608–1674

Music is another planet.

ALPHONSE DAUDET, 1840–1897

From ABT VOGLER

All we have willed or hoped or
    dreamed of good shall exist;
  Not its semblance, but itself, no
    beauty, nor good, nor power
Whose voice has gone forth, but each
    survives for the melodist
  When eternity affirms the concep-
    tion of an hour.
The high that proved too high, the
    heroic for earth too hard,
  The passion that left the ground to
    lose itself in the sky,
Are music sent up to God by the lover
    and the bard;
  Enough that He heard it once: we
    shall hear it by and by.

ROBERT BROWNING, 1812–1889

BUILT FROM MUSIC

Once upon a time there was a King
who lived in a plain house, although
he formerly had a palace of superlative
beauty. But it had been destroyed in
an earthquake. The King did not want
a new palace, because the old one had
been built from music, which was the
reason for its unearthly loveliness.

However, his people knew that such
an important sovereign ought to have
a palace. So one by one they invited
all the celebrated musicians in the
kingdom to come and play. They
hoped, of course, that the walls would
begin to rise up as before. But although each man outdid himself in
brilliance, skill, and technique, not a
single thing happened.

Then a little lame boy stepped forward and suggested that maybe if they
all played something together the walls
would rise, but they all laughed him
to scorn. What? Play something for
which no one man could ever possibly
get sole credit? No indeed! Not they!

But the little fellow found another
small lad, and they made foolish little
home-made whistles out of pieces of
wood. Then they began tootling the
national anthem as best they could.

When people recognized this familiar tune, they began to hum it in
sheer amusement at the pluck of two
boys.

The famous musicians caught the
contagion, seized their harps and
lyres and flutes and trumpets to join
in. Suddenly in this glorious harmony
lo! the walls began to rise, and the
King had a house not made with
hands, but from a marvelous hidden
spirit.

SPEECH OF ANGELS

Music is well said to be the speech of
angels.

THOMAS CARLYLE, 1795–1881

OFFICE DUET

As noon approaches every day,
Chimes from the church across the way
Ride o'er the city's busy din,
And climb to where the clouds begin.
Here in my office in the sky,
Old hymns plead their way in, and vie
With my insistent clicking keys
That type their brisk monotonies:
"Dear Sir: We have received your bill,
And when the merchandise is
    stored. . . ."
    "Faith of our fathers! living still
In spite of dungeon, fire and
    sword. . . ."

"We are indeed surprised to know
That you will never guarantee. . . ."
"O Love that will not let me go
I rest my weary soul in Thee. . . ."

They make a very strange duet—
The chimes and typewriter—and yet
I wonder why it should seem odd
To mix up offices and God.
                         LUCY CARRETH

IN PLYMOUTH

So through the Plymouth woods John
    Alden went on his errand;
Came to an open space, and saw the
    disk of the ocean,
Sailless, somber and cold with the
    comfortless breath of the east-wind;
Saw the new-built house, and people
    at work in the meadow;
Heard, as he drew near the door, the
    musical voice of Priscilla
Singing the hundredth Psalm, the
    grand old Puritan anthem,

Music that Luther sang to the sacred
    words of the Psalmist,
Full of the breath of the Lord, con-
    soling and comforting many.
Then, as he opened the door, he be-
    held the form of the maiden
Seated beside her wheel, and the
    carded wool like a snow-drift
Piled at her knee, her white hands
    feeding the ravenous spindle,
While with her foot on the treadle
    she guided the wheel in its motion.
Open wide on her lap lay the well-
    worn psalm-book of Ainsworth,
Printed in Amsterdam, the words and
    the music together,
Rough-hewn, angular notes, like stones
    in the wall of a churchyard,
Darkened and overhung by the run-
    ning vine of the verses,
Such was the book from whose pages
    she sang the Old Puritan Anthem.

Al peopull y^t on yirth do dwel,
Sjing to ye Lord wth chereful vojce;
Him serue wth mirthe, His prayse
    forth tel,
Come ye beefore Him and rejoyce.
    HENRY WADSWORTH LONGFELLOW,
                             1807–1882

From A PRAYER
FOR OLD AGE

God guard me from those thoughts
    men think
In the mind alone;
He that sings a lasting song
Thinks in the marrow-bone.
          WILLIAM BUTLER YEATS,
                             1865–1939

NATURE

It is His garment; and to them
Who touch in faith its utmost hem
He, turning, says again, "I see
That virtue has gone out of me."

JOHN BANISTER TABB, 1845–1909

From THE FIFTIETH BIRTHDAY OF AGASSIZ

And nature, the old nurse, took
  The child upon her knee,
Saying, "Here is a story book
  My father hath writ for thee.
Come, wander with me," she said,
  "In regions yet untrod
And read what is still unread
  In the manuscripts of God."

HENRY WADSWORTH LONGFELLOW,
1807–1882

Beauty is God's handwriting. Welcome
it in every fair face, every fair sky,
every fair flower.

CHARLES KINGSLEY, 1819–1875

POSTURE

Half a proper gardener's work is done
  upon his knees.

RUDYARD KIPLING, 1865–1936

THE SEA AROUND US

To stand at the edge of the sea,
to sense the ebb and flow of the tides,
to feel the breath of a mist over a great
  salt marsh,
to watch the flight of shore birds that
  have swept up and down the shore
  lines of the continents for untold
  thousands of years,
to see the running of old eels and the
  young shad to the sea,
is to have knowledge of things that are
  as nearly eternal as any earthly life
  can be.

RACHEL CARSON, 1907–1964

From SPRING LANDSCAPE

In many a flower, one can tell,
Nests a glittering parable.
In hedges, where the sunlight pours,
The bushes burst with metaphors.

LOUIS GINSBERG

The air is full of sounds;
the sky is full of tokens;
the ground is all memoranda and
 signatures;
and every object covered over with
 hints that speak to the intelligent.

RALPH WALDO EMERSON,
1803–1882

THE PATER-NOSTER OF NATURE

Look at Nature. She never wearies of saying over her floral pater-noster. In the crevices of Cyclopean walls, on the mounds that bury huge cities, in the dust where men lie, dust also— still that same sweet prayer and benediction. The amen of Nature is always a flower.

OLIVER WENDELL HOLMES,
1809–1894

SYMBOL

An Italian gardener once said that grapevines should not be planted so deep that they could not hear the church bells ringing. He had never lost his sense of wonder over holy earth, holy air, and holy water, for which the village altar and its mystic bell symbolized his utter dependence upon God.

What is lovely never dies, but passes into other loveliness, star-dust or sea-foam, flower or winged air.

THOMAS BAILEY ALDRICH,
1836–1907

THE URGE

The urge of the seed: the germ.
The urge of the germ: the stalk.
The urge of the stalk: leaves.
The urge of leaves: the blossom.
The urge of the blossom: to scatter pollen.
The urge of the pollen: the imagined dream of life.
The urge of life: longing for tomorrow.
The urge of tomorrow: pain.
The urge of pain: God.

EDGAR LEE MASTERS, 1869–1950

Who reaches
with a clumsy hand
for a rose
must not complain
if the thorns scratch.

HEINRICH HEINE, 1797–1856

LAW OF GROWTH

The word of God is in us. Given a hard-working farmer, it will thrive and grow up to God whose seed it is. And accordingly, its fruits will be God-Nature. Pear seeds grow into pear trees, nut seeds into nut trees, and God seeds into God.

MEISTER ECKHART, 1260–1328

GOD'S PURPOSE

Why should I start at the plough of my Lord, that maketh deep furrows in my soul? I know that He is no idle husband-man. He purposeth a crop!

SAMUEL RUTHERFORD, 1600–1661

From TINTERN ABBEY

This prayer I make,
Knowing that Nature never did betray
The heart that loved her; 'tis her
  privilege,
Through all the years of this our life,
  to lead
From joy to joy; for she can so inform
The mind that is within us, so impress
With quietness and beauty, and so feed
With lofty thoughts, that neither evil
  tongues,
Nor greetings where no kindness is,
  nor all
The dreary intercourse of daily life,
Shall e'er prevail against us, or disturb
Our cheerful faith that all which we
  behold
Is full of blessings.

WILLIAM WORDSWORTH, 1770–1850

GOD'S OTHER HYMNBOOK

Every race has seen more clearly than
we do now that Nature is God's other
hymnbook for all men where He sings
in the recurring rhythms of sun and
rain and tree and fruit and food.

The ancient Jews devoted six whole
days to their Feast of First Fruits.
People wore green garlands and
wreaths of flowers. They carried white
willow baskets of pomegranates, dates,
and figs. They bound their sheaves
with lilies. Even their oxen were gar-
landed with roses as the gay processional, led by a pipe-player and a
banner-bearer, climbed the steep streets
to the Temple.

They saw in the tree and its fruit
both their life and their Creator.

THE OTHER PLAYER

The chessboard is the world, the
pieces are the phenomena of the universe, and the rules of the game are
what we call the laws of Nature. The
player on the other side is hidden from
us. We know that his play is always
fair, just, and patient. But also we
know, to our cost, that he never over-
looks a mistake or makes the smallest
allowance for ignorance.

THOMAS H. HUXLEY, 1825–1885

Miracles are not in contradiction to
nature. They are only in contradiction
with what we know of nature.

ST. AUGUSTINE, 354–430

A SAFE HOME

God is the presence, warm, all-enfold-
ing, touching the drab world into brilliance, lifting the sad heart into song,
indescribable, beyond understanding,
yet by a bird's note, a chord of music,
a light at sunset, a sudden movement
of rapt insight, a touch of love, making
the whole universe a safe home for the
soul.

AN EARLY CHRISTIAN MYSTIC

ENTER, GOD!

Art and blue heaven,
April and God's larks,
Green reeds and sky-scattering river.
A stately music—
  Enter, God!

ROBERT LOUIS STEVENSON,
1850–1894

SWEEPINGS OF
HEAVEN'S FLOOR

Nature is full of genius, full of the divinity, so that not a snowflake escapes its fashioning hand. Nothing is cheap and coarse, neither dewdrops nor snowflakes.

Myriads of these little disks, so beautiful to the most prying eyes, are whirled down on every traveler's coat, the observant and the unobservant, on the restless squirrel's fur, on the far-stretching fields and forests, the wooded dells and mountain tops.

Far, far away from the haunts of men, they roll down some little slope, fall over and come to their bearings, and melt or lose their beauty in the mass, ready anon to swell some little rill with their contribution, and so, at last, the universal ocean from which they came. There they lie, like the wreck of chariot wheels after a battle in the sky.

Meanwhile the meadow mouse shoves them aside in his gallery, the school boy casts them in his snowball, or the woodman's sled glides smoothly over them, these glorious spangles, these sweepings of heaven's floor.

And they all sing, melting as they sing, of the mysteries of the number six, six, six, six.

He takes up the water of the sea in His hand, leaving the salt; He dispenses it in mist through the sky, He re-collects and sprinkles it like grain in six-rayed stars over the earth, there to lie till it dissolves in bonds again.

HENRY DAVID THOREAU,
1817–1862

From SONG OF MYSELF

A child said *What is the grass?* fetching it to me with full hands,
How could I answer the child? I do not know what it is any more than he.

I guess it must be the flag of my disposition, out of hopeful green stuff woven.

Or I guess it is the handkerchief of the Lord,
A scented gift and remembrancer designedly dropt,
Bearing the owner's name someway in the corners, that we may see and remark, and say *Whose?*
WALT WHITMAN, 1819–1892

THE EXCESSES OF GOD

Is it not by His high superfluousness we know
Our God? For to equal a need
Is natural, animal, mineral: but to fling
Rainbows over the rain
And beauty above the moon, and secret rainbows
On the domes of deep sea-shells,
And makes the necessary embrace of breeding
Beautiful also as fire,
Not even the weeds to multiply without blossom
Nor the birds without music:
There is the great humaneness at the heart of things,
The extravagant kindness, the fountain
Humanity can understand, and would flow likewise
If power and desire were perch-mates.
ROBINSON JEFFERS, 1887–1962

GARDEN OF THE LORD

The word of God came unto me,
Sitting alone among the multitudes;
And my blind eyes were touched with
  light,
And there was laid upon my lips a
  flame of fire.

I laugh and shout for life is good,
Though my feet are set in silent ways.
In merry mood I leave the crowd
To walk in my garden. Even as I walk
I gather fruits and flowers in my hands,
And with joyful heart I bless the sun
That kindles all the place with radiant
  life.
I run with playful winds that blow the
  scent
Of rose and jasmine in eddying whirls.

At last I come where tall lilies grow,
Lifting their faces like white saints
  to God.
While the lilies pray, I kneel upon the
  ground:
I have strayed into the holy temple of
  the Lord.

HELEN KELLER

THIS CONSPICUOUS WORLD

Anything that God makes is worth
looking at. We live in no chance
world. It has been all thought out.

Everywhere work has been spent on
it lavishly—thought and work—loving
thought and exquisite work. All its
parts together, and every part separ-
ately, are stamped with skill, beauty,
and purpose.

As the mere work of a Great Master
we are driven to look—deliberately
and long—at the things which are
seen.

More than that, God made me to
look at them. He who made light made
the eye. It is a gift of the Creator.

The whole mechanism of man is
made with reference to the temporal
world—the eye for seeing it, the ear
for hearing it.

Also God has made the world con-
spicuous; the whole temporal world
clamors for observation.

Nature is never and nowhere silent.
The bird will call to you, the sea will
change her mood for you, the flower
looks up appealingly from the wayside, and the sun, before he sets with
irresistible coloring, will startle you
into attention.

Had God feared that the visible
world had been a mere temptation to
us, He would have made it less con-
spicuous.

HENRY DRUMMOND, 1851–1897

ENOUGH

There is a dance of miracles holding
  hands in a chain around the Earth
  and out through space to the moon,
  and to the stars and beyond the stars;
And to behold this dance is enough;
So much brighter, and secret looking,
  and glimpses of wonder and dreams
  of terror.
It is enough! It is enough!

JAMES OPPENHEIM

Science has found that nothing disappears without a trace. Nature does not
know extinction. All it knows is trans-
formation.

WERNHER VON BRAUN

THE LAWS OF GOD

The law the lawyers know about
Is property and land;
But why the leaves are on the trees,
And why the winds disturb the seas,
Why honey is the food of bees,
Why horses have such tender knees,
Why winters come and rivers freeze,
Why faith is more than what one sees,
And hope survives the worst disease,
And charity is more than these,
They do not understand.
DOUGLAS PEPLER

THE ONE THOUSANDTH PSALM

O God, we thank Thee for everything!
For the sea and its waves, blue, green, and gray and always wonderful;
For the beach and the breakers and the spray and the white foam on the rocks;
For the blue arch of heaven; for the clouds in the sky, white and gray and purple;
For the green of the grass; for the forests in their spring beauty; for the wheat and corn and rye and barley.
For the brown earth turned up by the plow; for the sun by day, and the dews by night.

We thank Thee for all Thou hast made and that Thou hast called it good.
For all the glory and beauty and wonder of the world;
For the glory of springtime, the tints of the flowers and their fragrance;
For the glory of the summer flowers, the roses and cardinals and clethra;
For the glory of the autumn, the scarlet and crimson and gold of the forest;
For the glory of winter, the pure snow on the shrubs and trees.

We thank Thee that Thou hast placed us in the world to subdue all things to Thy glory,
And to use all things for the good of Thy children.
We thank Thee! We enter into Thy work and go about Thy business.
EDWARD EVERETT HALE, 1822–1909

From CROSS CREEK

Who owns Cross Creek? The redbirds, I think, more than I, for they will have their nests even in the face of delinquent mortgages. And after I am dead, who am childless, the human ownership of grove and field and hummock is hypothetical.

But a long line of redbirds and whippoorwills and blue-jays and ground doves will descend from the present owners of nests in the orange trees, and their claim will be less subject to dispute than any human heirs.

Houses are individual and can be owned, like nests, and fought for. But what of the land? It seems to me that the earth may be borrowed but not bought. It may be used, but not owned. It gives itself in response to love and tending, offers its seasonal flowering and fruiting. But we are tenants and not possessors, lovers but not masters.

Cross Creek belongs to the wind and the rain, to the sun and the seasons, to the cosmic secrecy of seed, and beyond all, to time.
MARJORIE KINNAN RAWLINGS,
1896–1953

MORNING THANKSGIVING

For earth's little secret and innumerable ways,
For the carol and color, Lord, we bring
What things may be of thanks, and
that Thou hast lent our days
Eyes to see and ears to hear and lips
to sing.

JOHN DRINKWATER, 1882–1937

THE DANDELION

The time has been when I'd have
walked right over that little flower and
not seen it, and now it grows yellower
each minute that I look at it, and each
minute I see it better than I did the
one before.

There's nothing in life, when you
come to think of it—not Columbus setting out to sea nor Napolean starting
on a march—more wonderful than that
brave little blossom putting up the
first of all through the earth.

ELLEN GLASGOW, 1874–1945

PRAYER IN APRIL

God grant that I may never be
A scoffer at Eternity—
As long as ever April brings
The sweet rebirth of growing things;
As long as grass is green anew,
As long as April's skies are blue,
I shall believe that God looks down
Upon His wide earth, cold and brown,
To bless its unborn mystery
Of leaf, and bud, and flower to be;
To smile on it from tender skies—
How could I think it otherwise?
Had I been dust for many a year,
I still would know when Spring was
near,

For the good earth that pillowed me
Would whisper immortality,
And I, in part, would rise and sing
Amid the grasses murmuring.
When looking on the mother sod,
Can I hold doubt that this be God?
Or when a primrose smiles at me,
Can I distrust Eternity?

SARA HENDERSON HAY

GOD IN NATURE AND SUPERNATURE

God is the author of, and God is variously reflected in, all innocent Nature
as well as in all Supernature.

He is the God revealed in high
heroisms, in the sincere forgiveness
of our enemies, and in the eager acceptance of suffering, and likewise in
the beauties of external nature and in
the honesties and decencies of common
human life.

He is the God not only of the Alpine
heights with the edelweiss and the
alpenrose, but also of the Lombard
plains with their cornfields and pota-
toes.

The recognition of this brings much
help in our prayers. For in prayer it
brings a tension, and also a relaxation. In both these movements of the
soul God can, and should be, envis-
aged—in the relaxation, the God of
nature, the source of all that is wholesome and homely; and in the tension,
the God of Supernature, the source of
all that is ardent and heroic.

We thus escape dullness and monotony—the subtle dangers of the spiritual life.

FRIEDRICH VON HÜGEL, 1852–1925

SPRING MELODY

Algernon Charles Swinburne has said
with rare beauty about William Blake
that all the tremulous and tender
splendor of spring is minted into his
melody. Every page has the smell of
the English April.

Over everything—the flocks of
sheep, the growth of leaves, the laughter in the divided lips of flowers, and
the music at the molded mouth of the
flute-player—there is cast a pure fine
veil of light, softer than sleep and
keener than sunshine.

The sweetness of sky, leaf, grass
and water, and the bright life of bird,
beast, and child are kept fresh by some
graver sense of faithful and mysterious love.

From MELAMPUS

With love exceeding the simple love
　　of the things
　　That glide in grasses and rubble of
　　　woody wreck;
Or change their perch on a beat of
　　quivering wings
　　From branch to branch, only restful
　　　to pipe and peck;
Or, bristled, curly at a touch
　　their snouts in a ball;
　　Or cast their web between
　　　bramble and thorny hook;
The good physician Melampus,
　　loving them all,
　　Among them walk'd as a scholar
　　　who reads a book.

For him the woods were a home and
　　gave him the key
　　Of knowledge, thirst for their
　　　treasuries in herbs and flowers.

The secrets held by the creatures
　　nearer than we
　　To earth he sought, and the link of
　　　their life with ours:
And where alike we are, unlike where,
　　and the vein'd
　　Division, vein'd parallel, of a blood
　　　that flows
In them, in us, from the source by
　　man unattain'd
　　Save marks he well what the mystical
　　　woods disclose.

　　GEORGE MEREDITH, 1828–1909

A SONG IN HUMILITY

Let me no more despise
Such creatures as comprise
Earth's lowliest, the least
Of life below the beast
Man binds, the bird brought low.

The ant on crowded crown
Of clay, the evening gnat:
Brief butterfly who set
On such a tiny twig
Her body blossomed big,
Wings balanced like a blade;
The worm split by my spade;
The midge, the mindless fly;
All things that live and die.

All quick things that are caught
All creatures come to naught
In parallel of these
Life's littler entities.

Nothing is old or new
In doing what all do,
So vast a thing as die.
None is more great than I,
And nothing is too small
To thus accomplish all.

　　CARLETON DREWRY

INFINITY

I lean over the rail of my porch to hear what is in the air liquid with the blue-bird's warble.

My life partakes of infinity.

I go forth to make new demands on life.

I wish to have my immortality now.

I am eager to report the glory of the universe.

HENRY DAVID THOREAU,
1817–1862

INSECTS AS SYMBOLS

To the Greeks the butterfly became the symbol of immortality because it emerged from its chrysalis and exquisitely changed from the crawling caterpillar which had wound a cocoon around itself.

To the early Egyptians the scarab became the same sort of sacred symbol of continuity, for the female beetle had laid her eggs in dung, yet there emerged this beautiful hard-shelled insect with transparent iridescent wings, immortalized by jewelers in gold and precious stones, engraved with eternal mottos, for use in pyramids and tombs.

Our early Church Fathers may have taken their clue about the bee from Ecclesiasticus 11:3–4: "The bee is little among such as fly, but her fruit is the chief of sweet things. Boast not of thy clothing and raiment, and exalt not thyself in the day of honor; for the works of the Lord are wonderful, and his works among men are hidden." In any case, altar candles have been made from beeswax from time out of mind, and at least one ancient prayer mentions "blessed Mother Bee" by name.

Because the Gospels tell how John the Baptist lived on locust and wild honey, a recent convert in Africa told the missionary he was first drawn to Christianity because he too found grasshoppers his favorite dish, and he felt one entered a new religion for simple reasons first.

In Africa some tribes feel that the constant fluttering of fireflies over their fields by night is a token that their tribal gods are protecting their crops and property.

The cricket on the hearth is more than just the title of a book for the British, for the cheerful chirping at their firesides spells a certain cozy comfort perpetuated through the generations.

Some of the experimental colonies of human beings, testing out the living and working together in brotherhoods, have quoted Solomon's proverb: "Go to the ant, thou sluggard, consider her ways, and be wise. She provideth her meat in the summer, and gathereth her food in the harvest."

Even the Mexican jumping-bean is a lively sermon to the peasant that God has put an instinct in the mother beetle to provide food for her young in this vegetable.

And as for modern superstitions: who fails to be pleased when a little black-dotted red ladybug lights on him? Someone is sure to predict: "You're in for some good fortune!" Here is one insect that is never known to work harm and is an expert in getting rid of pests.

In India there is an ancient saying: "The subtle anklets that ring on the feet of an insect when it moves are heard of God."

INSCRIPTION

We have loved
the stars
too fondly
to be fearful
of the night.

AN ASTRONOMER'S GRAVE
ALLEGHENY OBSERVATORY
UNIVERSITY OF PITTSBURGH

From EARTH

Grasshopper, your fairy song
And my poem alike belong
To the dark and silent earth
From which all poetry has birth;
All we say and all we sing
Is but as the murmuring
Of that drowsy heart of hers
When from her deep dream she stirs:
If we sorrow, or rejoice,
You and I are but her voice.

Deftly doth the dust express
In mind her hidden loveliness,
And from her cool silence stream
The cricket's cry and Dante's dream:
For the earth that breeds the trees
Breeds cities, too, and symphonies.
Equally her beauty flows
Into a saviour or a rose,—
Looks down in dream, and from above
Smiles at herself in Jesus' love.
Christ's love and Homer's art
Are lent the workings of her heart;
Through Leonardo's hand she seeks
Herself, and through Beethoven speaks
In holy thunderings around
The awful message of the ground.

*

All tenderness of all the ages,
Seraphic secrets of the sages,
Vision and hope of all the seers,

All prayer, all anguish, and all tears
Are but the dust, that from her dream
Awakes and knows herself supreme—
Are but earth when she reveals
All that her secret heart conceals
Down in the dark and silent loam,
Which is ourselves, asleep, at home.

Yes, and this my poem, too,
Is part of her as dust and dew,
Wherein herself she doth declare
Through my lips, and say her prayer.

JOHN HALL WHEELOCK

THE MYSTERY OF COLOR

However much we may learn of
chlorophyll, chromogen, and color cells
—the pigments of nature that are
made from earth and rain, air and sun,
somewhere in the dark habitation of
the roots and the airy galleries of the
leaves—we do not know why the same
ingredients should clothe one petal
with flame and another with blue.

We do not know what impulse
sends up the water lily from the stag-
nant ooze in glistening white and lays
a mauve mantle over the wistaria that
feeds upon corruption; nor why two
plants of the same genus in the same
condition should be so differently
colored as are the blue and yellow gen-
tian.

Color, like fragrance, is intimately
connected with light; and between the
different rays of the spectrum and the
color cells of plants there is a strange
telepathy.

These processes, so little explored,
seem in their deep secrecy and earthly
spirituality more marvelous than the
most radiant visions of the mystics.

MARY WEBB, 1881–1927

CANTICLE OF
THE CREATURES

O most high, almighty, good Lord God, to Thee belong praise, glory, honor, and all blessing!

Praised be my Lord God with all His creatures; and specially our brother the sun, who brings us the day, and who brings us the light; fair is he, and shining with a very great splendor: O Lord, to us he signifies Thee!

Praised be my Lord for our sister the moon, and for the stars, which He has set clear and lovely in heaven.

Praised be my Lord for our brother the wind, and for air and cloud, calms and all weather, by the which Thou upholdest in life all creatures.

Praised be my Lord for our sister water, who is very serviceable unto us, and humble, and precious, and clean.

Praised be my Lord for our brother fire, through whom Thou givest us light in the darkness; and he is bright and pleasant, and very mighty, and strong.

Praised be my Lord for our mother the earth, the which doth sustain us and keep us, and bringeth forth divers fruits, and flowers of many colors, and grass.

Praised be my Lord for all those who pardon one another for His love's sake, and who endure weakness and tribulation, blessed are they who peaceably shall endure, for Thou, O most Highest, shall give them a crown!

Praised be my Lord for our sister, the death of the body, from whom no man escapeth. Woe to him who dieth in moral sin! Blessed are they who are found walking by Thy most holy will, for the second death shall have no power to do them harm.

Praise ye, and bless ye the Lord, and give thanks unto him, and serve Him with great humility.

ST. FRANCIS OF ASSISI, 1182–1226

❧

CONSIDER THE BEE

The bee is small among flying creatures, but her product is the best of sweet things.

Do not boast about wearing fine clothes, nor exalt yourself in the day that you are honored,

for the works of the Lord are wonderful, and his works are concealed from men.

ECCLESIASTICUS 11:3–4

❧

A BARN IS A MIRACLE

Here is a miracle painted red,
A weathervane upon its head
With sliding panels in the walls,
The hidden doors and secret stalls.

The wheat upon this threshing floor
Once stood in acres, score on score;
And all of June stacked in this pile
Was hay and clover by the mile.

With summer high up in the mows
Above the sheep, above the cows,
The small teeth nibbling in the bin—
So winter's barn takes all things in.

Here, in this small and magic box,
The farmer crowds his fields and flocks;
Arithmetic can never tell
How one barn holds the farm so well.

RALPH W. SEAGER

PRAYER

The soul deep in prayer
As a hyacinth
Stretches forth its pillar of bloom;
Feelers of fragrance unseen
To the edge of the room.

EVELYN UNDERHILL, 1875–1941

QUIET MIRACLE

Prayer is a force as real as terrestrial gravity. As a physician, I have seen men, after all other therapy had failed, lifted out of disease and melancholy by the serene effort of prayer.

It is the only power in the world that seems to overcome the so-called "laws of nature"; the occasions on which prayer had dramatically done this have been termed "miracles."

But a constant, quieter miracle takes place hourly in the hearts of men and women who have discovered that prayer supplies them with a steady flow of sustaining power in their lives.

ALEXIS CARREL, 1873–1944

WHEN MAN PRAYS

God warms His hands at man's heart when he prays.

JOHN MASEFIELD, 1878–1967

SEEKING GOD

When you seek your own, you never find God, for you are not seeking him with purity of heart.

You are seeking something along with God, as if He were a candle with which one might look for something else, and having found it, one might throw the candle away.

Take it for granted that which you look for with God has no essential value, whatever it may be, whether profit, or reward, or spirituality, or whatever.

MEISTER ECKHART,
1260–1328

THE ANSWER

Trouble and perplexity drive me to prayer, and prayer drives away perplexity and trouble.

PHILIP MELANCHTHON,
1497–1560

PRAYER

Prayer, the Church's banquet, Angels'
  age,
  God's breath in man returning to his
  birth,
The soul in paraphrase, heart in pilgrimage,
  The Christian plummet sounding
  heav'n and earth;

Engine against th' Almighty, sinner's
  tower,
  Reversèd thunder, Christ-side-pierc-
  ing spear,
The six-days-world transposing in an
  hour,
  A kind of tune which all things hear
  and fear;

Softness, and peace, and joy, and love,
  and bliss,
  Exalted Manna, gladness of the best,
  Heaven in ordinary, man well
  dressed,
The milky way, the bird of Paradise,

  Church-bells beyond the stars heard,
  the soul's blood,
  The land of spices, something understood.

GEORGE HERBERT, 1593–1633

PRIVATE PRAYER

Private prayer, such as men secretly
offer unto God by themselves, requires
no special place, although Jesus Christ
commandeth when we pray to enter
into our chamber and to close the door
and to pray secretly unto our Father.

Whereby He would that we should
choose to our prayers such places as
might offer least occasion to call us
back from prayer, and also that we
should expel from our minds in time
of our prayer all vain thoughts.

Otherwise Jesus Christ Himself
doth observe no special place of
prayer, for we find him sometimes
praying in Mount Olivet, sometimes in
the desert, sometimes in the temple,
sometimes in the Garden.

Peter coveteth to pray upon the top
of the house. Paul prayed in prison and
was heard of God.

He also commandeth men to pray in
all faith in all places, lifting up unto
God pure and clean hands, as we find
that the prophets and most holy men
did whenever danger or necessity required.

Appointed places in which to pray
may not be neglected, but public and
common prayers should be used in
places appointed for the assembly.
From whence whomever neglects
themselves is in no wise excused. I
mean not that to be absent from that
place is sin because that place is more
holy than another, for the whole earth
created by God is equally holy.

JOHN KNOX, 1505?–1572

After having given myself wholly to
God, I renounced, for the love of Him,
everything that was not He; and I
began to live as if there were none
but He and I in the world.

And I make it my business to per-
severe in practicing the presence of
God.

One way to recollect the mind easily
in time of prayer, and preserve it more
in tranquility, is not to let it wander
too far at other times.

BROTHER LAWRENCE, 1611–1691

From THE BATTLE WITHIN

God, harden me against myself,
This coward with pathetic voice
Who craves for ease, and rest, and
    joys:
Myself, arch-traitor to myself;
My hollowest friend, my deadliest foe,
My clog whatever road I go.
Yet One there is can curb myself,
Can roll the strangling load from me,
Break off the yoke and set me free.

CHRISTINA GEORGIANA ROSSETTI,
1830–1894

ANCIENT GREEK PRAYER

O Zeus, our King, grant to us what is
good for us whether we pray for it or
not, and keep away from us whatever
is harmful however much we may pray
for it.

DIVINE MERCY

So weak is man, so ignorant and blind,
that did not God sometimes withhold
in mercy what we ask, we should be
ruined at our own request.

HANNAH MORE, 1745–1833

CONTINUOUS PRAYER

That we pray is a divine gift. There
is an interior prayer without ceasing,
yearning continually even though the
tongue is silent. The goal of all perfection is this, that the spirit is freed from
all carnal inclinations and is lifted up
into the spiritual until every word and
every volition becomes one continuous
prayer.

ST. AUGUSTINE, 354–430

INTERCESSION

There play upon all souls, at all times,
forces that are unseen, suggestions, sub-
liminal suggestions, allurements, warn-
ings, intuitive glimpses of undefined
truth, instinctive impulses to good or
ill, promptings of the divine and of
the devilish.

Into the moulding of each day's
conduct there enter a thousand untrace-
able factors, psychical, psychological,
social, religious, some from the long
past, others from the surrounding present.

To pray for another is to add to the
forces playing upon that soul for good,
not only by the sympathy and goodwill
of the one who prays, but by the rein-
forcement of divine energies since God
has so willed.

AUTHOR UNKNOWN

From AURORA LEIGH

God answers sharp and sudden to some
    prayers,
And thrusts the thing we have prayed
    for in our face,
A gauntlet with a gift in 't.

ELIZABETH BARRETT BROWNING,
1806–1861

DIALOGUE

We dream alone, we suffer alone, we
die alone, we inhabit the last resting
place alone. But there is nothing to
prevent us from opening our solitude
to God. And so what was an austere
monologue becomes dialogue.

HENRI FRÉDÉRIC AMIEL, 1821–1881

DEFINITION

Prayer, in its simplest definition, is merely a wish turned Godward.

PHILLIPS BROOKS, 1835–1893

Prayer is our lost language.

GEORGE A. BUTTRICK

LIFTING-UP PROCESS

Intercession is not asking God for difficult things for Mr. Jones and Mr. Smith (though as you say sometimes when we are deeply concerned we can't help doing this).

It is offering your will and love that God may use them as channels whereby His spirit of mercy, healing, power, or light, may reach them and achieve His purpose in them.

We can't do it unless we care, both for God's will and also for "the whole family of man," but that certainly does not involve knowing all the details about everyone who asks our prayers. God knows the details; we need not.

Probably the best kind of intercession is a quite general offering of oneself in union with our Lord, and that is what the total prayer of the Church for the world is.

He prays in and through us, lifting up into the supernatural world all souls and causes, and setting them before God's face. It is our privilege to share that "lifting-up" process.

Of course, there is and must be a wide variety in the way people pray. For some, "crude petition" about Tommy's examination or Aunt Jane's bronchitis is the only sort that is real. We each do what we can, mostly very badly.

The variousness with which Grace works is one of the most wonderful things about it. It is a living and personal energy, not a machine, and makes a response of love to all our movements of love, even the most babyish.

EVELYN UNDERHILL, 1875–1941

HIS PERFECT IMAGE

Sometimes I considered myself before God as a poor criminal at the feet of his judge; at other times I beheld Him in my heart as my Father, as my God.

Sometimes I consider myself there as a stone before a carver, wherefrom he is to carve a statue. Presenting myself thus before God, I ask Him to form His perfect image in my soul, and make me entirely like Himself.

BROTHER LAWRENCE, 1611–1691

DAILY BUSINESS

As a shoemaker makes a shoe,
and a tailor makes a coat,
so ought a Christian to pray.
Prayer is the daily business
of the Christian.

MARTIN LUTHER, 1463–1546

From MARKINGS

For all that has been—Thanks!
For all that shall be—Yes!

DAG HAMMARSKJÖLD, 1905–1961

PRAYING HANDS

Hands folded in prayer
open
in compassion.

THY WILL BE DONE

Every day we plead in the Lord's Prayer, "Thy will be done!" yet when His will is done, we grumble and are not pleased with it.

Whatever He does, we should be glad, and those who are glad will always live in peace.

Sometimes we think or say, "Ah, but it would have been so much better otherwise," or "If that had not happened, this would have turned out so much better."

As long as you see it that way, there will be no peace for you. You must take everything for the best.

MEISTER ECKHART, 1260–1328

ON WINGS OF PRAYER

St. Francis de Sales told his followers that some men who pray remind him of three kinds of birds:

The ostrich, of course, has wings but it remains earthbound, like a self-centered person who is interested only in things material.

The hen also has wings and sometimes flies over the fence, thereby releasing itself from an altogether earthbound existence.

The swallow has wings with which it soars into the heights where it is borne along gently on great currents of air.

FLIGHT AND SIGHT

Prayer is the wing wherewith the soul flies to heaven, and meditation the eye wherewith we see God.

ST. AMBROSE, 339?–397

CAUTION

Sometimes, perhaps, thou hearest another pray with much freedom and fluency, whilst thou canst hardly speak a few broken words. Hence thou art ready to accuse thyself and admire him, as though the gilding of the key made it open the door better.

WILLIAM GURNALL

PETITION

We would have working through our
    ineffectiveness thy quiet strength,
Through our blind folly thy clear-eyed
    discernment,
Through our changing impulses thy
    one direct and steady determination,
Through our indecision thine unswerv-
    ing judgment.
Transform us, therefore, by thine own
    presence within us,
That so, being mastered and possessed
    by thee,
We may find freedom in service,
Entire liberty of our wills in entire sub-
    jection to thy will.

JOHN SOMERVELL HOYLAND

REST IN SAFETY

Be off, Satan, from this door and from these four walls.

This is no place for you. There is nothing for you to do here.

This is the place for Peter and Paul and the Holy Gospel, and this is where I mean to sleep, now that my worship is done, in the name of the Father and of the Son and of the Holy Spirit.

ON THE DOOR OF THE SLAVONIC
MONASTERY OF MOUNT SINAI

MAKE ME

I am only a spark:
Make me a fire.

I am only a string:
Make me a lyre.

I am only a drop:
Make me a fountain.

I am only an ant hill:
Make me a mountain.

I am only a feather:
Make me a wing.

I am only a rag:
Make me a king.

AMADO NERVO

PRAYER AND PRACTICE

It is good to keep some account of our prayers, that we may not unsay them in our practice.

MATTHEW HENRY, 1662–1714

PRAYER

My language of worship,
 as a man;
of my dependence,
 as a creature;
of my submission,
 as a subject;
of my confession,
 as a sinner;
of my thankfulness,
 as a recipient of mercies;
of my supplication,
 as a needy person.

TYRON EDWARDS, 1809–1894

JOURNAL

My journal is that of me which would else spill over and run to waste.

It is a leaf which hangs over my head in the path.

I bend the twig and write my prayers on it, then letting it go, the bough springs up and shows my scrawl to heaven.

The crow, the goose, and the eagle carry my quill, and the wind blows the leaves as far as I go.

HENRY DAVID THOREAU,
1817–1862

RELIGION IN ACTION

Prayer is religion in action, that is, prayer is real religion. It is prayer that distinguishes the religious phenomenon from such similar or neighboring phenomena as purely moral or esthetic sentiment.

Religion is nothing if it is not the vital act by which the entire mind seeks to save itself by clinging to the principle from which it draws its life.

This act is prayer by which term I understand no vain exercise of words, no mere repetition of certain sacred formulae, but the very movement itself of the soul, putting itself in a personal relation of contact with the mysterious power of which it feels the presence. It may be even before it has a name by which to call it.

Wherever this interior prayer is lacking, there is no religion. Wherever, on the other hand, this prayer rises and stirs the soul, even in the absence of forms and doctrines, we have living religion.

WILLIAM JAMES, 1842–1910

CONFESSION

When we consider the manifold weakness of the strongest devotions in time of prayer, it is a sad consideration.

I throw myself down in my chamber, and I call in and invite God and His angels thither, and when they are there, I neglect God and His angels for the noise of a fly, for the rattling of a coach, for the whining of a door.

I talk on, knees bowed down as though I prayed to God; and if God and His angels should ask me, when I thought of God last in that prayer, I cannot tell.

JOHN DONNE, 1572–1631

THE MARTYRS' POSTURE

So we spread ourselves before God, while the hooks pierce us, the fires blaze on us, and the swords slit our throats, and the beasts leap on us. Even the posture of the Christian at prayer shows his readiness for every manner of torture.

TERTULLIAN, C. 150–C. 230

PRAYER AND ACTION

We should pray with as much earnestness as those who expect everything from God, and should act with as much energy as those who expect everything from themselves.

CHARLES CALEB COLTON,
1780?–1832

Who listens to the Divine voice is saved from many unnecessary notions.

THOMAS A KEMPIS, 1379–1471

AN ELEVENTH-CENTURY PRAYER

I have sought Thee daily at dawn and twilight,
I have stretched my hand to Thee, turned my face,
Now the cry of a heart athirst I will utter,
Like the beggar who cries at my door for grace.
The infinite heights are too small to contain Thee.
Yet perchance Thou canst niche in the clefts of me.
Shall my heart not treasure the hope to gain Thee,
Or my yearning fail till my tongue's last plea?
Nay, surely Thy name I shall worship, while breath in my nostrils be.

SOLOMON IBN GABIROL,
1021–1058

"SUNK IN GOD"

Mystics, trying to tell us of their condition, often say that they fell "Sunk in God like a fish in the sea."

Nothing in nature is so lovely and so vigorous, so perfectly at home in its environment, as a fish in the sea. Its surroundings give to it a beauty, quality, and power which is not its own. We take it out, and at once a poor, limp dull thing, fit for nothing, is gasping away its life.

So the soul, sunk in God, living his life of prayer, is supported, filled, transformed in beauty, by a vitality and power which are its own.

Far better to be a shrimp within that ocean, than a full-sized theological whale cast upon the shore.

EVELYN UNDERHILL, 1875–1941

Intercession is loving our neighbor on our knees.

CHARLES H. BRENT, 1862–1929

ENDURANCE

What seems fathomable, I fathom; what is unutterable, I utter, because I can pray. How do people endure anything on earth if they cannot have God?

THOMAS DOOLEY, 1927–1961

INWARD FERMENTATION

I pray on the principle that the wine knocks the cork out of a bottle. There is an inward fermentation and there must be a vent.

HENRY WARD BEECHER, 1813–1887

WITHDRAWN FROM THE WORLD

Lord, grant that from hence I may learn to withdraw my thoughts, affections, desires, and expectations entirely from the world, and may fix them upon the heavenly state,

where there is fulness of joy;

where reigns heavenly, sweet, calm, and delightful love without alloy;

where there are continually the dearest expressions of this life;

where there is the enjoyment of this love without parting;

and where those person, who appear so lovely in this world, will be inexpressibly more lovely, and full of love to us.

JONATHAN EDWARDS, 1703–1758

WATCHFUL PROVIDENCE

Of all duties, prayer certainly is the sweetest and most easy. There are some duties which may seem to occasion a troublesome opposition to the natural workings of flesh and blood—such as the forgiveness of injuries and the love of our enemies—but this duty of prayer and thanksgiving to God requireth no strength of parts or painful study, but just to know and have a true sense of our dependence and of the mercies by which we are upheld.

With this, in every place and posture of the body, a good man may lift up his soul unto the Lord his God.

For it seems to be the least that can be done to answer the demand of our duty in this point, successively to open and shut up the day in prayer and thanksgiving, since there is not a morning thou risest, or a night thou liest down, but thou are indebted for it to the watchful providence of Almighty God.

LAURENCE STERNE,
1713–1768

Prayer, like radium, is a source of luminous energy, and when we pray we link ourselves with the inexhaustible motive power that spins the universe.

ALEXIS CARREL, 1873–1944

NOBLEST FEELING

Does not every true man feel that he is himself made higher by doing reverence to what is really above him? No nobler or more blessed feeling dwells in man's heart.

THOMAS CARLYLE,
1795–1881

A HYMN TO GOD
THE FATHER

Wilt Thou forgive that sin where I begun,
  Which is my sin, though it were
  done before?
Wilt Thou forgive that sin, through
which I run,
  And do run still: though still I do
  deplore?
    When Thou hast done, Thou hast
    not done,
      For, I have more.

Wilt Thou forgive that sin by which I
have won
  Others to sin? and made my sin their
  door?
Wilt Thou forgive that sin which I did
shun
  A year, or two: But wallowed in, a
  score?
    When Thou hast done, Thou hast
    not done,
      For, I have more.

I have a sin of fear, that when I have
spun
  My last thread, I shall perish on the
  shore;
Swear by Thyself, that at my death Thy
Son
  Shall shine as He shines now, and
  heretofore;
    And, having done that, Thou hast
    done,
      I fear no more.

        JOHN DONNE, 1572–1631

Prayer is not hearing yourself talk,
but being silent, staying silent,
and waiting until you hear God.
    SØREN KIERKEGAARD, 1813–1855

FLIGHT

He who runs
from God
in the morning
will scarcely
find Him
the rest
of the day.
    JOHN BUNYAN, 1626–1688

AN HOUR IN THY PRESENCE

Lord, what a change within us one
short hour
Spent in Thy presence will prevail to
make,
What heavy burdens from our bosoms
take,
What parchéd grounds refresh, as with
a shower!
We kneel, and all around us seems to
lower;
We rise, and all, the distant and the
near,
Stands forth in sunny outline, brave
and clear;
We kneel how weak, we rise how full
of power.
Why therefore should we do ourselves
this wrong
Or others—that we are not always
strong,
That we are ever overborne with care,
That we should ever weak or heartless
be,
Anxious or troubled, when with us in
prayer,
And joy and strength and courage are
with Thee!
    RICHARD CHENEVIX TRENCH,
        1807–1886

S MATHEVS   S MARCVS

QVÆRITE PRIMM REGNVM   PARATE VIAM DOMINI
ET IVSTITAM EIVS ET HÆ   RECTAS FACITE SE
OMIA ADIICIENTVR VOB   MITAS EIVS · MARC · I

SAINTS

*We must not wish to become every-
thing at once, nor to become saints in
four days.*

ST. PHILIP NERI, 1515–1595

There are three orders of saints:
   those who are a glory on the mountain tops;
   those who are gleams on the sides of
the hills;
   and those who are just a few faint
lights down in the valleys.

ST. PATRICK, C. 385–461

WHY THEY ARE CALLED
SAINTS

Those whom we have agreed to remember by the word "saint" are so
called because they were:
Cheerful when it was hard to be cheerful;
Patient, when it was hard to be patient;
Because they pushed on when they
   wished to stand still;
Because they kept silent when they
   wished to speak;
And were agreeable when they wished
   to be disagreeable.

AUTHOR UNKNOWN

TORCH-BEARERS

The Saints, with their extravagance of
human tenderness, are the great torch-
bearers, the tip of the wedge, and the
clearers of the darkness.

   The world is not yet with them, so
they often seem in the midst of the
world's affairs to be preposterous; yet
they are the impregnators of the world,
and vivifiers and animators of the
goodness which, but for them, would
lie forever dormant.

   It is not possible to be quite as mean
as we naturally are, when they have
passed before us.

   One fire kindles another; and without that over-trust in human worth
which they show, the rest of us would
lie in spiritual stagnation.

WILLIAM JAMES, 1842–1910

A saint is a person who does almost
everything any other decent person
does, only somewhat better and with a
totally different motive.

COVENTRY PATMORE, 1823–1896

THE GREATEST SAINT

Would you know who is the greatest
saint in the world?
Not he who prays most or fasts most.
Not he who gives the most alms.
Not he who is most eminent for tem-
perance, chastity, or thankfulness to
God.
But he who wills everything God wills.

WILLIAM LAW, 1686–1761

One day, of holy days the crest,
I, though no churchman, love to
keep,
All Saints'—the unknown good that
rest
In Gods' still memory, folded deep:
The bravely dumb that did their deed,
And scorned to blot it with a name,
Men of the plain, heroic breed,
That loved heaven's silence more
than fame.

JAMES RUSSELL LOWELL,
1819–1891

GROWTH IN HOLINESS

The soul is a force or an energy: and
holiness is the growth of that energy
in love, in full being, in creative, spiritual personality.

FRIEDRICH VON HÜGEL, 1852–1925

FRIENDLY PERSPECTIVE

To the poet, to the philosopher and to
the saint, all things are friendly and
sacred, all events profitable, all days
holy, all men divine.

RALPH WALDO EMERSON,
1803–1882

AXIOM

Belong to God and become a wonder to
yourself.

AN EARLY MYSTIC

Rejoice, O heaven and earth! Truly!
Truly! By God! By God! Be as sure of
it as you are that God lives.

At the least good deed, the least bit
of goodwill, or the least good desires,
all the saints in heaven and on earth
rejoice, and together with the angels,
their joy is such that all the joy in this
world cannot be compared to it.

The more exalted a saint is, the
greater his joy; but the joy of them all
put together amounts to as little as a
bean when compared to the joy of God
over good deeds.

For truly God plays and laughs in
good deeds. Then He says: Rejoice, O
ye heavens. For the Lord hath comforted His people. Notice that He will
have mercy on His afflicted ones, His
poor ones.

MEISTER ECKHART, 1260–1328

GOD'S WAY

Do not think that God will make thee
just by a miracle. If He wished a beautiful rose to grow in the stark cold of
winter He might do it well, but He
doeth no such thing, for He deemeth
it His will that it be done in true order
in May after the frost, by dew and
many a rainfall ordained and framed
to accomplish it.

HEINRICH SUSO, 1300?–1366

PERFECT HARMONY

Within! within, O turn
Thy spirit's eyes, and learn
Thy wandering senses gently to con-
trol;
Thy dearest Friend dwells deep within
thy soul,
And asks thyself of thee,
That heart, and mind, and sense, He
may make whole,
In perfect harmony.

GERHARD TERSTEEGEN,
1697–1769

TOWARD SAINTLINESS

The saint is one who begins with himself and with what he must do, not
with denunciations of society and its
wrongs.

He is a witness to the personal revolution, although he seldom stops there.

He approves of the sentiments of
the old Negro spiritual that chants,
" 'Tain't the preacher nor the deacon,
but 'tis me, O Lord, a-standin' in the
need of prayer."

And he would well understand Unamuno's remark that the way to get rid
of lying is to get rid of one liar, although he would be confident that he
could never do this in his own strength
alone.

As the saint finds his life laid open
before the scrutiny of the All-Loving
One, he is acutely aware that all of the
projected sins of society are present
within himself.

And with God's help he is concerned
to begin from within, in Maritain's
words, "To purify the springs of history within his own heart."

DOUGLAS V. STEERE

SHINING LIGHTS

Stars are of mighty use; the night
Is dark and long;
The road foul; and where one goes
right,
Six may go wrong.
One twinkling ray,
Shot o'er some cloud,
May clear much way,
And guide a crowd.

God's saints are shining lights: who
stays
O'er dark hills, swift streams, and
steep ways
As smooth as glass:
But these all night,
Like candles, shed
Their beams, and light
Us into bed.

They are—indeed—our pillar fires,
Seen as we go;
They are that City's shining spires
We travel to.

HENRY VAUGHAN, 1621–1695

He who is educated and eloquent must
not measure his saintliness merely by
his fluency.

Of two imperfect things, holy rusti-
city is better than sinful eloquence.

ST. JEROME, 340–420

THE BEST TIME
TO BE BEST

A saint is a sinner
living his best
in a world at its worst.

JOSEPH PARKER,
1830–1902

GOD'S MASTERPIECES

The world has known saints, and has forsaken them. Emerson rightly said that when man tires of the saints, he turns to the artists.

Man certainly has produced great masterpieces: the paintings of Fun Huang Grottos, a Cathedral of Chartres, a counterpoint of Palestrina. But these were possible because man had before him the living ideal of God's masterpieces—the saints.

Where there are no saints, there is no vital art. Where there are no living examples of love and accepted suffering, of life and growth, there can be no living artistic utterance.

When the creative spirit in man becomes dormant, the engineers take over. When the engineers become masters, contempt for the spiritual life quickly germinates. And it will continue to germinate in our time so long as so much of contemporary religion remains merely a matter of dogma and private salvation or an act of sentimentalism, totally out of contact with the whole of mankind.

From THE PATH OF THE SAINT

To have friends whose lives we can elevate or depress by our influence is sacred.

To be entrusted with little children is sacred.

To have powers by which we can make this earth a more decent place is sacred.

To be a child of God is sacred.

And honor, honesty, truthfulness, fidelity, and love are sacred.

HARRY EMERSON FOSDICK

THIRTEENTH-CENTURY RELIGIOUS INSTRUCTIONS

At some time in the day or night think upon and call to mind all who are sick and sorrowful, who suffer affliction and poverty, and the pain which prisoners endure who lie heavily fettered with iron.

Think especially of the Christians who are among the heathen, some in prison, some in as great thralldom as an ox or an ass.

Have compassion for those who are under strong temptation.

Take thought of all men's sorrows and sigh to our Lord that He may take care of them.

THE ANCREN RIWLE

The martyrs shook the powers of darkness with the irresistible power of weakness.

JOHN MILTON, 1608–1674

A BLESSING ON EVERY CHURCH

When the Franciscan brethren came upon a church or a cross, they bowed in prayer and said devoutly: "We adore Thee, O Christ, and we bless Thee in all Thy churches that are in all the world, for that by Thy holy Cross Thou has redeemed the world."

IN AND OUT OF FOCUS

Where I left myself, I found God.
Where I found myself, I lost God.
Our eyes are not in focus for the
Reality, until they are out of focus for
our own petty concerns.

MEISTER ECKHART, 1260–1328

POSSESSION

He who says, "What is mine is yours
 and what is yours is yours," is a
 saint.
He who says, "What is yours is mine
 and what is mine is mine," is a
 wicked man.

BABYLONIAN TALMUD

MIRACLE OF LOVE

Ten thousand muses never would
Stir an image out of wood,
But let love knock at the church door,
And saints in niches, gray with lore,
Step from their haloes to the floor,
And laugh, and are alive once more.

AUTHOR UNKNOWN

WRITTEN IN A COPY OF EMERSON'S ESSAYS

                    The will is free;
Strong is the soul, and wise and beautiful;
The seeds of godlike power are in us
 still;
Gods are we, bards, saints, heroes, if
 we will!

MATTHEW ARNOLD, 1822–1888

PATHS OF LIGHT

You go to your saint and find God
working and manifest in him. He got
near to God by some saint of his that
went before him, or that stood beside
him, in whom he saw the Divine
Presence. That saint again lighted his
fire at some flame before him. And so
the power of the sainthoods animates
and fills the world.

PHILLIPS BROOKS, 1835–1893

DESIRING THE GOOD

By desiring what is perfectly good,
even when we do not quite know what
it is and cannot do what we would, we
are part of the power against evil,
widening the skirts of light, and making the struggle with darkness nar-
rower.

GEORGE ELIOT, 1819–1880

WHAT THE LORD SAID

I am He who made all the saints.
I gave them grace; I bestowed on them
 glory.
I know what every one hath deserved.
I have kept them from evil with the
 blessings of my goodness.
I foreknew my beloved ones before the
 ages.
I chose them out of the world; they
 chose not me first.
I called them by grace; I drew them
 by mercy; I led them safely through
 sundry temptations.
I made both the small and the great.
Nothing can turn them back or press
 them down, for being full of the
 eternal Truth, they burn with the
 fire of unquenchable charity.

THOMAS A KEMPIS, 1379–1471

SANCTUARY

I love Thy Church, O God;
Her walls before Thee stand,
Dear as the apple of Thine eye,
And graven on Thy hand.

TIMOTHY DWIGHT, 1752–1817

OVER THREE DOORWAYS

All that which pleases thee is but for
the moment.
All that which troubles thee is but for
the moment.
That only is which is eternal.

MILAN CATHEDRAL

To all who are weary and seek rest,
To all who mourn and long for com-
fort,
To all who struggle and desire victory,
To all who sin and need a Savior,
To all who are idle and look for ser-
vice,
To all who are strangers and want
fellowship,
To all who hunger and thirst after
righteousness—
The church opens wide her doors and
offers her welcome in the name of
Jesus Christ her Lord.

AUTHOR UNKNOWN

GOD'S TRANSLATORS

The Church is catholic, universal. So
are all her actions. For all mankind is
of one Author and is one volume.

When one man dies, one volume is
not torn out of the book, but translated
into a better language. And every chapter must be so translated.

God employs several translators.
Some pieces are translated by age and
some by justice, but God's hand is in
every translation, and His hand will
bind up all our scattered leaves again
for that library where every book shall
lie open to one another.

JOHN DONNE, 1572–1631

FAVORITE SCENERY

I never weary of great churches. It is
my favorite kind of mountain scenery.
Mankind was never so happily inspired
as when it made a cathedral.

ROBERT LOUIS STEVENSON,
1850–1894

UNFAILING LOVE

Sometimes from our mad world, where men so trust in force, I come into this church alone and look at the cross above the altar.

It seems to say to me: "I am a symbol of apparent failure, and I represent the crucifixion of love by men and violence. But long ago they passed away, and the empires which by violence they founded passed away, and I still am here waiting.

"There is no way out of human misery but by love. Whoever believes in violence trusts in a god who cannot create or organize anything permanent. In the long run, it is only love that does not fail."

HARRY EMERSON FOSDICK

CHURCH ETIQUETTE

Let not this house be desecrated by a religion of show.

Let it not degenerate into a place of forms.

Let not your pews be occupied by lifeless machines.

Do not come here to take part in lethargic repetitions of sacred words.

Do not come from a cold sense of duty with the thought of having paid a debt to God.

Do not come to perform a present task to insure a future heaven.

Come to find heaven now, to anticipate the happiness of that better world by breathing its spirit, to bind your souls indissolubly to your Maker.

WILLIAM ELLERY CHANNING,
1780–1842

The business of the church is to afflict the comfortable and to comfort the afflicted.

AUTHOR UNKNOWN

INSCRIPTION

He who would enter the divine temple must be pure; and purity is to have a mind which thinks holy thoughts.

TEMPLE OF AESCULAPIUS
IN ANCIENT GREECE

BEYOND FASTIDIOUSNESS

The touching, entrancing beauty of Christianity consists, as much as in anything else, in its freedom from all fastidiousness.

A soul that is fastidious is as yet only hovering around the precincts of Christianity, but it has not entered its sanctuary, where heroism is always homely, where the best always acts as stimulus towards being (in a true sense) but one of the semiarticulate, bovine, childish, repulsively second-third-fourth-rate crowd.

When I told you of my choking emotion in reading that scene of Jesus, the Light of the World (that He is this is a historic fact), as the menial servant at the feet of those foolish little fishermen and tax-gatherers, what is it that moves me but just that huge life-and-love-bringing paradox, here in its fullest activity?

The heathen philosophies, one and all failed to get beyond fastidiousness: only Christianity—a deeply costingly realized Christianity—got beyond it.

FRIEDRICH VON HÜGEL, 1852–1925

TEST OF A SERMON

The test of a preacher is that his congregation goes away saying, not "What a lovely sermon," but "I will do something!"

ST. FRANCIS DE SALES, 1562–1622

ON THIS BOOK OF STONE

Churchmen understood perfectly well the power of art over minds still childish and unenlightened.

For the vast masses of the unlettered, for the populace who possessed neither psalter nor missal, and who remembered only as much of Christianity as they could see with their own eyes, the idea had to be given substance, clothed in perceptible form.

In the twelfth and thirteenth centuries the doctrinal truths were incarnated in the personages of the liturgical plays. Christian thought created its organs of expression with miraculous power.

Victor Hugo was right: The cathedral is a book of stone for the untutored, and a book which the printed book gradually rendered obsolete. "The Gothic sun set behind the great printing press at Mainz."

ÉMILE MÂLE, 1862–1954

DIVINE CONDUCTOR

We should think of the church as an orchestra in which the different churches play on different instruments while a Divine Conductor calls the tune.

WILLIAM RALPH INGE,
1860–1954

SUNDAY DRESS

Why did I once come walking down the center aisle in church? Why was I wearing the loveliest white gown of my entire lifetime? Why shall I treasure this dress to hand down to my daughters and granddaughters as something precious and almost sacred?

Surely because I loved someone enough to want his name to be my name, his home to be my home, his family to be my family.

I understood perfectly that the new name was binding me "for richer, for poorer, for better, for worse, in sickness and in health, till death do us part."

Exactly! Then how much more tender and troubling and eternal is the tie which the minister pronounces upon me as I walk out of church every Sunday of my life: "And now may the grace of our Lord Jesus Christ, and the love of God, and the fellowship of the Holy Spirit be and abide with you, now and forever. Amen."

I dare not make light of such grace, such love, and such fellowship, which my name "Christian" has bestowed on me. For his words bind me for life and eternity to every other Christian in every other country on earth—a family which is the largest single human fellowship.

Even my most ordinary Sunday-go-to-meeting dress can take on ecumenical beauty, reminding me of John's description in the Book of Revelation: "For the fine linen, dazzling white, is the righteous conduct of the saints."

I look more closely at my Sunday dress. What a heritage it holds, and what a future. Grace, love, fellowship, and "righteous conduct."

HOW GOD COMES TO US

Throughout His ministry our Lord emphasized the idea of feeding as something intimately connected with His love and care of souls.

The mystery of the Eucharist does not stand alone if it is the crest of a great wave, a total sacramental disclosure of the dealings of the transcendent God with men.

The hunger of man is the matter of Christ's first temptation. The feedings of the four thousand and the five thousand are more than miracles of practical compassion. We feel that in them something of deep significance is done, one of the mysteries of eternal life a little bit unveiled. So too in the Supper at Emmaus, when the bread is broken the holy one is known.

It is peculiar to Christianity, indeed part of the mystery of the Incarnation, that it constantly shows us this coming of God through and in homely and fugitive things and events, and puts the need and dependence of the creature in the very heart of prayer.

EVELYN UNDERHILL, 1875–1941

You may find a city without walls and gates, without a palace or a theater, but you will not find a city without a temple.

PLUTARCH, 46?–C. 120

The Church is composed of sinners who are trying to do the best things in the worst times.

THEODORE PARKER, 1810–1860

WANTED: A PARSON

An American once tried to found a town without a church. He bought 1,000 acres in a beautiful place. He laid out his town with every known convenience—schools, hospitals, theaters, dance hall, club house, playgrounds, parks. He built charming houses on lovely streets with lovely trees. He started businesses with matchless opportunities for profit. But to keep the curse of religion forever away from this little paradise, there was a clause in every deed making it impossible to use the property for religious purposes.

Within several years, 5,000 persons had settled there. But from the very beginning decent women hesitated to come. Parents in particular were reluctant to rear their children in such a place. Furthermore, the public schools had trouble getting the right kind of teachers.

Because good people held back from coming, bad people flocked in. Toward the end of five years, the man began to fear for his investment. So he published in every paper and pasted on every billboard in town this amazing manifesto:

"To whom it may concern: God knows that there is no such person as God, and my motto has always been 'To Hell with religion.' But for some fool reason, which no man can fathom, I have found by experience that we cannot do business in this country on any other basis than that silly bit of sentiment which we stamp on our coins: 'In God we trust.' Therefore, infernal foolishness though it all is, I have sent out for a parson and we are going to build a church."

From THE SERVANT IN THE HOUSE

The pillars of the Church go up like
the brawny trunks of heroes:
the sweet human flesh of men and
women is moulded about its bul-
warks, strong, impregnable:
the faces of little children laugh out
from every cornerstone:
the terrible spans and arches of it are
the joined hands of comrades;
and up in the heights and spaces there
are inscribed the numberless mus-
ings of all the dreamers of the
world.
It is yet building—building and built
upon.
Sometimes the work goes forward in
deep darkness:
sometimes in blinding light:
now beneath the burden of unutterable anguish:
now to the tune of a great laughter
and heroic shoutings like the cry of
thunder.
Sometimes, in the silence of the night-
time,
one may hear the tiny hammerings of
the comrades at work up in the
dome—
the comrades that have climbed ahead.

CHARLES R. KENNEDY, 1871–1950

WAY TO HEAVEN

I can hardly think that any man was
ever scared into heaven. They go the
fairest way to heaven that would serve
God without a hell. Other mercenaries
that crouch before God in fear of hell,
though they term themselves His servants, are, indeed, the slaves of the
Almighty.

SIR THOMAS BROWNE, 1605–1682

Persecution has not crushed the church;
power has not beaten it back;
time has not abated its forces;
and what is most wonderful of all,
the abuses of its friends have not
shaken its stability.

HORACE BUSHNELL, 1802–1876

From INSIDE OF KING'S COLLEGE CHAPEL, CAMBRIDGE

Give all thou canst; high Heaven re-
jects the lore
Of nicely-calculated less or more;
So deemed the man who fashioned for
the sense
These lofty pillars, spread that branch-
ing roof
Self-poised, and scooped into ten
thousand cells,
Where light and shade repose, where
music dwells
Lingering—and wandering on as loth
to die;
Like thoughts whose very sweetness
yieldeth proof
That they were born for immortality.

WILLIAM WORDSWORTH,
1770–1850

ST. MARK'S, VENICE

The whole edifice is to be regarded
less as a temple wherein to pray, then
as itself a Book of Common Prayer, a
vast illuminated missal, bound with
alabaster instead of parchment, stud-
ded with porphyry pillars instead of
jewels, and written within and without
in letters of enamel and gold.

JOHN RUSKIN, 1819–1900

CIRCUIT RIDER

My mother's Uncle David brought the
   Word
And founded churches in the wilder-
   ness;
His only scimitar the faith that spurred
Him on to ford the swollen streams
   and press
Still further in the forests, caring less
For the risk of death than for the
   spider's cord
That brushed this mighty servant of
   the Lord,
In homespun woven to a parson's
   dress.
For forty years he rode beneath the
   trees
And left as footprints on the winding
   trails
White meeting-houses in the wooded
   vales
New Canaans, Olivets, and Galilees;
And as he rode I think there followed
   him
Another David and his cherubim.

RACHEL ALBRIGHT

THE CHURCH IN THE
WILDWOOD

There's a church in the valley by the
   wildwood,
No lovelier spot in the dale;
No place is so dear to my childhood,
As the little brown church in the vale.

Oh, come to the church in the wildwood,
To the trees where the wild flowers
   bloom;
Where the parting hymn will be
   chanted,
We will weep by the side of the tomb.

How sweet on a clear Sabbath morning,

To list to the clear ringing bell;
Its tones so sweetly are calling,
Oh, come to the church in the vale.

From the church in the valley by the
   wildwood,
When day fades away in the night,
I would fain from this spot of my
   childhood
Wing my way to the mansion of light.

WILLIAM S. PITTS

AN EINSTEIN TESTIMONY

Being a lover of freedom, when the
revolution came in Germany, I looked
to the universities to defend it, knowing that they had always boasted of
their devotion to the cause of truth;
but, no, the universities immediately
were silenced.

Then I looked to the great editors
of the newspapers whose flaming edi-
torials in days gone by had proclaimed
their love of freedom; but they, like
the universities, were silenced in a
few short weeks.

Then I looked to the individual
writers, who, as literary guides of Germany, had written much and often
concerning the place of freedom in
modern life; but they, too, were mute.

Only the Church stood squarely
across the path of Hitler's campaign
for suppressing truth. I never had any
special interest in the Church before,
but now I feel a great affection and
admiration because the Church alone
has had the courage and persistence to
stand for intellectual truth and moral
freedom.

I am forced to confess that what I
once despised I now praise unreserv-
edly.

ALBERT EINSTEIN, 1879–1955

THE DWELLING PLACE

What happy secret fountain,
Fair shade or mountain,
Whose undiscovered virgin glory
Boasts it this day, though not in story,
Was then Thy dwelling? did some
    cloud
Fix'd to a tent, descend and shroud
My distrest Lord? or did a star,
Beckoned by Thee, though high and
    far,
In sparkling smiles haste gladly down
To lodge light and increase her own?
My dear, dear God! I do not know
What lodged Thee then, nor where,
    nor how;
But I am sure Thou now dost come
Oft to a narrow, homely room,
Where Thou too hast but the least
    part,
My God, I mean my sinful heart.

HENRY VAUGHAN, 1621–1695

⚜

THE BUILDING OF
CHARTRES CATHEDRAL

Who has ever seen or heard, in all the
ages of the past, that kings and princes
and lords, swollen with riches and
honor, men and women of all sorts, of
noble birth, have bowed their necks to
the yoke of such labor and harnessed
themselves to carts like beasts and
drawn them laden with all the materials needful for the construction of a
church, even to the doors of the
church?

What is more astonishing is that a
thousand or more men and women are
attached to one cart, so vast is the mass
and so heavy the machine, yet so deep
a silence reigns that not a voice or
whisper can be heard.

When there is a halt called on the
way, there is no sound save that of the
confession of sin and the prayers to
God for pardon. There, while the
priests are speaking and praying, hatred is lulled asleep and quarrels are
banished, debts are forgiven, and the
union of hearts re-established.

If anyone is so hardened that he cannot bring himself to forgive his enemies or to beg the admonitions of
the priests, then his offering is with-
drawn from the stock of materials and
it is accounted unclean and he himself
is separated from the society of the
people who have built the church.

You might think these were the
Children of Israel crossing Jordan and,
indeed, for them as for the Children
of Israel, it is as if miracles are being
wrought.

When they come to the church, they
set their wagons in a circle and form
a spiritual pact, and all the following
night this whole army sings its songs
of praise and offers prayer to Almighty
God.

LETTER WRITTEN BY
THE ABBOT HAIMON

⚜

LIFE'S SANCTUARIES

A person, if he is to be spiritually
healthy, ought to worship more than
once a week and in more than one
sanctuary. There should be more than
one place in everyone's life where he is
refreshed, restored, and rebuilt. A soul
can no more maintain robust spiritual
health on one worship experience per
week than he can live on one meal each
week. The soul of man must eat regularly or sicken and die.

HAROLD E. KOHN

CARVED REMINDER

Inscribed in an ancient European cathedral is this reminder for worshipers:

Deus absconditus heic.
(God is hidden here.)

WHAT IS THE CHURCH?

The church is many things. It is weddings and holy vows spoken in love and reverence. It is funerals and the promise of life eternal. It is babies being baptized. It is comfort and hope for a better tomorrow. It is Easter lilies. It is worn hymn books. It is work and sacrifice and holy communion.

The church is little children singing, "Jesus Loves Me." It is robed choirs singing anthems of praise. It is Christmas carols and little boys in bathrobes being wise men and shepherds, little girls in nightgowns portraying angels.

The church is stained glass windows. It is an altar, a pulpit, and God's word in a big leather book. It is fellowship dinners and foreign missions. It is a helping hand. It is a sermon that lifts the spirit. It is the sound of chairs scraping the floor in the Sunday school rooms. It is a bell ringing clear on a crisp, still morning. It is an organ's deep tones. It is heads bowed in prayer, a warm, friendly handclasp, a solemn whispered benediction.

The church is giving and receiving. It is budgets and figures. It is wood and bricks and stone. It is goodness and mercy. It is a manger bed, a star, and a cross. It is a way of life.

CHARLES O. AUSTIN, JR.

SOCIETY OF SINNERS

The Christian Church is a society of sinners. It is the only society in the world, membership in which is based upon the single qualification that the candidate shall be unworthy of membership.

CHARLES CLAYTON MORRISON,
1874–1966

OUR LORD'S DREAM

Our Lord's entire dream of His mission on earth is a dream tremendous, thrilling, and tender:

"And they shall come from the east, and from the west, and from the north, and from the south, and shall sit down in the Kingdom of God."

Meeting together. Sitting together. Elbow to elbow. Shoulder to shoulder. Sharing hymnbooks. Standing together. Kneeling together. Praying together.

One in Him who made them, and loved them, and gave His only Son to make them one family. Unbreakably one. Indestructibly one. Everlastingly one.

One in prayer to Him for whom this same mind which was in Christ Jesus may be in them also. That wider, deeper, kinder, and richer mind. So that His Kingdom may come, beginning with each of us, here and now. Inescapably and eternally.

Your parish is Christ's body,
Your offering is His hands,
Your prayer is His heart,
Your sins are His thorns.

AUTHOR UNKNOWN

AMERICA'S FIRST CHURCH

When I first went to Virginia, I well remember, we did hang an awning (which is an old sail) to three or four trees to shadow us from the sun, our walls were rails of wood, our seats unhewed trees, till we cut planks; our pulpit a bar of wood nailed to two neighboring trees; in foul weather we shifted into an old rotten tent, for we had few better, and this came by the way of adventure for new. This was our church, till we built a homely thing like a barn, set upon cratchets, covered with rafts, sedge, and earth; so was also the walls; the best of our houses of the like curiosity, but the most part far much worse workmanship, that could neither well defend wind nor rain, yet we had daily common prayer morning and evening, every Sunday two sermons, and every three months the holy communion, till our minister died. But our prayers daily, with an homily on Sundays, we continued two or three years after, till more preachers came. Moreover, every man was required to attend, or pay a fine of so many pounds of tobacco—which was the currency of that day.

CAPTAIN JOHN SMITH, 1580–1631

and new glories upon the face of men.

It is a seed stirring, if we do not choke it.

It is the Shekinah of the soul, the Presence in the midst.

The basic response of the soul to the Light is internal adoration and joy, thanksgiving and worship, self-surrender and listening.

The secret places of the heart cease to be our noisy workshop. They become a holy sanctuary of adoration, if our minds are stayed on Him.

Powerfully are the springs of our will moved to an abandon of singing love toward God.

In this center of creation all things are ours, and we are Christ's and Christ is God's.

This practice is the heart of religion. It is the secret, I am persuaded, of the inner life of the Master of Galilee.

He expected this secret to be freshly discovered in everyone who would be His follower.

It creates an amazing fellowship, the church catholic and invisible, and institutes group living at a new level, a society grounded in reverence, history rooted in eternity, colonies of heaven.

THOMAS KELLY, 1893–1941

OUR INNER SANCTUARY

Deep within us all is an amazing inner sanctuary of the soul, a holy place, a divine center, a speaking voice, to which we can continuously return.

Eternity is at our hearts, pressing upon our time-torn lives, warming us with intimations of an astounding destiny, calling us home unto itself.

It is a light within which illumines the face of God and casts new shadows

GOD'S ALTAR

There is in all the sons of men
   A love that in the spirit dwells,
That panteth after things unseen,
   And tidings of the future tells.
And God hath built His altar here
   To keep this fire of faith alive,
And sent His priests in holy fear
   To speak the truth, for truth to strive.

RALPH WALDO EMERSON, 1803–1882

SCHOOL

*To know that we know what we
know, and that we do not know what
we do not know is true knowledge.*

HENRY DAVID THOREAU,
1817–1862

SCHOOLROOM

The mother's heart is the child's schoolroom.

HENRY WARD BEECHER, 1813–1887

When you educate a man, you educate an individual.

When you educate a woman, you educate a whole family.

CHINESE PROVERB

FOUR CHARACTERS

There are four characters in scholars:
Quick to hear and quick to forget,
  his gain is cancelled by his loss;
Slow to hear and slow to forget,
  his loss is cancelled by his gain;
Quick to hear and slow to forget,
  he is wise;
Slow to hear and quick to forget,
  this is an evil lot.

SAYINGS OF THE JEWISH
FATHERS

From A SONG OF THE ROLLING EARTH

The song is to the singer, and comes
  back most to him,
The teaching is to the teacher, and
  comes back most to him,
The love is to the lover, and comes
  back most to him.

WALT WHITMAN, 1819–1892

He who knoweth not what he ought to know is a brute beast among men.

He that knoweth no more than he hath need is a man among brute beasts.

He that knoweth all that may be known is a god among men.

PYTHAGORAS, C. 582–C. 507 B.C.

SCHOOLBOY'S PRAYER IN INDIA

O Lord, help me to pass my examination;
O Lord, help the whole school to pass;
O Lord, help the whole world to pass.

A TEACHER'S PRAYER

O Lord of learning and of learners, we are at best but blunderers in this Godlike business of teaching.

Our shortcomings shame us, for we are not alone in paying the penalty for them. They have a sorry immortality in the maimed minds of those whom we, in our blundering, mislead.

We have been content to be merchants of dead yesterdays, when we should have been guides into unborn tomorrows.

Help us to be more interested in stimulating the builders of modern cathedrals than in retailing to students the glories of ancient temples.

May we be shepherds of the spirit, as well as masters of the mind.

Give us, O Lord of learners, a sense of the divinity of our undertaking.

GLENN FRANK

ON BEGINNING TO TEACH

Read much. Learn much. Yet you must come to one beginning: "I am He that teacheth man knowledge. I give a clearer understanding to the little ones than can be given by man. I, even I, lift up in a flash the ways of the eternal truth more than if a man had studied in the school ten years."

THOMAS A KEMPIS, 1379–1471

HIGHEST ACCOMPLISHMENT

A teacher who can arouse a feeling for one single good action, for one single good poem, accomplishes more than he who fills our memory with rows on rows of natural objects, classified with name and form.

JOHANN WOLFGANG VON GOETHE, 1749–1832

UNFORGETTABLE EXAMPLE

The greatest and most lasting impression made upon me at Hampton was that made by General Armstrong, the noblest, rarest human being I have ever met.

The older I grow, the more I am convinced that there is no education one can get from books and costly apparatus that is equal to that which can be gotten from contact with great men and women.

From his example I learned the lesson that great men cultivate love, and that only little men cherish a spirit of hatred.

BOOKER T. WASHINGTON, 1858–1915

From A MAN FOR ALL SEASONS

SIR THOMAS MORE: Why not be a teacher, you'd be a fine teacher. Perhaps a great one.

RICHARD RICE: And if I was, who would know it?

MORE: You, your pupils, your friends, God. Not a bad public, that.

ROBERT BOLT

From PASSAGE TO INDIA

Lo, soul, seest thou not God's purpose from the first?

The earth to be spann'd, connected by network,

The races, neighbors, to marry and be given in marriage,

The oceans to be cross'd, the distant brought near,

The lands to be welded together.

WALT WHITMAN, 1819–1892

COUNSELING VOLCANOES

Just now I cannot speak an exhortation
To thrill your class upon graduation.
I first must act as ethical adviser
To fourteen young volcanoes and a
    geyser;
Reprove a hurricane, while also show-
    ing
The Mississippi how to do its flowing;
Instruct a thunderhead in lightning-
    making
And teach an earthquake due restraint
    in quaking.
Then, having calmed some waterspouts
    and squalls,
And preached a sermon to Niagara
    Falls,
I may feel better qualified to give
Advice to Youth on How It Ought to
    Live.

ARTHUR GUITERMAN, 1871–1943

ON TEACHING

Then said a teacher, Speak to us of
Teaching.

And he said:

No man can reveal to you aught but
that which already lies half asleep in
the dawning of your knowledge.

The teacher who walks in the
shadow of the temple, among his followers, gives not of his wisdom but
rather of his faith and his lovingness.

If he is indeed wise he does not bid
you enter the house of his wisdom, but
rather leads you to the threshold of his
own mind.

The astronomer may speak to you
of his understanding of space, but he
cannot give you his understanding.

The musician may sing to you of the
rhythm which is in all space, but he
cannot give you the ear which arrests
the rhythm nor the voice which echoes
it.

And he who is versed in the science
of numbers can tell of the regions of
weights and measures, but he cannot
conduct you thither.

For the vision of one man lends not
its wings to another man.

And even as each one of you stands
alone in God's knowledge, so must
each one of you be alone in his knowledge of God and in his understanding
of the earth.

KAHLIL GIBRAN, 1883–1931

USE OF BOOKS

He who learns and makes no use of his
learning is a beast of burden with a
load of books. Does the ass comprehend whether he carries on his back a
library or a bundle of faggots?

SAADIA, 892?–942

A PRAYER FROM CHILE

Lord, Thou didst teach, forgive me for
teaching, for bearing the name of
teacher which Thou didst bear upon
earth.

Give me supreme love for my
school.

Make me more a mother than mothers are, that I may be able to love and
defend as they do what is not flesh of
my flesh.

May I succeed in making of one of
my girls my perfect stanza, and in her
bequeath Thee my most enduring
melody against the day when these my
lips shall sing no more.

GABRIELA MISTRAL, 1889–1957

MY ALTAR

I have worshipped in churches and
    chapels;
  I've prayed in the busy street;
I have sought my God and have found
    Him
    Where the waves of His oceans beat;
I have knelt in the silent forest,
    In the shade of some ancient tree;
But the dearest of all my altars
    Was raised at my mother's knee.

I have listened to God in His temple;
  I've caught His voice in the crowd;
I have heard Him speak when the
    breakers
    Were booming long and loud;
Where the winds play soft in the tree-
    tops
    My Father has talked to me;
But I never have heard Him clearer
    Than I did at my mother's knee.

The things in my life that are worthy
    Were born in my mother's breast;
And breathed into mine by the magic
    Of the love her life expressed.

The years that have brought me to
    manhood
    Have taken her far from me;
But memory keeps me from straying
    Too far from my mother's knee.

God, make me the man of her vision
    And purge me of selfishness;
God, keep me true to her standards,
    And help me to live to bless.
God, hallow the holy impress
    Of the days that used to be,
And keep me a pilgrim forever
    To the shrine at my mother's knee.
                    JOHN H. STYLES, JR.

BEYOND OURSELVES

Tho' growing with scarce a showing,
Yet, please God, we are growing.

The twig teacheth,
The moth preacheth,
The plant vaunteth,
The bird chanteth,
God's mercy overflowing,
Merciful past man's knowing.
Please God to keep us growing.
            CHRISTINA GEORGINA ROSSETTI,
                            1830–1894

Seize the moment
of excited curiosity
on any subject
to solve your doubts,
for if you let it pass,
the desire may never return,
and you may remain in ignorance.
        WILLIAM WIRT, 1772–1834

PATIENCE ABOUT HIS BOOK

The German astronomer Johannes
Kepler, whose book on the planetary
motions is now a classic, said, "It may
wait a century for a reader, as God
has waited six thousand years for an
observer."

QUESTIONS NEED ANSWERS

Curiosity in children is but an appetite
for knowledge. One great reason why
children abandon themselves wholly
to silly pursuits and trifle away their
time insipidly is because they find their
curiosity balked and their inquiries
neglected.

        JOHN LOCKE, 1632–1704

HE WAS MY TEACHER

He harrowed minds with curving question marks,
Teaching as much outside the book as in;
He'd listen out the window for Spring's larks,
Postponing Euclid's chalky discipline.

He kept the burr of "Why?" beneath the tail
Of every sluggard slouched down in his seat;
Our spines came straight—we did not dare to fail,
And we survived by thinking on our feet.

He was my teacher—wise—yet hard as knots;
I tried to pick him loose and so undo him;
But he was miles ahead of all my plots:
I've found instead that he has tied me to him.

RALPH W. SEAGER

HEROIC NORWEGIAN TEACHERS

From the side streets of Norway, during World War II, came more than 5,000 magnificent women teachers, for during the years of the Nazi Occupation, the conquerors destroyed Norwegian primers, histories, geographies, etc., substituting their own textbooks full of twisted notions, falsified information and subtle Nazi propaganda.

Instantly these Lutheran schoolteachers refused to use the new books. Their spokesman said courageously to the Gestapo, "We cannot and will not teach our pupils your doctrine of Nazi superiority and Jewish inferiority, for we have a precious old Norwegian folk song which says, 'Every child's heart we unfold is another province added to our fatherland.' We will not betray that trust!"

All 5,000 of them were loaded into a wretched old steamer, and in the dead of winter it sailed northward to an Arctic concentration camp where, as slave laborers, the teachers might repent in frozen isolation.

But more and more brave women continued this same courageous opposition. During all the war years, the school children of Norway grew up understanding fully what superb business it was to dare carry Christ through Norway.

You cannot teach a man anything. You can only help him to find it for himself.

GALILEO, 1564–1642

PERPETUAL PERSISTENCE

We must study geography until there is for us no foreign land.

We must study humanity until there is for us no foreign man.

EDWARD MCDOWELL

All teaching depends on a certain presentiment and preparation in the taught. We can only teach others profitably what they already virtually know. We can only give them what they had already.

HENRI FRÉDÉRIC AMIEL,
1821–1881

SCRIPTURES

*The Bible is God's chart for you to
steer by, to keep you from the bottom
of the sea, and to show you where the
harbor is, and how to reach it without running on rocks and bars.*

HENRY WARD BEECHER, 1813–1887

Everyone who has a thorough knowledge of the Bible may truly be called
educated; and no other learning or culture, no matter how extensive or elegant, can, among Europeans and
Americans, form a proper education.

Western civilization is founded
upon the Bible; our ideas, our wisdom,
our philosophy, our literature, our art,
our ideals, come more from the Bible
than from all other books put together.

I thoroughly believe in a university
education for both men and women;
but I believe a knowledge of the Bible
without a college course is more valuable than a college course without the
Bible.

WILLIAM LYON PHELPS, 1865–1943

The Bible is alive; it speaks to me.
The Bible has feet; it runs after me.
The Bible has hands; it lays hold on
    me.

MARTIN LUTHER, 1483–1546

THIS DIVINE REACH
The Bible not only mirrors our long-
ings; it also resolves them. If it is true
that a hand reaches up wistfully out of
the night, it is also true that a hand
reaches down to us. It is never enough
to know that man seeks God; what he
wants to know is if there is Someone
somewhere who hears and answers.

JOSEPH R. SIZOO

From THE BOOK OF
COMMON PRAYER
Blessed Lord, who hast caused all Holy
Scriptures to be written for our learning, grant that we may in such wise
hear, read, mark, learn, and inwardly
digest them, that by patience and comfort of Thy Holy Word, we may embrace and ever hold fast the blessed
hope of everlasting life which Thou
hast given us in our Savior Jesus Christ.

THOMAS CRAMNER, 1489–1556

THREE INESCAPABLE
GUIDELINES

I take the whole Christ for my Savior.
I take the whole Bible for my staff.
I take the whole Church for my family.

ST. AUGUSTINE, 354–430

❧

From THE PROBLEM

Out from the heart of nature rolled
The burdens of the Bible old;
The litanies of nations came,
Like the volcano's tongue of flame,
Up from the burning core below,—
The canticles of love and woe:
The hand that rounded Peter's dome
And groined the aisles of Christian
    Rome
Wrought in a sad sincerity;
Himself from God he could not free;
He builded better than he knew;—
The conscious stone to beauty grew.

*

These temples grew as grows the grass;
Art might obey, but not surpass.
The passive Master lent His hand
To the vast soul that o'er Him planned;
And the same power that reared the
    shrine
Bestrode the tribes that knelt within.
Ever the fiery Pentecost
Girds with one flame the countless
    host,
Trances the heart through chanting
    choirs,
And through the priest the mind in-
spires.

RALPH WALDO EMERSON,
1803–1882

❧

We Protestants claimed proudly, and
with justice, that we are the people of
the Book. So we once were. But are we
now as universally and obviously so?

In certain services the Roman Catho-
lics give a huge place to Scripture, passage upon passage. And always their
approach to the reading of the Gospels
is movingly reverent and lowly. It is
with awed hearts they take the words
and deeds of Jesus Christ into their
hands and on their lips.

The deacon kneels before the altar,
and with joined hands says, "Cleanse
my heart and my lips, O God Almighty, who didst cleanse the lips of
the prophet Isaias with a live coal;
vouchsafe of Thy gracious mercy, so to
cleanse me, that I may worthily proclaim Thy holy Gospel through Jesus
Christ our Lord."

He takes the book from the altar,
kneels again, and asks the priest for his
blessing. The priest answers, "The
Lord be in thy heart, and on thy lips,
that thou mayest worthily, and in a becoming manner, announce the holy
Gospel."

When the lesson is finished, the sub-
deacon takes the book to the priest,
who kisses the Gospel, and says, "By
the words of the Gospel may our sins
be blotted out."

All of which seems to me more
likely to result in genuine worship
than this "bright brief brotherly" idea,
which impatiently crowds the holy
Word of God into a narrow corner of
the service, and so hurries on.

JAMES S. STEWART

❧

All history is an inarticulate Bible.

THOMAS CARLYLE, 1795–1881

From MIRIAM

We search the world for truth. We cull
The good, the pure, the beautiful,
From graven stone and written scroll,
From all old flower-fields of the soul;
And, weary seekers of the best,
We come back laden from our quest,
To find that all the sages said
Is in the Book our mothers read.

JOHN GREENLEAF WHITTIER,
1807–1892

BIBLE MIRROR

These books bring back the living image of the most Holy Mind, and Christ Himself, the whole of Him, is here so rendered present that you would see no more of Him if you beheld Him before you.

DESIDERIUS ERASMUS, 1469?–1536

RELEASE OF FOUR PRISONERS

On the way to her coronation, Queen Elizabeth I received a Bible handed to her, which she kissed and pressed to her heart.

It being the custom to release prisoners at the inauguration of a prince, one of her courtiers besought her with a loud voice to release four or five principal prisoners.

When she asked who they were, the answer was: the four Evangelists—Matthew, Mark, Luke, and John—and the Apostle Paul, who had been shut up for a long time in the unknown Latin, so that they could not converse with the common people in the "modir tonge."

Holy Scripture is a stream of running water, where alike the elephant may swim and the lamb may walk without losing its footing.

POPE GREGORY THE GREAT,
590–604

THE ANVIL OF GOD'S WORD

I paused last eve beside the black-
smith's door,
And heard the anvil ring, the vesper's
chime,
And looking in I saw upon the floor
Old hammers, worn with beating
years of time.
"How many anvils have you had?" said
I,
"To wear and batter all these ham-
mers so?"
"Just one," he answered. Then with
twinkling eye:
"The anvil wears the hammers out,
you know."
And so, I thought, the anvil of God's
Word
For ages skeptics' blows have beat
upon,
But though the noise of falling blows
was heard
The anvil is unchanged; the hammers
gone.

JOHN CLIFFORD, 1836–1923

BASIS OF BELIEF

If you believe what you like in the Gospel, and reject what you do not like, it is not the Gospel you believe, but yourselves.

ST. AUGUSTINE, 354–430

MEDIEVAL THERAPY

When I am tired, the Bible is my bed;
Or in the dark, the Bible is my light.

When I am hungry, it is vital bread;
Or fearful, it is armor for the fight.

When I am sick, 'tis healing medicine;
Or lonely, thronging friends I find
   therein.

If I would work, the Bible is my tool;
Or play, it is a harp of happy sound.

If I am ignorant, it is my school;
If I am sinking, it is solid ground.

If I am cold, the Bible is my fire;
And wings, if boldly I aspire.

Should I be lost, the Bible is my guide;
Or naked, it is raiment, rich and warm.

Am I imprisoned, it is ranges wide;
Or tempest-tossed, a shelter from the
   storm.

Would I adventure, 'tis a gallant sea;
Or would I rest, it is a flowery lea.

Does gloom oppress? The Bible is a
   sun.
Or ugliness? It is a garden fair.

AUTHOR UNKNOWN

AN UNUSUALLY
LONG LETTER

Scripture is a long letter sent to us
from our eternal country, and we who
hope in time to reach its shores should
learn what we can about it, and about
the conditions of reaching it while we
may.

ST. AUGUSTINE, 354–430

Oliver Cromwell wrote on the flyleaf
of his Bible:
   "He who ceases to be better, ceases
to be good."

From BIBLIOLATRES

Slowly the Bible of the race is writ,
And not on paper leaves nor leaves of
   stone;
Each age, each kindred adds a verse to
   it,
Texts of despair and hope, of joy or
   moan.
While swings the sea, while mists the
   mountains shroud,
While thunder's surges burst on cliffs
   of cloud,
Still at the prophet's feet the nations
   sit.

JAMES RUSSELL LOWELL,
1819–1891

PERILS OF TRANSLATION

Henry VIII and Cardinal Wolsey did
their best to keep William Tyndale's
Bibles, translated into the English
tongue, out of England.
   Signs at street corners warned:
   "No women, no artificers, no ap-
prentices, journeymen, yeomen, hus-
bandmen, or laborers shall read the
Bible in English to himself or another,
privately or openly, on pain of a
month's imprisonment."
   John Foxe's *The Book of Martyrs*
states: "For though they digged up
Wyclif's body, burned his bones, and
drowned his ashes, yet the Word of
God, and the truth of His doctrine,
with the success thereof, they could not
burn, which do yet remain."

REDEMPTION

Having been tenant long to a rich lord,
　Not thriving, I resolved to be bold,
　And made a suit unto him to afford
A new small-rented lease and cancel th'
　old.
In heaven at his manor I him sought.
　They told me there that he was lately
　　gone
　About some land which he had
　　dearly bought
Long since on earth, to take possession.
I straight returned, and knowing his
　great birth,
　Sought him accordingly in great re-
　　sorts,
　In cities, theaters, gardens, parks,
　　and courts.
At length I heard a ragged noise and
　mirth
　Of thieves and murderers; there I
　　him espied,
　Who straight, Your suit is granted,
　　said, and died.

GEORGE HERBERT, 1593–1633

SUCH SEVERE CENSURE

On its publication in 1611, the King James Version endured bitter attacks.

One noted Hebrew scholar sent word to King James that he would rather be "rent in pieces by wild horses" than consent to its use in the churches.

It was denounced as theologically unsound and ecclesiastically biased, as truckling to the King and unduly deferring to his belief in witchcraft, as untrue to the Hebrew text, on relying too much on the Septuagint.

The personal integrity of the translators was impugned. Among other things, they were accused of "blasphemy," "most damnable corruptions," "intolerable deceit," and "vile imposture," the critic who used these epithets being careful to say that they were not "the dictates of passion, but the just resentment of a zealous mind."

Thou wert the first put in my hand,
When yet I could not understand,
And daily did'st my young eyes lead
To letters, till I learnt to read.
But as rash youth, when once grown
　strong,
Fly from their nurses to the throng,
So with that first light gained from
　thee
Ran I in chase of vanity,
Tried dross for gold, and never
　thought
My first cheap book had all I sought.
Long reigned this vogue; and thou,
　cast by,
With meek, dumb looks did'st woo
　mine eye,
And oft left open, would'st convey
A sudden and most searching ray
Into my soul, with whose quick touch,
Refining still, I struggled much.
By this mild art of love at length
Thou overcam'st my sinful strength,
And having brought me home, did'st
　there
Show me the pearl I sought elsewhere.

HENRY VAUGHAN, 1621–1695

Christianity takes oversight of the whole world. The Bible interferes with everybody and everything. The Bible will let nothing alone.

JOSEPH PARKER, 1830–1902

From THE COTTER'S
SATURDAY NIGHT

The cheerfu' supper done, wi' serious
  face,
    They round the ingle form a circle
    wide;
The sire turns o'er with patriarchal
  grace
    The big ha'-bible,[1] ance his father's
    pride;
His bonnet rev'rently is laid aside,
His lyart haffets[2] wearing thin and
  bare;
    Those strains that once did sweet in
    Zion glide,
He wales[3] a portion with judicious
  care;
And, "Let us worship God," he says
  with solemn air.

        ROBERT BURNS, 1759–1796

[1] hall-Bible
[2] grey temples
[3] chooses

A MAJOR DIFFERENCE

What makes the difference
is not how many times
you have been
through the Bible,
but how many times
and how thoroughly
the Bible has been through you.

    GIPSY RODNEY SMITH, 1860–1947

ON UNDERSTANDING
THE BIBLE

Some people are troubled by things in
the Bible which they cannot understand, but as for me, I am troubled by
the things I can understand.

    MARK TWAIN, 1835–1910

LIVING MONITOR

Time can take nothing from the Bible.
It is the living monitor. Like the sun,
it is the same in its light and influence
to man this day which it was years ago.
It can meet every present inquiry and
console every present loss.

    RICHARD CECIL, 1748–1810

OUR EVER-LIVING BOOK

Generations follow generations,
  yet it lives;
Nations rise and fall,
  yet it lives;
Kings, dictators, and presidents come
  and go,
  yet it lives;
Torn, condemned, and burned,
  yet it lives;
Doubted, suspected, and criticized,
  yet it lives;
Damned by atheists,
  yet it lives;
Exaggerated by fanatics,
  yet it lives;
Misconstrued and misrepresented,
  yet it lives;
Ranted and raved about,
  yet it lives;
Its inspiration denied,
  yet it lives;
Even now it lives:
  a lamp to our feet,
  a light to our paths,
  a standard for childhood,
  a guide for youth,
  a comfort for the aged,
  food for the hungry,
  water for the thirsty,
  rest for the weary,
  and salvation for the sinner.

I AM THE BIBLE

I was fused into being in the hot forge of human experience, where hearts are sensitive and where God can best speak to mankind.

I have through the centuries challenged men when their souls were absorbed in the murky swamps of life's low levels.

I have lifted their eyes to the sunlit summits where prayer and faith work their magic spell upon the soul.

Across my pages march the spiritual masters of the centuries, and in me they still speak.

If you read me tonight, I will prick your conscience and shed light upon your play or your task tomorrow.

I will speak to you of something other than bread and clothing and the physical wherewithal of life.

I will lift your soul from the muddy vista of life's low levels and fix it upon the upper and sunlit peaks of faith and prayer.

PERCY R. HAYWARD

BOOK OF THE AGES

While nations, kings, philosophers, systems, and institutions have died away, the Bible engages men's deepest thoughts, is examined by the keenest intellects, stands revered before the highest tribunals, is more assailed, more defended, more denied, more industriously translated, and more freely given to the world, more honored, more abused, more forgotten, more neglected, more searched, and more loved than any other book the world has ever known.

Down across the ages, each Sunday throughout Christendom, uncounted ministers have based uncounted sermons on some verse, for this has been their tool of tools, and uncounted children have learned some "golden text" by heart, until, even if every Bible in all the world should be destroyed by edict, instantly it could be reproduced from the memories of those Christians in whose minds whole chapters are indelibly inscribed, beyond loss and beyond obliteration.

It survives all changes, itself unchanged. It moves all minds, yet is moved by none. It sees all things decay, itself incorruptible. It sees myriads of other books engulfed in the stream of time, yet it is borne along till the mystic angel shall plant his foot upon the sea and swear by him that liveth forever and ever that time shall be no more.

H. L. LANE

The Bible does not profess to make men omniscient, but simply to tell them enough to make them happy and good, if they will believe it and live up to it.

HENRY VAN DYKE, 1852–1933

When Mary Queen of Scots arrived in Scotland from France in 1561, she reached a temporary gateway where "certane barneis sange in the maist hevinlie wyis; and ane bonny barne discendit doun as it had been ane angell, and deliverit to hir Hieness the keyes of the toun togidder with ane Bybill and Psalme Buik coverit with fyne purpourit velvet in Scots vers."

A SINGLE HERO

We sometimes speak of heroes of the Bible; in fact the entire Biblical literature has a single Hero. A variety of interesting and colorful men and women walk across its pages, but everything of lasting significance is done by God alone. It is a library of "the mighty acts of God."

HENRY SLOANE COFFIN,
1877–1954

⚜

PRIVATE JUBILATE

To walk through life to the rhythms of music may become a private Jubilate, as it was after that Miserere morning when Feodor Dostoevski was being marched off to slave labor in Siberia. A Russian peasant rushed out of her house to give her Bible to this passing prisoner.

During his twelve years of frightful cold and subhuman treatment, this precious Book became his inner joy until he emerged from the Arctic experience to become one of the world's most magnificent novelists.

"My hosanna had passed through whirlwinds of doubt," he wrote. "Each of us bears the guilt of all and of everything on earth, not merely the general world-guilt, but each one individually for all and each on the earth.

"I believe that there is nothing lovelier, deeper, more sympathetic, and more perfect than the Savior. I say to myself with jealous love that not only is there no one else like Him, but there could be but one figure of absolute beauty: Christ. That infinitely lovely figure is, as a matter of course, a marvel."

THEY DREW THE INFERENCES

A century ago John Inglis went home to Scotland after twenty-five years of patient constant labor on the Island of Aneityum in the New Hebrides.

He was asked to give a brief speech to the General Assembly of the Free Church, and he had the wit to do it unforgettably.

"Fathers and brethren, we are told that missionaries should content themselves with facts, and leave the church to draw the inferences.

"I wish to bring these facts to your notice:

"First, I place on your table the *Shorter Catechism,* translated into the language of Aneityum.

"Second, I place on your table *Pilgrim's Progress,* translated into the language of Aneityum.

"Third, I place on your table the *Holy Scriptures,* Old and New Testaments, translated into the language of Aneityum.

"Now leave the Church to draw the inference!"

Needless to say, that sedate audience went wild with applause, for everybody could guess the years of danger and of pluck in learning the new language, dealing with difficulties of teaching, preaching, building, counseling, translating, faithfully year in and year out.

⚜

SELF-EXAMINATION

The New Testament holds up
a strong light by which
a man can read
even the small type
of his soul.

JOHN A. HUTTON, 1868–1947

From THE SYNAGOGUE

The Bible? That's the Book. The Book
  indeed,
  The Book of books;
  On which who looks,
As he should aright, shall never need
  Wish for a better light
  To guide him in the night.

        GEORGE HERBERT, 1593–1633

SERIOUS READING

Robinson Crusoe had been brought up
in church, but when he found himself
in the dismaying disaster of shipwreck,
alone on a desert island, his immediate
comfort was in the Bible which he had
salvaged from the sea.

"In the morning," he wrote, "I
took the Bible and beginning at the
New Testament, I began seriously to
read it, and imposed upon myself to
read a while every morning and every
night."

Three things favored his piety: solitude; a religious tradition back of him;
and an overwhelming personal need
for definite new strength if he were
to face this strange ordeal.

One morning these three factors
came together. He wrote, "I threw
down the book," and with his heart as
well as his hands lifted to heaven, he
prayed. "This was the first time I could
say, in the true sense of the word, that
I prayed in all my life."

MY PERSONAL LETTER

The Bible is essentially a letter from
God with my personal address on it.

LIGHTING A FLAME OF COMPASSION

Maria Millis, a housemaid in an English nobleman's castle, was concerned
that the small son in the household
should be permitted to grow up with
no knowledge of the Bible.

Her own delight in its pages being
so great, she taught the boy to read the
Book and to fall in love with Jesus
Christ for the rest of his life.

The flame of compassion which
Maria Millis lighted in the conscience
of Lord Shaftesbury made him dedicate
himself tirelessly to pass laws to rescue
boys and girls from working in coal
mines twelve hours a day and to keep
small chimney-sweep boys from such
a dangerous occupation, to accomplish
all sorts of needed prison reforms
throughout Great Britain; and to encourage him in the establishing of
"Ragged Schools" throughout England
to provide free education to poor children.

THE BOOK

Softly I closed the Book as in a dream
And let its echoes linger to redeem
Silence with music, darkness with its
  gleams.
That day I worked no more. I could not
  bring
My hands to toil, my thought to traf-
  ficking.
A new light shone on every common
  thing.
Celestial glories flamed before my
  gaze.
That day I worked no more. But, to
  God's praise,
I shall work better all my other days.

        WINFRED ERNEST GARRISON

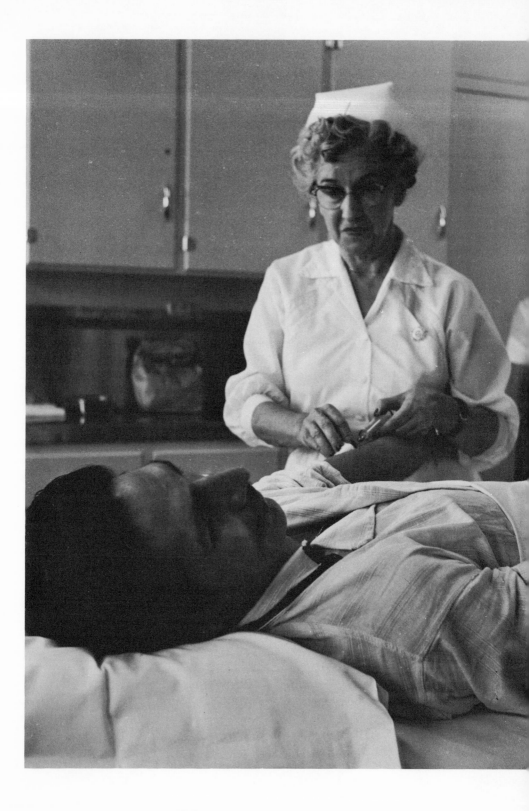

SERVICE

The greatest use of life is to spend
it for something that will outlast it.

WILLIAM JAMES, 1842–1910

CALLED OF GOD

The world is to be cleaned by some-body, and you are not called of God if you are ashamed to scrub.

HENRY WARD BEECHER,
1813–1887

THREE CHINESE PROVERBS

Wherever you go, employ all your heart.

The pleasure of doing good is the only one which will never wear out.

To do one good deed near home is bet-ter than to build a seven-story pagoda.

WORK FOR A GOD

To make some nook of God's creation a little fruitfuller, better, more worthy of God, to make some human hearts a little wiser, manfuller, happier, more blessed, less accursed! It is work for a god.

THOMAS CARLYLE, 1795–1881

We can only give what we have. Happiness, grief, gaiety, and sadness are by nature contagious.

Bring your health and your strength to the weak and sickly, and so you will be of use to them. Give them not your weakness, but your energy.

What others claim from us is not our thirst and our hunger, but our bread and our gourd.

HENRI FRÉDÉRIC AMIEL, 1821–1881

TRACING THE LOST IMAGE

Consecrate with Thy presence the way our feet may go, and the humblest work will shine, and the roughest place be made plain.

Lift us above unrighteous anger and mistrust, into faith and hope and charity, by a simple and steadfast re-liance on Thy sure will.

In all things draw us to the mind of Christ, that Thy lost image may be traced again, and that Thou mayest own us at one with Him and Thee, to the glory of Thy great name.

JAMES MARTINEAU, 1805–1900

RIPE FRUIT

Without sacrifice there is no resurrection. Nothing grows and blooms save by giving. All you try to save in yourself wastes and perishes. How do you know the fruit is ripe? Because it leaves the bough. All things ripen for giving's sake and in the giving are consummated.

ANDRÉ GIDE, 1869–1951

PROMPT REPAYMENT

He is base—and that is the one base thing in the universe—to receive favors and render none. The benefit we receive we must be rendered again, line for line, deed for deed, cent for cent, to somebody. Beware of too much good staying in your hand. Pay it away quickly in some sort.

RALPH WALDO EMERSON,
1803–1882

THE BLESSED COOLIES

Who are these
That run along the highways of the world,
And seek its meanest suburbs with their feet?
They are the troubadours of God,
Blowing an airy melody along earth's aisles,
As solid as the masonry of dreams.
They are the wise eccentrics,
Who reason with divine hilarity.
They are the canny merchants,
Who buy the hearts of nations for their Prince.
They are the weird tailors
Who push the threads of ages through their hands,

Who take no blood, to spill it, save their own.
They are the blessed coolies
Who lift the loads of folly on their backs
And dump them into truth's dissolving streams.
They are the blithe outrunners,
Who trek the world's long reaches for old trails
Whereon to lay the pavement of new years.
They are the grave cross-carriers,
Who bear stern wooden gibbets on their backs,
And nail their loves and treasures to the beams.
They are our princely brothers,
Born of the womb which bore us,
Who speak for Christ amid the courts of life.

JEAN KENYON MAC KENZIE,
1874–1936

TO EXPANDING GOODNESS

It was Jesus' faith that,
if you get into the world anywhere,
a seed of the Kingdom,
a nucleus of persons
who exhibit the blessed life,
who are dedicated to expanding goodness,
who rely implicitly on love and sympathy,
who try in meek patience the slow patience that is right,
who still feel clasping hands of love even when they go through pain and trial and loss—
this seed will enlarge and create a society.

RUFUS M. JONES, 1863–1948

A MEDIEVAL PRAYER

Help us this day, O God,
to serve Thee devoutly,
and the world busily.
May we do our work wisely,
give succour secretly,
go to our meat appetitely,
sit thereat discreetly,
arise temperately,
please our friend duly,
go to bed merrily,
sleep surely,
for joy of our Lord Jesus Christ.

A PORTION OF THYSELF

The poet brings his poem;
The shepherd, his lamb;
The farmer, corn;
The miner, a gem;
The sailor, coral and shells;
The painter, his picture;
The girl, a handkerchief of her own
sewing.

RALPH WALDO EMERSON, 1803–1882

CONTAGIOUS HERITAGE

Every soul that touches yours—
Be it the slightest contact—
Gets therefrom some good;
Some little grace; one kindly thought;
One aspiration yet unfelt;
One bit of courage
For the darkening sky;
One gleam of faith
To brave the thickening ills of life;
One glimpse of brighter skies
Beyond the gathering mists—
To make this life worth while
And heaven a surer heritage.

GEORGE ELIOT, 1819–1880

BY OUR STAIRS

When we lie down worn out,
Other men will stand young and
fresh.
By the steps that we have cut they will
climb;
By the stairs that we have built they
will mount.
They will never know the names
Of the men who made them.
At the clumsy work they will laugh;
And when the stones roll they will
curse us.
But they will mount, and on our work;
They will climb, and by our stairs!
No man liveth to himself,
And no man dieth to himself.

OLIVE SCHREINER, 1855–1920

To save one life is better than to build
a seven-story pagoda.

CHINESE PROVERB

From DISCOVERY

That a secret plan
Is hid in my hand;
That my hand is big,
Big,
Because of this plan.
That God,
Who dwells in my hand,
Knows this secret plan
Of the things He will do for the world
Using my hand!

TOYOHIKO KAGAWA, 1888–1960

A Christian is someone to whom God
entrusts all his fellowmen.

DWIGHT L. MOODY, 1837–1899

EARLY ENGLISH EPITAPH

What wee gave, wee have;
What wee spent, wee had;
What wee left, wee lost.

TIVERTON CHURCHYARD

From STANZAS ON FREEDOM

They are slaves who fear to speak
For the fallen and the weak,
They are slaves who will not choose
Hatred, scoffing, and abuse,
Rather than in silence shrink
From the truth they needs must think;
They are slaves who dare not be
In the right with two or three.

JAMES RUSSELL LOWELL,
1819–1891

TRUE GREATNESS

No man has come to true greatness
who has not felt in some degree that
his life belongs to his race, and that
which God gives him He gives him for
mankind.

PHILLIPS BROOKS, 1835–1893

From JERUSALEM

He who would do good to another
    must do it in
Minute Particulars:
General Good is the plea of the scoun-
    drel, hypocrite & flatterer,
For Art & Science cannot exist but in
    minutely organized Particulars
And not in generalizing Demonstra-
    tions of the Rational Power.

WILLIAM BLAKE, 1757–1827

All that is needed for the success of
evil is that good people do nothing.

EDMUND BURKE, 1729–1797

SPITALFIELDS COVENANT, 1775

I am no longer my own but Thine.
Put me to what Thou wilt; rank me
    with whom Thou wilt.
Put me to doing; put me to suffering.
Let me be employed by Thee, or laid
    aside by Thee.
Let me be exalted for Thee, or brought
    low for Thee.
Let me be full; let me be empty.
Let me have all things; let me have
    nothing.
I freely and heartily yield all things to
    Thy pleasure and disposal.
Now, O glorious and blessed God,
    Father, Son, and Holy Spirit, Thou
    art mine and I am Thine.
The covenant which I have made on
    earth, let it be ratified in heaven.

JOHN WESLEY, 1703–1791

JOHN WESLEY'S TOMBSTONE INSCRIPTION

God buries
His workmen,
but carries on
His work.

Most people are other people.
Their thoughts are someone else's opin-
    ions,
their lives a mimicry,
their passions a quotation.

OSCAR WILDE, 1854–1900

None shall usurp the heights but he to whom the miseries of the world are misery and will not let him rest.

JOHN KEATS, 1795–1821

SALT OF ALL THE ELEMENTS

Be of good cheer, brave spirit; stead-
fastly
Serve that low whisper thou hast
    served; for know,
God hath a select family of sons
Now scattered wide thro' earth, and
    each alone,
Who are thy spiritual kindred, and
    each one
By constant service to that inward law,
Is weaving the sublime proportions
Of a true monarch's soul. Beauty and
    strength,
The riches of a spotless memory,
The eloquence of truth, the wisdom got
By searching of a clear and loving eye
That seeth as God seeth. These are
    their gifts,
And Time, who keeps God's word,
    brings on the day
To seal the marriage of these minds
    with thine,
Thine everlasting lovers. Ye shall be
The salt of all the elements, world of
    the world.

RALPH WALDO EMERSON,
1803–1882

There are three kinds of people in the world:

the immovable,
the movable,
and those that move.

PERSIAN PROVERB

CREED AND CROSS

No man can believe in "the brotherhood of man" and be comfortable. It
is a creed that takes away all cushions
and leaves us with a cross.

G. A. STUDDERT-KENNEDY,
1883–1929

PRONOUNS

The Lord said,
"Say, 'We' ";
But I shook my head,
Hid my hands tight behind my back
    and said,
Stubbornly,
"I."

The Lord said,
"Say, 'We' ";
But I looked upon them, grimy and all
    awry.
Myself in all those twisted shapes?
    Ah, no!
Distastefully I turned my head away,
Persisting,
"They."

The Lord said,
"Say, 'We' ";
And I
At last,
Richer by a hoard
Of years
And tears,
Looked in their eyes and found the
    heavy word
That bent my neck and bowed my
    head:
Like a shamed schoolboy then I
    mumbled low,
"We,
Lord."

KARLE WILSON BAKER

THY TREASURES

O Lord, the children of my people are
Thy peculiar treasures,
Make them mine, O God, even while I
have them
My lovely companions, like Eve in
Eden!
So much my treasure that all other
wealth is, without them, but dross
and poverty.
Do they not adorn and beautify the
world,
And gratify my soul which hateth soli-
tude!
Thou, Lord, hast make Thy servant a
sociable creature for which I praise
Thy name,
A lover of company, a delighter in
equals;
Replenish the inclination which Thy-
self hath implanted,
And give me eyes to see the beauty of
that life and comfort
Wherewith those by their actions in-
spire the nations!
Their markets, tillage, courts of judi-
cature, marriages, feasts, and assemblies,
Navies, armies, priests, and sabbaths,
trades and business,
The voice of the bridegroom, musical
instruments, the light of candles
and the grinding of mills
Are comfortable, O Lord, let them not
cease.
The riches of the land are all the materials of my felicity in their lands;
They are my factors, substitutes, and
stewards,
Second selves, who by trade and business animate my wealth,
Which else would be dead, and rust in
my hands.
But when I consider, O Lord, how they

come unto Thy temples, fill Thy
courts, and sing Thy praises,
O, how wonderful they then appear!
What stars,
Enflaming suns,
Enlarging seas of divine affection,
Confirming patterns,
Infusing influence do I feel in these
Who are the shining light of all the
land (to my very soul):
Wings and streams
Carrying me unto Thee,
The sea of goodness from whence they
came.

THOMAS TRAHERNE, 1637–1674

No man can sincerely try to help another without helping himself.

J. B. WEBSTER

From THE NAMELESS SAINTS

Is there some desert or some pathless
sea
Where Thou, good God of angels,
wilt send me?
Some oak for me to rend; some sod,
Some rock for me to break;
Some handful of His corn to take
And scatter far afield,
Till it, in turn, shall yield
Its hundred fold
Of grains of gold
To feed the waiting children of my
my God?
Show me the desert, Father, or the sea,
Is it thine enteprise? Great God, send
me.
And though this body lie where ocean
rolls,
Count me among all Faithful Souls.

EDWARD EVERETT HALE, 1822–1909

GAELIC RUNE OF HOSPITALITY

I saw a stranger yestereen,
I put food in the eating place,
Drink in the drinking place,
Music in the listening place;
And in the sacred name of the Triune
He blessed myself and my house,
My cattle and my dear ones;
And the lark sang in her song,
"Often, often, goes the Christ in the
    stranger's guise;
Often, often, often, goes the Christ in
    the stranger's guise."

Gilbert Keith Chesterton says of the Franciscan friars that they were perpetually coming and going in all the highways and byways of Italy seeking to ensure that any man who met one of them by chance should have a spiritual adventure.

Suppose we could, with the help of the Spirit, let loose into our country a group of men and women, from every walk in life, caught by the infection of radiant religion, changed and transformed in their hearts, seeking to ensure that every man meeting them by chance should have a spiritual adventure.

So that when you touched them you got a spark? So that you felt their religion had made them not less human but more human.

SAMUEL M. SHOEMAKER, 1893–1963

CURE FOR BOREDOM

If you ever feel bored, go out on the street and do one good deed ten times.

CARRIE CHAPMAN CATT,
1859–1947

AN APOSTOLATE OF AFFECTION

The very word "apostolate" is crammed with color, charm, and a conscious concern for every living creature.

Adopt Apostolate into a life and that life will be literally house-cleaned. To become an Apostle has always meant to be sent out on Christ's errands: Go! Preach! Teach! Heal! Give ye them to eat!

Every stranger is suddenly the Lord Himself: therefore, an apostolate of affection toward all the underloved, the lost, the last, and the least.

A CUP OF WARM MILK

The world itself is a child,
Appalled, bewildered,
Exhausted, supperless,
Roared at and threatened
By drunken old war.
The world needs a cup of milk,
Warm with kindness,
In a fireside corner,
On a low footstool;
A reassuring arm
And a homelike voice.
Quiet; comfort; mothering.

SUSAN CLEGHORN

Think of the importance of friendship in the education of men. It will make a man honest; it will make him a hero; it will make him a saint. It is the state of the just dealing with the just, the magnanimous with the magnanimous, the sincere with the sincere, man with man.

HENRY DAVID THOREAU, 1817–1862

BLESSED IS THE MATCH

During World War II, a wealthy young Hungarian girl, named Hannah Senesch, went to Palestine to help escaping Jewish refugees.

When parachutists were asked for, she volunteered, persuading the officers that since the enemy would never expect a girl to be in such a dangerous business, she might prove more useful than a man.

On her first flight to Yugoslavia, she became hopelessly entangled in parachute cords, was captured, imprisoned, and eventually executed.

In her cell she wrote a song which was destined to make her beloved by other Jews the whole world over:

Blessed is the match that is consumed in kindling flame.
Blessed is the flame that burns within the human heart.
Blessed is the heart with strength to stop its beating for honor's sake.
Blessed is the match!

From TODAY

To be alive in such an age!
With every year a lightning page
Turned in the world's great wonderbook
Whereon the leaning nations look.
Where men speak strong for brotherhood,
For peace and universal good,
When miracles are everywhere,
And every inch of common air
Throbs a tremendous prophecy
Of greater marvels yet to be.
  O thrilling age,
  O willing Age!
When steel and stone and rail and rod

Become the avenue of God—
A trump to shout His thunder through
To crown the work that man may do.

      *

To be alive in such an age—
  To live in it!
  To give to it!
Rise, soul, from thy despairing knees.
What if thy lips have drunk the lees?
Fling forth thy sorrow to the wind
And link thy hope with humankind—
The passion of a larger claim
Will put thy puny grief to shame.
Breathe the world thought, do the world deed.
Think hugely of thy brother's need.
And what thy woe, and what thy weal?
Look to the work the times reveal!
Give thanks with all thy flaming heart—
Crave but to have in it a part.
Give thanks and clasp thy heritage—
To be alive in such an age!

ANGELA MORGAN,
1874–1957

SYMPATHY

Ask God to give thee skill
  In comfort's art,
That thou may'st consecrated be
  And set apart
Upon a life of sympathy,
For heavy is the weight of ill
  In every heart;
And comforters are needed much
  Of Christlike touch.

ANNA E. HAMILTON, 1846?–1876

This only is charity, to do all, all that we can.

JOHN DONNE, 1572–1631

REPORT OF THE CARNEGIE HERO FUND COMMISSION

If there be something peculiar in the blood and fiber of an individual who does an heroic deed, it has not been discovered by the Commission in over thirty years of contacts.

In appearance and behavior the hero resembles the rest of mankind.

He has the same strength, weaknesses, ills, and frailties that flesh is heir to.

He comes from all the races into which mankind is divided.

Riches, poverty, sex, youth, or age hold no distinguishing characteristics that set a hero apart from other men.

One lives in splendor in a city mansion. Another shares a squalid cabin with a half dozen tattered brothers and sisters on a mountain side.

One is a girl of ten years who struggles with a little boy in the water and then has the rare discretion to tell him to take hold of her long braided hair while she swims with him to safety.

Another is an aged man who fails, through lack of strength to lift a woman from the tracks in time to save their lives.

Negroes, whites, and men of other races share alike the moment of supreme self-sacrifice.

HEROES OF PEACE

❧

THE TRIED AND THE UNTRIED

The Tried

To build a world of brotherhood by the machinery of war;

To establish fellowship by feeding racial rancor and by keeping the Negro and immigrant in place;

To use force and violence in guaranteeing national security;

To dispose of the criminal by a prison system;

To put money first in the purpose of life;

To be a Christian without following Christ.

The Untried

To build a friendly world by faith and understanding and to put love where there is now hate;

To lead the race toward a juster, wiser, and more merciful social order, where each individual is evaluated in terms of his true worth;

To fortify the nation by the armaments of faith and the long range canons of love;

To give guidance to those who err and in time redeem the environment of every little child;

To work for the good of all and not for the gain of wealth;

To make an earnest trial of Jesus' way of Life.

ROY A. BURKHART, 1895–1964

GIVE ME THY HARDER PART

O Love, give me a passionate heart
That my heart may be pure.
Give me, O Love, thy harder part,
The daring to endure.
Lead me not in ways too green,
Lest my faith cease to strive.
Keep thou thy sword for ever keen
To stab my soul alive.
O give me thy deep strength to hold
Thy peace within my breast,
All sick and sorrowing hearts to fold
In thy enfolding rest.

IRENE RUTHERFORD MC LEOD

SIMPLICITY

Simplicity, simplicity, simplicity!
I say, let your affairs be as two or
three, and not a hundred or a thou-
sand.
Simplify! Simplify!

HENRY DAVID THOREAU, 1817–1862

From PUCK OF POOK'S HILL
Father in Heaven, who lovest all,
O help Thy children when they call;
That they may build from age to age
An undefiled heritage.

*

Teach us delight in simple things,
And mirth that hath no bitter springs;
Forgiveness free of evil done
And love to all men 'neath the sun!

RUDYARD KIPLING, 1865–1936

SIMPLE ADMIRATION

I used to like to hear my father, Charles
Darwin, admire the beauty of a flower.
It was a kind of gratitude to the flower
itself, and a personal love for its delicate form and colour. I remember him
gently touching a flower he delighted
in. It was the same simple admiration
that a child might have.

FRANCIS DARWIN, 1848–1925

The only simplicity that matters is the
simplicity of the heart. If that be gone,
it can be brought back by no turnips
or cellular clothing, but only by tears
and terror and the fires that are not
quenched.

GILBERT KEITH CHESTERTON,
1874–1936

THE LOVELY LITANIES

A noble life, a simple faith, an open
    heart and hand—
These are the lovely litanies which
    all men understand.

The cries of clashing creeds are heard,
    on every side they sound,
But no age is degenerate in which such
    lives are found.

These are the firm-knit bonds of
    grace, though hidden from the view,
Which bind in sacred brotherhood all
    men the whole world through.

AUTHOR UNKNOWN

DEO OPTIMO MAXIMO

All else for use, One only for desire;
Thanksgiving for the good, but thirst
for Thee:
Up from the best, whereof no man
need tire,
Impel Thou me.

Delight is menace if Thou brood not
by,
Power is a quicksand, Fame a gathering jeer.
Oft as the morn (though none of earth
deny
These three are dear),

Wash me of them, that I may be re-
newed,
And wander free amid my freeborn
joys:
Oh, close my hand upon Beatitude!
Not on her toys.

LOUISE IMOGEN GUINEY, 1861–1920

THE DIVINE CENTER

Our lives in a modern city grow too
complex and overcrowded.

Even the necessary obligations which
we feel we must meet grow overnight,
like Jack's beanstalk, and before we
know it we are bowed down with burdens, crushed under committees,
strained, breathless, and hurried, pant-
ing under a never-ending program of
appointments.

Our complex living, we say, is due
to the complex world we live in with
its radios and autos, which give us
more stimulation per square hour than
used to be given per square day to our
grandmothers.

Nor will simplification of life follow simplification of program.

The outer distractions of our interest
reflect an inner lack of integration
in our own lives. We are trying to be
several selves at once, without all our
selves being organized by a single
mastering Life within us.

Each of us tends to be, not a single
self, but a whole committee of selves.
There is the civic self, the parental
self, the financial self, the religious
self, the society self, the professional
self, the literary self.

We feel honestly the pull of many
obligations and try to meet them all.

Life is meant to be lived from a
center, a divine center. Each of us can
live such a life of amazing power and
peace and serenity, of integration and
confidence and simplified multiplicity,
on one condition—that is, if we really
want to.

There is a divine abyss within us all,
a holy Infinite Creator, a Heart, a Life
who speaks in us and through us to the
world. We have heard this Holy
Whisper at times, but too many of us
have heeded the Voice only at times.

We have not counted this Holy
Thing within us to be the most precious thing in the world.

THOMAS KELLY, 1893–1941

A NOBODY

I'm nobody! Who are you?
Are you nobody, too?
Then there's a pair of us—don't tell!
They'd banish us, you know.

How dreary to be somebody!
How public, like a frog
To tell your name the livelong day
To an admiring bog!

EMILY DICKINSON, 1830–1886

In his book, *Purity of Heart,* Søren Kierkegaard shows that while purity of heart comes from willing one thing, a man can defeat this by wanting variety.

For though a man seems to desire one thing—honor or riches or pleasure or power—each of them turns out to be a multitude of separate things.

To seek change continually makes the man seek pleasure, pleasure, pleasure, until he is bored. And to be bored with life means being bored with the Eternal.

"The love of repetition is the daily bread that satisfies with benediction. He who wills repetition is matured in seriousness."

❧

George Bernard Shaw once said that there are only two tragedies in life: one, not to get your heart's desire; the other, to get it.

❧

OUR SPIRITUAL HOME

Everything we do, if we learn to do it simply for God, is, here and now, the one means of growing in love for Him.

Today is cooking and scrubbing; tomorrow it may be utterly different. Let us practice a genial concentration upon just the one thing picked out for us by God.

More than half our life goes in wishing for things other than these sent us; yet it is these things, as sent, and when willed and at last loved as sent, that train us for home, that can form a spiritual home for us even here and now.

FRIEDRICH VON HÜGEL, 1852–1925

THE FINE ART OF OMISSION

Beauty rides on a lion. This means that beauty rests on necessities.

The line of beauty is the result of perfect economy.

The cell of the bee is built at the angle which gives the most strength with the least wax.

The bone or quill of the bird gives the most strength with the least weight.

"It is the purgation of superfluities," said Michelangelo.

There is not a particle to spare in natural structures.

There is a compelling reason in the uses of the plant for every novelty of color or form; and our art saves material by more skillful arrangement, and reaches beauty by taking every superfluous ounce that can be spared from a wall, and keeping all its strength in the poetry of columns.

In rhetoric, this art of omission is a chief secret of power, and in general, it is proof of high culture to say the greatest matter in the simplest way.

RALPH WALDO EMERSON,
1803–1882

❧

MAN'S TWO WINGS

Purity and simplicity
are the two wings
with which man soars
above the earth
and all temporary nature.
Simplicity is the intention;
purity is the affection.
Simplicity turns to God;
purity unites with
and enjoys Him.

THOMAS A KEMPIS, 1379–1471

EXPRESSION
IN INDIVIDUALITY

The matter of simplicity comes into literary style, into building, into dress, into life, individualized always by one's personality. In each we aim at the expression of the best that is in us, not at imitation or ostentation.

CHARLES DUDLEY WARNER,

1829–1900

THE WAY OF QUIETNESS

The distinguishing trait of people accustomed to good society is a calm, imperturbable quiet. They eat in quiet, move in quiet, live in quiet, and lose even their money in quiet; while low persons cannot take up either a spoon or an affront without making an amazing noise about it.

EDWARD BULWER-LYTTON,

1803–1873

THE HOUSEWIFE

Jesus, teach me how to be
Proud of my simplicity.

Sweep the floors, wash the clothes,
Gather for each vase a rose.

Iron and mend a tiny frock,
Keeping one eye on the clock.

Always having time kept free
For childish questions asked of me.

Grant me wisdom Mary had
When she taught her little Lad.

CATHERINE CATE COBLENTZ,

1897–1951

FLAMING BLOSSOMS

At some time, perhaps many times in his life, every man is likely to meet with a thing in art or nature or human life or books which astonishes, and gives him a profound satisfaction not so much because it is rich or beautiful or strange, as because it is a symbol of a thing which, without the symbol, he could never grasp and enjoy.

The glory of purple that has flown from a painted church window and settles upon peasant's shoulders for an hour;

the eloquence, as of an epigram rich in anger and woe;

one bare branch that juts out from a proud green wood into the little midnight stars and makes them smaller with its splendid pang;

a woodman felling one by one the black and golden oak trees in the spring and slaying their ancient shadows;

or, in a discreet and massive crowd, one jet of laughter, so full of joy or defiance or carelessness that it seems to cut through the heavy air like the whistle of a bullet.

The world is one flame of these blossoms, could we but see.

EDWARD THOMAS

From THE BREWING OF SOMA

Drop Thy still dews of quietness,
    Till all our strivings cease;
Take from our souls the strain and
    stress,
And let our ordered lives confess
    The beauty of Thy peace.

JOHN GREENLEAF WHITTIER,

1807–1892

From EPISTLE
TO MRS. HIGGINS

Happy the man, of mortals happiest
he,
Whose quiet mind from vain desires
is free;
Whom neither hopes deceive, nor fears
torment,
But lives at peace, within himself con-
tent;
In thought, or act, accountable to none
But to himself, and to the gods alone.

GEORGE GRANVILLE, 1667–1735

I can conceive the subtlest and pro-
foundest sage desiring nothing better
than to retain, ever undiminished, a
childlike capacity for simple pleasures.

NORMAN DOUGLAS, 1868–1952

THE INWARD LIFE

This mystery of an inward life hidden
in man is his most precious treasure.
What a miserable mistake it is, therefore, to place religious goodness in
outward observances, in notions and
opinions which good and bad men can
equally receive and practice, and to
treat the ready, real power and opera-
tion of an inward life of God in the
birth of our souls as "fanaticism and
enthusiasm"!

WILLIAM LAW, 1685–1761

A man is rich in proportion to the
number of things he can do without.

HENRY DAVID THOREAU,
1817–1862

LEISURE

What is this life if, full of care,
We have no time to stand and stare?

No time to stand beneath the boughs
And stare as long as sheep or cows:

No time to see, when woods we pass,
Where squirrels hide their nuts in
grass:

No time to see, in broad daylight,
Streams full of stars, like skies at
night:

A poor life this if, full of care,
We have no time to stand and stare.

WILLIAM HENRY DAVIES,
1871–1940

From MY MIND TO ME
A KINGDOM IS

Some have too much, yet still do crave,
I little have, and seek no more:
They are but poor, though much they
have,
And I am rich with little store:
They poor, I rich; they beg, I give;
They lack, I leave; they pine, I live.

EDWARD DYER, 1540–1607

RICHNESS IN YOUR LIFE

Do not pray for easy lives. Pray to be
strong men.

Do not pray for tasks equal to your
powers but for powers equal to your
tasks.

Then the doing of your work will be
no miracle, but you shall be a miracle.

Every day you shall wonder at yourself, at the richness of life which has
come to you by the grace of God.

PHILLIPS BROOKS, 1835–1893

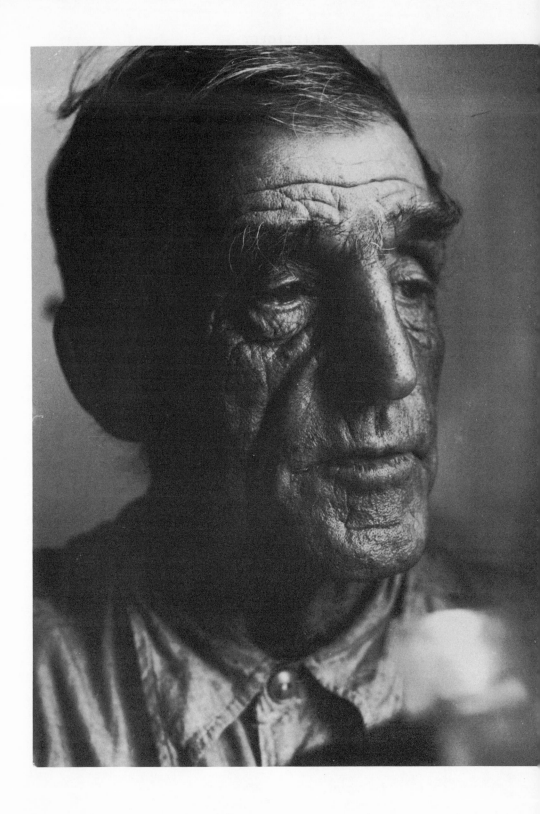

SPIRITUALITY

From IN NO STRANGE LAND
O world invisible, we view thee,
O world intangible, we touch thee,
O world unknowable, we know thee,
Inapprehensible, we clutch thee!

FRANCIS THOMPSON, 1859–1907

NECESSITY

It takes solitude, under the stars, for us to be reminded of our eternal origin and our far destiny.

ARCHIBALD RUTLEDGE

Back of the loaf is the snowy flour,
  And back of the flour the mill;
And back of the mill is the wheat, and
    the shower,
  And the sun, and the Father's will.

MALTBIE D. BABCOCK, 1858–1901

Every part of an element separated from its mass desires to return to it by the shortest way.

LEONARDO DA VINCI, 1452–1519

FIRSTHAND NEED

What this parish needs, what every parish needs, is a man who knows God at more than second hand.

THOMAS CARLYLE, 1795–1881

SIGHT

Thou hast an eye within thee, far more piercing than thy outer eye, an eye that beholds at once the past, the present, and the future;

which diffuses through all things the brightness of its vision;

which penetrates what is hidden, investigates what is impalpable;

which needs no foreign light wherewith to see, but gazes with a light of its own peculiar to itself—

the eye of the mind, the inner eye which sees invisibles.

HUGH OF ST. VICTOR, d. 1141

BASIC LESSON

The mystery of the universe and the meaning of God's world are shrouded in hopeless obscurity until we learn to feel that all laws suppose a lawgiver and that all working involves a divine energy.

ALEXANDER MACLAREN, 1826–1910

TRUE RELIGIOUSNESS

The most beautiful thing we can experience is the mysterious. It is the source of all true art and science.

He to whom the emotion is a stranger, who can no longer pause to wonder and stand rapt in awe, is as good as dead: his eyes are closed.

To know that what is impenetrable to us really exists, manifesting itself as the highest wisdom and the most radiant beauty which our dull faculties can comprehend only in their more primitive forms—this knowledge, this feeling is at the center of true religiousness.

ALBERT EINSTEIN, 1879–1955

UNEXPECTED GUEST

Let mystery have its place in you. Do not be always turning up your whole soil with the plough-share of self-examination, but leave a little fallow corner in your heart ready for any seed the winds may bring, and reserve a nook of shadow for the passing bird.

Keep a place in your heart for the unexpected guest, an altar for the unknown God.

HENRI FRÉDÉRIC AMIEL, 1821–1881

DIVINE UNITY

God takes to Himself as an instrument a part of the whole, the human body, and unites Himself with that, in order that since men could not look up to His invisible power, they might be able at any rate, from what resembled themselves, to reason to Him and to contemplate Him.

ST. ATHANASIUS, 295–373

THE DIVINE GOOD

How generously does the Divine display His good.

We look for Him, but do not see Him.

We listen to Him, but do not hear Him.

Yet He enters into all, and without Him there is nothing.

CONFUCIUS, 500 B.C.

ABSTRACTION

Today people, even people in the churches themselves, think of religion, not as that which is relevant to, and informs, all activities, but as just one activity among others for those who happen to be inclined that way, like folk-dancing. It is something apart. The whole business of religion begins and ends in a situation of abstraction from the things that actually fill men's lives.

HERBERT H. FARMER

RELIGIOUS OUTLOOK

Among all my patients in the second half of life—that is to say, over thirty-five, there has not been one whose problem in the last resort was not that of finding a religious outlook on life. It is safe to say that every one of them fell ill because he had lost that which the living religious of every age have given to their followers, and none of them has been really healed who did not regain his religious outlook.

CARL G. JUNG, 1875–1961

HEALING PERFUMES

The whole world is a thurible heaped with incense, afire with the divine, yet not consumed.

This is the most spiritual of earth's joys, too subtle for analysis, mysteriously connected with light and whiteness, for white flowers are sweetest— yet it penetrates the physical being to its depths.

Here is a symbol of the material value of spiritual things.

If we washed our souls in these healing perfumes as often as we wash our hands, our lives would be infinitely more wholesome.

The old herbalists were wise in their simplicity in the making of marigold potions, medicaments of herbs, pillows for the sick from rosemary and basil, beechleaf mattresses for the weary.

A thousand homely plants send out their oils and resins from the still places where they are in touch with vast forces, to heal men of their foulness.

MARY WEBB, 1881–1927

DIVINE FIRE

This Fire is at the root and about the root—I mean, about the center of all things, both visible and invisible. It is in water, earth, and air; it is in minerals, herbs, and beasts; it is in men, stars, and angels. But originally it is in God Himself for He is the Fountain of heat and fire, from Him it is derived to the rest of the creatures in a certain stream of sunshine. It is an influence of the Almighty God, and it comes from the land of the Living Ones.

HENRY VAUGHAN, 1621–1695

ESSENCE OF GOOD BREEDING

It has been said that true religion will make a man a more thorough gentleman than all the courts of Europe. And it is true that you may see simple laboring men as thorough gentlemen as any duke, simply because they have learned to fear God, and fearing Him, to restrain themselves, which is the very root and essence of all good breeding.

CHARLES KINGSLEY, 1819–1875

UNITY

From hand to hand the greeting flows,
From eye to eye the signals run,
From heart to heart the bright hope
    glows,
The seekers of the truth are one.

One in the freedom of the truth,
One in the joy of paths untrod,
One in the soul's perennial youth,
One in the larger thought of God.

The freer step, the fuller breath,
The wide-horizon's grander view,
The sense of life that knows no death,
The life that maketh all things new.

SAMUEL LONGFELLOW, 1819–1892

SEEING ETERNITY

Yet to live always as though time were a bridge is precisely what the saints do. Their eyes are forever on the Eternal, that Beyond which is also here and now and within, because they have cultivated the art of seeing eternity through that narrow slit—the ever now moment.

From THE PATH OF THE SAINT

LAST LETTER BY A
THIRD-CENTURY MARTYR

O feet most blessedly bound with irons, not to be loosed by the iron-smith, but by the Lord!

O feet most blessedly bound, guiding me along the way of salvation to Paradise!

O feet which are bound to the world for the present time, only to be made free by the Lord!

O feet which linger awhile among the fetters and the prison-bars, only to run more quickly to Christ along a blessed road!

Let envy, malice, or cruelty hold you here in chains as long as they will, yet from the earth and from these sufferings you shall speedily enter the Kingdom of Heaven.

The body is not comforted in mines with soft chairs and cushions, yet it is comforted with the peace and solace of Christ.

The body weary with labor lies prostrate at last, but there is no evil in lying down with Christ.

Your unbathed limbs are foul and discolored with filth, yet within they are spiritually cleansed.

The bread is scarce, but men live not by bread; they live by the word of God. Shivering you look for clothing, but he who puts on Christ is abundantly clothed and adorned.

ST. CYPRIAN, d. 258

PREFERENCE

The gospel doesn't pat the world on the back. It doesn't try to get along with the world. It wants to turn the world upside down!

Did anything of the sort ever occur to you during the festivities of the Christmas season? Somewhere in the candlelight, between the carols, was there any upsetting discordant note?

Writes Matthew, "When Herod the king had heard these things he was troubled." Could it be that the only trouble God has with Christmas is that it troubles us so little?

We set it to music, but we seem more than a little shy about setting it to work! With its preference for the commonplace and the humble. That isn't my preference!

And the love that comes not as Lord but as servant. That isn't the role I choose to play!

"Follow me!" There seems to be no remedy for it but some annual ritual of interment with robed choirs!

PAUL SCHERER

From ST. PAUL

Only as souls I see the folk thereunder,
    Bound who should conquer, slaves
      who should be kings,
Hearing their one hope with an empty
    wonder,
    Sadly contented with a show of
      things.

Then with a thrill the intolerable
    craving
    Shivers through me like a trumpet
      call—
O to save these, to perish for their
    saving,
    Die for their life, be offered for
      them all!

FREDERICK W. H. MYERS, 1843–1901

QUESTIONS

I had a thousand questions to ask God;
but when I met him, they all fled and
didn't seem to matter.

CHRISTOPHER MORLEY,

1890–1957

⚜

GOD'S ALMIGHTY POWER
AT WORK

A housewife should stand in sheer
amazement if she really thought about
this: today she has a set of fifteen eggs
and she places them under a hen or
goose. In four or six weeks she has a
basket full of little chickens or goslings. They eat, and drink, and grow
until they are full grown.

Where do they come from? The
eggs open when the time is come, and
inside sit the chicks or goslings. They
poke their little beaks through the
shell and at last creep out. The mother
hen or goose does nothing but sit on
the eggs and keep them warm.

It is God's almighty power that is
at work within those eggs, making
them turn into hens and geese.

Similarly with the fish in the water
and with all the plants which grow
from the earth. Where do they come
from? Their first beginning is the
spawn which floats in the water, and
from this grow, by the Word and
power of God, carp, trout, pike, and all
kinds of fish, so that the water is
swarming with fish.

An oak, beech, or fir-tree grows out
of the earth many feet thick and many
yards high. What is its first beginning?
Water and earth.

It is the Word and omnipotence of
God that brings it all about.

MARTIN LUTHER, 1483–1546

MEASURE OF RICHES

It is pitiful the things by which we
are rich—a matter of coins, coats, and
carpets; a little more or less stone,
wood, or paint; the fashion of a cloak
or hat; like the luck of the naked Indians, of whom one is proud in the
possession of a glass bead or red
feather, and the rest miserable for
want of it. If N. has a breakfront
desk, you want one, of course, but a
bigger, richer more glamorous one.

RALPH WALDO EMERSON, 1803–1882

⚜

From THE EXCURSION

I have seen
A curious child, who dwelt upon a
tract
Of inland ground, applying to his ear
The convolutions of a smooth-lipped
shell;
To which, in silence hushed, his very
soul
Listened intensely; and his countenance
soon
Brightened with joy; for within were
heard
Murmurings, whereby the monitor ex-
pressed
Mysterious union with his native sea.
Even in such a shell the universe itself
Is to the ear of faith; and there are
times,
I doubt not, when to you it doth im-
part,
Authentic tidings of invisible things;
Of ebb and flow, and ever-during
power;
And central peace, subsisting at the
heart
Of endless agitation.

WILLIAM WORDSWORTH,

1770–1850

FROM THE CHINESE

I would not paint a face, a rock, nor
   brooks nor trees,
Mere semblances of things, but something more than these.

I would not play a tune upon the sheng
   or lute,
Something that did not sing meanings
   that else were mute.

That art is best which to the soul's
   image gives no bound,
Something beside the form, something
   beyond the sound.

LI PO, C. 700–762

HIS SIGNATURE

There is a signature of wisdom and
power impressed on the works of God,
which evidently distinguishes them
from the feeble imitations of men. Not
only the splendor of the sun, but the
glimmering light of the glowworm,
proclaims His glory.

JOHN NEWTON, 1725–1807

WINGED SEEDS

Every moment and every event of every
man's life on earth plants something
in his soul.

For just as the wind carries thousands of invisible and visible winged
seeds, so the stream of time brings
with it germs of spiritual vitality that
come to rest imperceptibly in the minds
and wills of men.

Most of these unnumbered seeds
perish and are lost, because men are
not prepared to receive them: for such
seeds as these cannot spring up anywhere except in the good soil of liberty
and desire.

The mind that is the prisoner of its
own pleasure and the will that is the
captive of its own desire cannot accept
the seeds of a higher pleasure and a
supernatural desire.

THOMAS MERTON

THE CHURCH IS
HIS GARMENT

O blessed Lord, in whose garment was
variety, but no rent or seam, have
mercy upon Thy holy church; and so
unite all hearts and affections by the
union of faith and charity, that we be
not torn into factions and schisms, but
being anointed by Thy Spirit from
above, may keep the unity of the Spirit
in the bond of peace.

JEREMY TAYLOR, 1613–1667

INVISIBLE WIRES

It seems certain that, as cells of an immense organism, we are connected with
everything that exists by an inextric-
able network of vibrations, waves, and
influences of nameless, numberless,
and uninterrupted fluids. Nearly always in nearly all men, everything
carried along by these invisible wires
falls into the depths of unconscious-
ness, and passes unperceived, which
does not mean that it remains inactive.

MAURICE MAETERLINCK, 1862–1949

God often visits us, but most of the
time we are not at home.

JOSEPH ROUX, 1834–1886

From A DEATH IN THE DESERT

I say, the acknowledgment of God in
Christ
Accepted by thy reason, solves for thee
All questions in the earth and out of
it.

ROBERT BROWNING, 1812–1889

Whate'er thou lovest, man,
That, too, become thou must:
God, if thou lovest God,
Dust, if thou lovest dust.

ANGELUS SILESIUS, 1624–1677

GODHEAD

The most high nature of the Godhead
may thus be perceived, and beheld:
how it is simplicity and onefoldness,
inaccessible height and bottomless
depth, incomprehensible breadth and
eternal length, a dark silence, a wild
desert, the rest of all saints in the
unity, and a common fruition of Himself and of all saints in eternity.

Many other marvels may be seen in
the abysmal Sea of the Godhead: and
though, because of the senses to which
they must be shown from without, we
must use sensible images, yet in truth,
these things are perceived and beheld
from within, as an abysmal and uncon-
ditioned good.

The enlightened man shall also mark
and behold the attributes of the Father
in the Godhead: how He is omnipotent
power and might, creator, mover, pre-
server, beginning and end, the origin
and being of all creatures.

WILLIAM LAW, 1686–1761

THE ETERNAL FORCES

I am against bigness and greatness in
all their forms, and with the invisible
molecular moral forces that work from
individual to individual, stealing in
through the crannies of the world like
so many soft rootlets, or like the
capillary oozing of water, and yet
rending the hardest monuments of
man's pride, if you give them time.

The bigger the unit you deal with,
the hollower, the more brutal, the
more mendacious is the life displayed.

So I am against all big organizations
as such, national ones first and fore-
most; against all big successes and big
results; and in favor of the eternal
forces of truth which always work in
the individual and immediately unsuc-
cessful way, under-dogs always, till
history comes, after they are long dead,
and puts them on the top.

WILLIAM JAMES, 1842–1910

From ANCIENT EPISTLE TO DIOGNETUS

In a word, what the soul is in the body,
the Christians are in the world.

The soul is spread through all the
members of the body, and Christians
through the divers of the world. So
Christians have their abode in the
world, and yet they are not of the
world.

The soul which is invisible is
guarded in the body which is visible.
So Christians are recognized as being in
the world, and yet their religion remaineth invisible.

Christians hold the world together.

WHAT IS
TIMELESS LIVING?

The mystery of immortality is very great. Any way that one looks at it, this is a mysterious universe, but I beg of you to get the mystery in the right place. It is not so much the survival of the spiritual life that is mysterious. It is the arrival of such a life in the first place, that is here now in souls whom we have known and loved. There is the mystery—the arrival of a quality of living essentially timeless and eternal. Would it not be a mystery if, having arrived, it did not survive?

HARRY EMERSON FOSDICK

CHRIST THE KING

When we deliberate, He reigns.
When we decide wisely, He reigns.
When we decide foolishly, He reigns.
When we serve Him in humble loyalty, He reigns.
When we serve Him self-assertedly, He reigns.
When we rebel and seek to withhold our services, He reigns.
He is the Alpha and Omega, which is and which was and which is to come, the Almighty.

WILLIAM TEMPLE, 1881–1944

O God, plan our lives for us
better than we can plan them for ourselves,
and don't let us get in the way.

WILLIAM BRAISTED

OUR DAILY HOPE
AND GLORY

No poem is written, no picture painted, no music made, no sinner forgiven, no child born, no man loved, no truth known, no stone shaped, no peace attained, except grace took a risk, bore a burden, absorbed the evil, and suffered the pain. This is believing in God, too.

Indeed, there are two things about God perennially unavoidable. He is most certain in the deepest mystery; though he grants no information, he does give his presence.

And secondly, we never see him directly; he is always mediated by the very things that seem to deny him. What these things mean is that the incarnation and the crucifixion and the resurrection are not separate events; they are phases of believing in God.

We share in the world, ineluctably; we bear its sins, its shame, and its agony, for good or ill; and if by the power of the spirit we know what we are doing, the resurrection is our daily hope and glory.

SAMUEL H. MILLER

Clay is fashioned into vessels; it is on their empty hollowness that their use depends. Doors and windows are cut out to make a dwelling, and on the empty space within its usefulness depends. Thus, while the existence of things may be good, it is the nonexistent in them that makes them serviceable.

LAO-TSE, C. 604 B.C.

DEITY

He-Who-Has-No-Second holds the universe in His grasp, yet He is handless.

He is present everywhere, yet He has no feet.

He is sightless, yet He sees all.

Though earless, all the heartbeats of men are audible to Him.

Smaller than the smallest, taller than the tallest, yet even the Himalayas are but a dwarf's leap beside Him.

Yet He, who has humbled us all, is humble enough to dwell in your hearts.

HINDU SCRIPTURES

HOW LONG?

O Lord, how long
Shall we say we are all brethren,
That we love our Father in heaven,
And our life give it the lie?

O Lord, how long
Shall we speak of love,
Of our hearts going out to mankind,
And our love be asleep?

O Lord, how long
Shall we talk of prayer,
And rejoice in the beauty of worship,
And our prayer be a dream?

O Lord, how long
Shall we bow down to Christ,
Call Him Lord, preach His Word,
And He know us not?

O Lord, how long
Is the light of truth flashing,
The Son of Man coming,
To be rejected, too, of this generation?

AUTHOR UNKNOWN

O world, thou choosest not the better part!
It is not wisdom to be only wise,
And on the inward vision close the eyes;
But it is wisdom to believe the heart.
Columbus found a world, and had no chart
Save one that faith deciphered in the skies;
To trust the soul's invincible surmise
Was all his science and his only art.
Our knowledge is a torch of smoky pine
That lights the pathway but one step ahead
Across a void of mystery and dread.
Bid, then, the tender light of faith to shine
By which alone the mortal heart is led
Unto the thinking of the thought divine.

GEORGE SANTAYANA, 1863–1952

THE WAY OF HOLINESS

One eats in holiness, tastes the taste of food in holiness, and the table becomes an altar.

One works in holiness, and he raises up the divine sparks which hide themselves in all tools.

One walks in holiness across the fields, and the soft songs of all herbs, which they voice to God, enter into the song of our soul.

One drinks in holiness to each other with one's companions, and it is as if they read together in the Torah.

One dances the roundelay in holiness and a brightness shines over the gathering.

MARTIN BUBER, 1872–1965

SIMILITUDE

Consider the matter in the following similitude. A grain of wheat has the air and light of this world enclosed or incorporated in it. This is the mystery of its life, this is its power of growing, by this it has a strong continual tendency of uniting again with that ocean of light and air whence it came forth, and so it helps to kindle its own vegetable life. On the other hand, that great ocean of light and air, having its own offspring hidden in the heart of grain, has a perpetual strong tendency to unite and communicate with it again. From this desire of union on both sides, the vegetable life arises and all the virtues and powers contained in it.

WILLIAM LAW, 1686–1761

MANY VOICES
IN THE WORLD

Fragrance is the voice of inanimate things.

The air is full of the cries of leaves and grass, softer than those of the flowers.

In the dark night of the cedar there is a different atmosphere from that within the dusks of the beeches or the green gloom of April larchwoods.

Sometimes, in places where there are no flowers, aromas dart upon one like little elves with sharp teeth, from corn and fir-cones, damp soil and toadstools, keen grass and pungent bracken.

Even rock sends out a curious redolence in hot weather which unites with dried herbs to form an undercurrent to the mellowness of gorse.

In a shower, unsuspected sweets rush out of ambush with a laugh, overpowering and imprisoning us.

In the dewy summer dark, clover and night-flowering stock conspire with the sleepless honeysuckle to invade the drenched garden and to conquer and possess the dreaming house.

MARY WEBB, 1881–1927

Live unto the dignity of thy nature, and leave it not disputable at last whether thou has been a man.

Dost not thy title lead to a divine particle and union with invisibles?

Let true knowledge and virtue tell the lower world thou art a part of the higher.

Let thy thoughts be of things which have not entered into the hearts of beasts.

Think of things long past and long to come, acquaint thyself with the stars, and consider the vast expansion beyond them.

Let intellectual tubes give thee a glance of things, which visive organs reach not.

Have a glimpse of incomprehensibles, and thoughts of things which thoughts but tenderly touch.

Lodge immaterials in thy head; ascend into invisibles; fill thy spirit with spirituals, with the mysteries of faith, the magnalities of religion, and thy life with the honor of God, without which, though giants in wealth and dignity, we are but dwarfs and pigmies in humanity.

SIR THOMAS BROWNE, 1605–1682

We of the clergy make our bread and butter on the fact that Christ was crucified, yet very few of us are crucified with Him.

SØREN KIEKEGAARD, 1813–1855

OMNISCIENCE

God is the fact of the fact,
   the life of the life,
   the soul of the soul,
   the incomprehensible,
   the sum of all contradictions,
   the unity of all diversity.
He who knows Him, knows Him not.
He who is without Him is full of Him.
Turn your back on Him,
   and you turn your back
   upon gravity,
   upon air,
   upon light.
He cannot be seen,
   but by Him all seeing comes.
He cannot be heard,
   but by Him all hearing comes.
He is not a being,
   but apart from Him there is no
   being.
There is no apart from Him.

      JOHN BURROUGHS, 1837–1921

From ALONE

I paused to listen to the silence. My breath, crystallized as it passed my cheeks, drifted on a breeze gentler than a whisper. The wind vane pointed toward the South Pole. Presently the wind cups ceased their gentle turning as the cold killed the breeze. My frozen breath hung like a cloud overhead.

The day was dying, the night was being born—but with great peace. Here were the imponderable processes and forces of the cosmos, harmonious and soundless. Harmony, that was it! That was what came out of the silence—a gentle rhythm, the strain of a perfect chord, the music of the spheres, perhaps.

It was enough to catch that rhythm, momentarily to be myself a part of it. In that instant I could feel no doubt of man's oneness with the universe. The conviction came that that rhythm was too orderly, too harmonious, too perfect to be a product of blind chance —that, therefore, there must be purpose in the whole and that man was part of that whole and not an accidental offshoot. It was a feeling that transcended reason; that went to the heart of man's despair and found it groundless. The universe was a cosmos, not a chaos; man was as rightfully a part of that cosmos as were the day and night.

      RICHARD E. BYRD, 1888–1957

ST. PAUL'S AFFIRMATION

Great is the mystery of godliness:
God was manifest in the flesh,
justified in the Spirit,
seen of angels,
preached unto the Gentiles,
believed on in the world,
received up unto glory.

      I TIMOTHY 3:16

GOD

Within but not enclosed;
without but not excluded;
above but not raised up;
below but not depressed;
wholly above, presiding;
wholly beneath, sustaining;
wholly without, embracing;
wholly within, filling.

      HILDEBERT, 1055–1133

TRAVEL

What is traveling? Changing your place? By no means! Traveling is changing your opinions and your prejudices.

ANATOLE FRANCE, 1844–1924

IN SECURITY

He who loves Thee
truly travels in security
along a wide and royal road.

ST. TERESA, 1515–1582

FOR JOURNEYING MERCIES

O Divine Wayfarer,
Whose first shelter was a stable,
Whose first journey was a flight for life,
And who traveling oft hadst not where to lay Thy head:
Be to those who carry Thy message a sure guide and unfailing rest.
Clothe them in the garment of charity which is strange to no man,
And teach them the language of sympathy which is understood by all,
That, whilst strangers in every land,
They may yet be welcomed as citizens of the soul of man
And as brothers of the human heart.

AUTHOR UNKNOWN

Darest thou now, O Soul,
Walk out with me toward the Unknown Region,
Where neither ground is for the feet, nor any path to follow?
No map, there, nor guide,
Nor voice sounding, nor touch of human hand,
Nor face with blooming flesh, nor lips, nor eyes, are in that land.
I know it not, O Soul;
Nor dost thou, all is a blank before us,—
All waits, undreamed of, in that region—that inaccessible land.
Till, when the tie is loosened,
All but the ties eternal, Time and Space,
Nor darkness, gravitation, sense, nor any bounds bound us.
Then we burst forth, we float,
In Time and Space, O Soul! prepared for them;
Equal, equipped at last (O joy! O fruit or all!) them to fulfill, O Soul!

WALT WHITMAN, 1819–1892

From PILGRIM'S PROGRESS

I have loved to hear my Lord spoken of, and, wherever I have seen the print of His shoe in the earth, therein I have delighted to place my foot also.

JOHN BUNYAN, 1628–1688

THE TWO TORCHES

Now the tale of the two torches did happen on this wise: how when they did fare forth on their long journey through the Whole World, the one torch did go unlighted, whilst the other did burn with great brightness.

All in good time they did get back to that place from the which they made start, to give reports of all which they had seen.

So the first torch said that the whole world lay in dense darkness, and lamented sadly how the general state were now so bad as could not be worse.

But the second torch said quite contrariwise: how that wheresoever he had gone he had found much light shining, and that the general state of the earth be such as to give just cause for hearty rejoicing.

Whereat the sender-forth of these twain did put a question to the first torch: "Mayhap thou willst do well to ask thyself, 'How much of the darkness around me be of mine own making?'"

OLD ENGLISH LEGEND

I am not born for one corner; the whole world is my native land.

SENECA, 3 B.C.–A.D. 65

CHARTLESS

I never saw a moor,
I never saw the sea;
Yet know I how the heather looks,
And what a wave must be.

I never spoke with God,
Nor visited in heaven;
Yet certain am I of the spot
As if the chart were given.

EMILY DICKINSON, 1830–1886

ANCIENT GAELIC RUNE

King of the elements, Love, Father of
    Bliss,
In my pilgrimage from airt to airt,
    From airt to airt,
May each evil be a good to me,
May each sorrow be a gladness to me,
And may Thy Son be my foster-
    brother,
Oh, may Thy Son be my foster-brother.

Holy Spirit, Spirit of Light,
A pilgrim I, throughout the night,
    Throughout the night.
Love my heart pure as the stars,
Love my heart pure as the stars,
Nor fear I then the spells of evil,
    The spells of evil.

Jesus, Son of the Virgin pure,
Be Thou my pilgrim-staff throughout
    the land,
    Throughout the land.
Thy love in all my thought,
Thy likeness in my face,
May I heart-warm to others and they
    heart-warm to me,
For the love of Thee,
For the love of Thee.

AUTHOR UNKNOWN

THE GOLDEN AGE

The Golden Age is in my heart today.
Who are you, anyone, who can remain
    unmoved when the light breaks
    upon you?
Who can say it is just as well to see
    as not to see?
Who can ever be the same child or
    woman or man again after the day
    has broken?
Who can admit there is anything else
    in the world after this has come to
    the world?

I brushed aside all obstructions from
    my doorsill and stepped into the
    road;
And though so many cried to me, I did
    not turn back;
And though I was very sorrowful at
    having to leave my friends behind,
    I did not turn back;
And though the ground was rough and
    I was overtaken by fierce storms, I
    did not turn back;
For when the soul is started on the
    soul's journey it cannot turn back.
Can you go on with your old life as if
    nothing had happened?
The whole universe has happened!

All of love in all of life has happened;
All your forgotten kinship to the
    people has happened;
All the terrible thirst for justice has
    happened;
All the sad things have happened in
    gladness at last;
And all things out of place have hap-
    pened in place at last;
And all old enmity has happened in
    friendship at last;
The Golden Age is on my soul today.

AUTHOR UNKNOWN

We often think of ourselves as living
in a world which no longer has any un-
explored frontiers.

We speak of pioneering as a thing
of the past.

But in doing so we forget that the
greatest adventure of all still chal-
lenges us—what Mr. Justice Holmes
called "the adventure of the human
mind."

Men may be hemmed in geographically, but every generation stands on
the frontiers of the mind.

In the world of ideas, there is always pioneering to be done, and it can
be done by anyone who will use the
equipment with which he is endowed.

The great ideas belong to everyone.

MORTIMER J. ADLER

From THE ADVENTURES
OF A MOUNTAINEER

Many people ask: "What is the use of
risking life and limb in attempting to
climb Mount Everest?"

The real reason behind an expedition is the same spirit of inquiry and
adventure that lies behind all mountaineering and exploration. Were man
not an inquirer and an adventurer, he
would never have risen to his present
status.

In mountaineering, and on Mount
Everest in particular, a man sees himself for what he is. He learns the value
of comradeship and of service.

Out of Nature's strength we gather
our own strength. And it is good to be
strong, to be able to endure, not as a
brute beast, but as a thinking man im-
bued with the spirit of a great ideal.

FRANK S. SMYTHE

MORE THAN A LEGEND

Some knights were traveling one night through a mysterious country, when in crossing a dry riverbed, a voice seemed to tell them: "Pick a handful of the pebbles under your feet and you will be both glad and sorry."

Each knight, therefore, scooped up a handful of pebbles and rode on in the dark.

But in the morning when they took the pebbles from their pockets, lo! they were diamonds and emeralds and sapphires, and they were indeed glad they had had sense enough to take so many, yet sorry they had not taken more.

FROM GERMAN LORE

AN INDIAN EDUCATOR
ADDRESSES A
WORLD YOUTH CONFERENCE

We are on a journey and to us comes God's question, "Adam, where art thou?" And since we represent the youth of the countries from which we come we also have to face the question, "Where is thy brother?"

In the spirit we show and the imagination we display depends the fruitfulness of our coming together.

Let us not be too clever in our cleverness, nor yet too fearful in our littleness. But let us be humble in our ignorance, depending on "the foolishness of God which is wiser than the wisdom of me."

Like the Magi let us seek the King with confidence, bringing as royal gifts the best body, mind, soul, and strength.

Let us cast aside with courage our preconceived notion as to where He can be found.

Let us be ready to be sent forth from His presence to wherever He may send us.

SARAH CHAKKO, 1905–1959

TO THE BRITISH PARLIAMENT

Gentlemen, you should study larger maps! A great empire and little minds go ill together!

EDMUND BURKE, 1729–1797

MUCH ADO

It is storied of that prince (Pyrrhus, King of Epire) that having conceived a purpose to invade Italy, he sent for Cineas, a philosopher and the King's friend, to whom he communicated his design, and desired his counsel.

Cineas asked him to what purpose he would invade Italy?

He said to conquer it.

And what will you do when you have conquered it?

Go into France, said the King, and conquer that.

And what will you do when you have conquered France?

Conquer Germany.

And what then? I presume, said Cineas, you mean to conquer the whole world. What will you do when you have conquered all?

Why then, said the King, we will return and enjoy ourselves at quiet in our own land.

So you may now, said the philosopher, without all this ado.

THOMAS TRAHERNE, 1637–1674

ROOM IN THE HEART

I stand before the map of the world; before its countries stretched wide and its waters deep. I stand before the rivers lying like long crooked fingers across the land, fed forever from the streams, the snows and the rains of the mountains, pouring endlessly into the seas.

Up and down the rivers people have their mansions and their squatted huts. Children are born and families fish the waters for food, or till the soil of the valleys and country sides. Some families work in factories and some in the dark interior of the earth.

How alike we are around the world; living in our families, working and playing, having fun and having sorrow, knowing fear and security, needing food and clothing.

On this day I send into families of the world my wishes for good will. I will make room in my heart for all my brothers and sisters everywhere.

ABBIE GRAHAM

GAELIC PRAYER

I am going out on Thy path.
God be behind me,
God be before,
God be in my footsteps.

From SALUT AU MONDE!

I see African and Asiatic towns,
I see Algiers, Tripoli, Derne, Moga-
dore, Timbuctoo, Monrovia,
I see the swarms of Pekin, Canton,
Benares, Delhi, Calcutta, Tokio . . .
I see the picturesque crowds at the fairs
of Khiva and those of Herat,
I see Teheran, I see Muscat and Me-
dina, and the intervening sands, I
see the caravans toiling onward . . .
I see ranks, colours, barbarisms, civili-
sations, I go among them, I mix in-
discriminately,
And I salute all the inhabitants of the
earth.

WALT WHITMAN, 1819–1892

RESOLUTION

I have resolved to run when I can, to go when I cannot run, and to creep where I cannot go. As to the main, I thank Him who loved me, I am fixed; my way is before me, my mind is beyond the River that has no bridge.

JOHN BUNYAN, 1628–1688

From HOPE EVERMORE AND BELIEVE

Go from the east to the west, as the
sun and the stars direct thee,
Go with the girdle of man, go and
encompass the earth.
Not for the gain of the gold; for the
getting, the hoarding, the having,
But for the joy of the deed; but for
the Duty to do.
Go with the spiritual life, the higher
volition and action,
With the great girdle of God, go
and encompass the earth.

ARTHUR HUGH CLOUGH,
1819–1861

I met a thousand men on the road to Delhi. They were all my brothers.

HINDU PROVERB

ROAD TO SMITHVILLE

A traveler, heading for Smithville came to a fork in the road where the arm of a signpost reading "Five miles to Smithville" pointed up a steep, rocky hill.

The other fork led down a delightful, tree-lined road, running beside a cool, babbling brook.

It seemed sensible to him at the moment to climb up and change the sign around, so that the Smithville marker pointed down the comfortable path.

The traveler walked and walked, but he never got to Smithville.

From ULYSSES

I am become a name;
For always roaming with a hungry
heart
Much have I seen and known,—cities
of men
And manners, climates, councils, governments,
Myself not least, but honor'd of them
all,—
And drunk delight of battle with my
peers,
Far on the ringing plains of windy
Troy.
I am a part of all that I have met;
Yet all experience is an arch wherethro'
Gleams that untravell'd world whose
margin fades
For ever and for ever when I move.
How dull it is to pause, to make an
end,
To rust unburnish'd, not to shine in
use!
As tho' to breathe were life! Life piled
on life
Were all too little, and of one to me
Little remains; but every hour is saved

From that eternal silence, something
more,
A bringer of new things; and vile it
were
For some three suns to store and hoard
myself,
And this gray spirit yearning in desire
To follow knowledge like a sinking
star,
Beyond the utmost bound of human
thought.

ALFRED TENNYSON, 1809–1892

Who indeed knows the secret of the earthly pilgrimage? Who indeed knows why there can be comfort in a world of desolation?

Now God be thanked that there is a beloved one who can lift up the heart in suffering, that one can play with a child in the face of such misery.

Now God be thanked that the name of a hill is such music, that the name of a river can heal. Aye, even the name of a river that runs no more.

Who indeed knows the secret of the earthly pilgrimage?

Who knows for what we live, and struggle, and die?

Who knows what keeps us living and struggling, while all things break about us?

Who knows why the warm flesh of a child is such comfort, when one's own child is lost and cannot be recovered?

Wise men write many books, in words too hard to understand. But this, the purpose of our lives, the end of all our struggle, is beyond all human wisdom.

ALAN PATON

From CRY, THE BELOVED COUNTRY

WANTING TO GO SOMEWHERE

You may suppose that you can dodge God; but you merely get away from one place where matters are bad, to another place where matters are worse: and with the same wistful eyes staring at you. You may be unconscious of it all.

You are unconscious of a great deal that goes on in this amazing universe: your return trip, for example, about the earth's axis from dawn to dawn, at the rate of something over a thousand miles an hour; not to mention that other trip year after year, with Mars and Saturn, Jupiter and Neptune, around the sun; or still that third mad rush through space in company with all the starry heavens, at who knows how many of thousands of miles an hour.

And you, forsooth are eternally wanting to go somewhere!

PAUL SCHERER

A PARABLE

Whereunto shall I liken this generation of church members? I will liken them unto a world traveler buying a compass; the clerk gave him one used in mathematics. Whereupon the traveler did say: "But I am in dire need of a compass which will help me to go by a sure star in a sure sky through unknown seas and across uncharted areas. Have you nothing for my guidance?" "No," said the clerk, "the only compasses I keep on hand are those for describing big and little circles. I don't have any call for compasses for going places."

AUTHOR UNKNOWN

PIONEERS OF PEACE

Who are these that go about the streets of the city and upon the paths of the world? The Word of God is in their mouths, the bread in their hands they share, they bind up the wounded, and they comfort them that mourn. Who are these?

These are the stewards of the loving-kindness of God, and day laborers in His kingdom.

They are the harvesters of children, the saviors of the sick, and the consolers of the desperate, friends of the prisoner and the family of the poor.

They are of every race and every tongue, and they are indestructibly one.

They are the pioneers of peace, and the fellows of Christ in action.

JEAN KENYON MAC KENZIE,
1874–1936

Though it may be unessential to the imagination, travel is necessary to an understanding of men.

Only with long experience and the opening of his wares on many a beach where his language is not spoken, will the merchant come to know the worth of what he carries, and what is parochial and what is universal in his choice.

Such delicate goods as justice, love and honor, courtesy, and indeed all the things we care for, are valid everywhere; but they are variously molded and often differently handled, and sometimes nearly unrecognizable if you meet them in a foreign land; and the art of learning fundamental common values is perhaps the greatest gain of travel to those who wish to live at ease among their fellows.

FREYA STARK

MISJUDGMENT?

Daniel Webster once said that he would not give a single dollar to bring California one inch nearer to Boston: plenty of land there, but all desert, and no water. Tell that to the airplanes, the railroads, the vacationists, and the Californians!

THE GROWTH OF A BYWORD

The word "saunter" dates back to the Middle Ages in Europe when hundreds of thousands of crusaders and pilgrims were headed toward the Holy Land, to gain merit for their souls.

A number of the pious who went on foot were too poor to finance all of the 1500-mile trip across France and Austria and the Near East. When they needed food or lodging, they would knock timidly at a door and explain, *"A la Sante Terre!"* ("To the Holy Land!")

The householder, touched by their earnest air and travel-stained appearance, gladly offered hospitality, for it was a period when all men secretly longed to gain this merit. If the trip itself was impossible, surely generosity was a good second best in the sight of high heaven.

But there were chiselers in medieval days. These men, observing the ease of a pilgrim's journey, began also to knock boldly at any house, saying in a brisk whine: *"A la Sante Terre!"* But their utter lack of knowledge about their supposed destination became a byword throughout Europe, and householders said, "There goes a *Sante-Terrer"*—a Saunterer!

WINDSHIELD STICKER

I resolve to examine my habits of driving on the highways in the light of our Lord's commandment to love my neighbors as myself, to the end that acts of selfishness which endanger the lives of my fellow men may be eliminated in me, and that I may offer to God each time I drive a record of thoughtfulness and consideration for the safety of others.

AN OBSERVATION

There is a certain relief in change, even though it ebb from bad to worse; as I have found in traveling in a stagecoach, that it is often a comfort to shift one's position and be bounced in a new place.

WASHINGTON IRVING, 1783–1859

From THE EXPLORER

"There's no sense in going further—
　　it's the edge of civilization,"
　　So they said, and I believed it—
　　broke my land and sowed my
　　crop—
Built my barns and strung my fences in
　　the little border station
　　Tucked away below the foothills
　　where the trails run out and stop.

Till a voice, as bad as Conscience, rang
　　interminable changes
　　On one everlasting Whisper, day
　　and night repeated—so:
"Something hidden. Go and find it. Go
　　and look behind the Ranges—
　　Something lost behind the Ranges.
　　Lost and waiting for you. Go!"

RUDYARD KIPLING, 1865–1936

THE LOCOMOTIVE

I like to see it lap the miles,
And lick the valleys up,
And stop to feed itself at tanks;
And then, prodigious, step

Around a pile of mountains,
And, supercilious, peer
In shanties by the sides of roads;
And then a quarry pare

To fit its sides, and crawl between,
Complaining all the while
In horrid, hooting stanza;
Then chase itself down hill

And neigh like Boanerges;
Then, punctual as a star,
Stop—docile and omnipotent—
At its own stable door.

EMILY DICKINSON, 1830–1886

THE ART OF TRAVELING

When you pack your bags to explore the beauties of your own country or to travel around the world, consider these keys to a happy journey:

Travel lightly. You are not traveling for people to see you!

Travel slowly. Jet planes are for getting places, not seeing places. Take time to absorb the beauty and inspiration of a mountain or a cathedral.

Travel expectantly. Every place you visit is like a surprise package to be opened. Untie the strings with an expectation of high adventure.

Travel hopefully. "To travel hopefully," wrote Robert Louis Stevenson, "is better than to arrive."

Travel humbly. Visit people and places with reverence and respect for their traditions and ways of life.

Travel courteously. Consideration for your fellow travelers and your hosts will smooth the way through the most difficult days.

Travel gratefully. Show appreciation for the many things that are being done by others for your enjoyment and comfort.

Travel with an open mind. Leave your prejudices at home.

Travel with curiosity. It is not how far you go, but how deeply you go that mines the gold of experience. Thoreau wrote a big book about tiny Walden Pond.

Travel with imagination. As the old Spanish proverb puts it: "He who would bring home the wealth of the Indies must carry the wealth of the Indies with him."

Travel fearlessly. Banish worry and timidity. The world and its people belong to you just as you belong to the world.

Travel relaxed. Make up your mind to have a good time. Let go and let God.

Travel patiently. It takes time to understand others, especially when there are barriers of language and custom. Keep flexible and adaptable to all situations.

Travel with the spirit of a world citizen. You'll discover that people are basically much the same the world around. Be an ambassador of good will to all people.

WILFERD A. PETERSON

It is better to do a good deed
near home than to travel
a thousand miles to burn incense.

FROM THE CHINESE

TREES

From A BALLAD OF TREES
AND THE MASTER

Into the woods my Master went,
Clean forspent, forspent.
Into the woods my Master came,
Forspent with love and shame.
But the olives they were not blind to
  Him;
The little gray leaves were kind to
  Him;
The thorn-tree had a mind to Him,
When into the woods He came.

SIDNEY LANIER, 1842–1881

PROVISION

When you are crossing the desert, plant trees, for you may be coming back the same way in your old age when you will be glad of the shade.

PERSIAN PROVERB

SWINGING PERFUME

A man ought to carry himself in the world as an orange tree would if it could walk up and down in the garden, swinging perfume from every little censer it holds up in the air.

HENRY WARD BEECHER,
1813–1887

BRAID SCOTS VERSION

Anither parable set He afore them saying: "The Kingdom of Heaven is like a wee mustard seed, whilk a mon took and plantit in his yaird. Whilk in sooth is muckle wee o' a' seeds, but whan it is growit up is the biggest o' a' yerbs, and comes to be a tree sae that all the burdies o' the luft come and howff in its branches.

Father, enlarge my sympathies. Give me a roomier heart! May my life be like a great hospitable tree, and may weary wanderers find in me a rest.

JOHN HENRY JOWETT, 1865–1923

From A FOREST HYMN

The groves were God's first temples.
     Ere man learned
To hew the shaft, and lay the archi-
     trave,
And spread the roof above them—ere
     he framed
The lofty vault, to gather and roll back
The sound of anthems; in the darkling
     wood,
Amid the cool and silence, he knelt
     down,
And offered to the Mightiest solemn
     thanks
And supplication. For his simple heart
Might not resist the sacred influence
Which, from the stilly twilight of the
     place,
And from the gray old trunks that high
     in heaven
Mingled their mossy boughs, and from
     the sound
Of the invisible breath that swayed at
     once
All their green tops, stole over him,
     and bowed
His spirit with the thought of bound-
     less power
And inaccessible majesty. Ah, why
Should we, in the world's riper years,
     neglect
God's ancient sanctuaries, and adore
Only among the crowd, and under
     roofs
That our frail hands have raised? Let
     me, at least,
Here, in the shadow of this aged wood,
Offer one hymn—thrice happy, if I
     find
Acceptance in His ear.

WILLIAM CULLEN BRYANT,
1794–1878

FRAGRANCE

The sandalwood tree imparts its fragrance even to the axe that hews it.

HINDU PROVERB

THE PICTURE

GARDENER: We shall have to cut you
     down.
THE TREE: But why? I have been
     standing here for many years.
GARDENER: We are landscaping
     around this mansion. You're too big.
THE TREE: Maybe your picture is too
     small.

ARTHUR B. RHINOW

PLANTING TREES

Martin Luther, when every authority in
Germany was up in arms to silence
him, managed to write calmly, "Even
if I knew that tomorrow the world
would go to pieces, I would still plant
my apple tree!"

In desperate danger, he dared. In
calamitous circumstances, he cared. In
sudden shocks, he shared. Ring by ring,
to picture his tree growing up. Apple
by apple, to visualize its fruits feeding
tomorrow's families.

GREEN GLORY

For in the true nature of things, if we
will rightly consider, every green tree
is far more glorious than if it were
made of gold and silver.

MARTIN LUTHER, 1483–1546

PARABLE OF THREE TREES

Three trees once grew on a hillside, and as they swayed in the breeze they would dream what they would like to be.

"I should like to be cut down one day," said the first tree, "and turned into a baby's cradle."

"I should like to be cut down one day," said the second tree, "and become a great ship sailing the seas, carrying treasure and precious stones."

And the third said, "I should like to stand on a hill-top and point people to heaven."

One day the woodcutters came along and cut down the first tree. "Let's make it into a cattle stall," they said.

"But I do not wish to be a cattle stall," cried the tree. "I want to be a baby's cradle." But they turned it into a cattle stall. And when the child Jesus was born, they laid Him gently in the cattle stall, for there was nowhere else to put Him. And the tree said, "Why, this is far, far more wonderful than ever I dreamed."

The woodcutters said of the second tree, "Let's make this tree into a fishing boat." But the tree said, "No! I don't wish to be a fishing boat. I want to be a great ship carrying treasure and precious stones." But they turned the tree into a fishing boat, and put it on an inland lake. A fisherman named Simon Peter bought the boat, and Jesus sailed in the boat and taught the people from it. And the tree said, "Why this is far, far more wonderful than ever I dreamed."

And of the third tree they said, "Let's make it into a cross." But the tree said, "I don't want to be a cross, a thing of shame on which men die. I want to stand on a hilltop and point people to heaven." But they turned the tree into a cross and Jesus was nailed to that cross. And all down the years, men have looked to that cross, and it has pointed them to God.

KENNETH D. HARVEY

What unnumbered cathedrals has God reared in the forest shades, vast and grand, full of curious carvings, and haunted evermore by tremulous music! In the heavens above, how do stars seem to have flown out of His hand faster than sparks out of a mighty forge!

HENRY WARD BEECHER, 1813–1887

He is part of the blossomless crabtree who doth not the will of the King.

FROM THE IRISH

From UNDER A WILTSHIRE APPLE TREE

Some folks as can afford,
So I've heard say,
Set up a sort of cross
Right in the garden way
To mind 'em of the Lord.
But I, when I do see
Thik apple tree
An' stoopin' limb
All spread wi' moss,
I think of Him
An' how He talks wi' me.
He never pushed the garden door,
He left no foot mark on the floor;
I never heard 'Un stir nor tread
And yet His Hand do bless my head,
And when 'tis time for work to start
I takes Him with me in my heart.

ANNA BUNSTON DE BARY

OUTDOOR PRAYER

Almighty One, in the woods I am
blessed. Happy is everyone in the
woods. Every tree speaks through
Thee, O God! What glory is in the
woodland! On the heights is peace,
peace to serve Him.

LUDWIG VAN BEETHOVEN,
1770–1827

THE LOVE OF TREES

To the great tree-loving
fraternity we belong.
We love trees
with universal and
unfeigned love,
and all things that do grow
under them or around them—
the whole leaf
and root tribe.
Not alone when
they are in their glory,
but in whatever state they are—
in leaf,
or rimed with frost,
or powdered with snow,
or crystal-sheathed in ice,
or in severe outline stripped
and bare against a November sky—
we love them.

HENRY WARD BEECHER, 1813–1887

TWO CHINESE PROVERBS

I

When one leaf trembles, the whole
bough moves.

II

All the wood for a temple does not
come from one tree.

ANNUAL MIRACLE

Some people who say they can't possibly accept miracles—in church, that
is, or theologically—actually accept
miracles agriculturally every day of
their lives.

Suppose such a person drops a small
brown apple seed in the good black
earth of his own back yard.

He waits for a green sprout to come
up.

But why *green,* sir? Out of black
and brown?

He watches downpours of rain practically drown his sprout, tornadoes of
wind wrestle with it, dry spells threaten
to parch it, and insects pester and peck
it.

Nonetheless, it is plucky enough to
weather trouble and becomes a frail
sapling.

Another year and the trunk thickens. Thickens again, ring by ring.
Branches wave overhead.

Then one amazing Spring morning
—apple blossoms!

Yet how in the world could such
frivolous, fragile pinkness and whiteness — totally unbusinesslike — ever
come from out of black earth, brown
trunk, brown twigs, with bewitching
fragrance thrown in? Also hundreds of
green leaves suddenly pushing the blossoms out of the way?

Another wait from Spring to Fall,
then lo! a juicy apple, brilliant red outside, dazzling white inside, with its
own tantalizing aroma.

What Artist could possibly manage
to secrete an interchangeable palette of
pinks, greens, reds, and whites, inside
one ridiculous little brown seed? And
not just once, but repeating this miracle
annually?

A B C'S IN GREEN

The trees are God's great alphabet:
With them He writes in shining green
Across the world His thoughts serene.

He scribbles poems against the sky
With a gay, leafy lettering,
For us and for our bettering.

The wind pulls softly at His page,
And every star and bird
Repeats in dutiful delight His word,
And every blade of grass
Flutters to class.

Like a slow child that does not heed,
I stand at summer's knees,
And from the primer of the wood
I spell that life and love are good,
I learn to read.

LENORA SPEYER

DAILY DRAMA

A tree is a daily drama of God at work in nature for the guidance of mankind. There it stands: a pillar of starch by day and a pillar of sugar by night!

But the man of God is often too blind to see through the trunk to the sap and too deaf to hear the little leaves clapping their hands, as the Psalmist said.

Not in applause, however. But because each leaf is the kind of economical engine which any manufacturer would give his eyeteeth to know how to build and run from a distant dynamo ninety-three million miles away, without a penny of "overhead." Each tiny leaf is a factory, all day creating starch and all night creating sugar, ever sending them down the trunk to feed the twigs, the branches, and the roots.

In its public life, each leaf is an obvious windmill, innocently twirling away for all the world to see what fun it is to do its tremendous task in this nonchalant merry-go-round. But in its purely private life, it is a starch factory, quietly absorbing every particle of sunlight, packing it away until darkness falls. Then without observing union hours, that same leaf labors till morning converting the starch into sugar by some secret formula, which has been in the family ever since Eden, and shooting the sugar down the stalks and stems and trunk to furnish all the material needed by the growing parts of the tree.

Green chlorophyll is the only thing on earth with power to trap the sun's energy and use it for the manufacture of foods.

Hundreds of thousands of humble leaves on each tree, no one of which could work alone, all properly placed for the catching of sunrays.

From CHILDE HAROLD

The thorns which I have reap'd are of
    the tree
I planted; they have torn me, and I
    bleed.
I should have known what fruit would
    spring from such a seed.

GEORGE GORDON BYRON, 1788–1824

If all the trees on earth were pens, and if there were seven oceans full of ink, they would not suffice to describe the wonders of the Almighty.

MOHAMMED, 570?–632

ROMANTIC ABANDON

I have always loved willows, because they are the only trees who have wantonly escaped from the classic idea of a tree; because instead of growing straight up into the air they lean sideways at all sorts of sad and desperate angles, their branches jutting out of them anywhere, like soft green spray, instead of being placed symmetrically on each side of the trunk, and because sometimes even four or five trunks grow fanwise out of one root.

This waywardness in their structure gives willows a look of wild romantic abandon, as though they were changelings and held the spirits of people who have been crossed in love.

I like them, too, because they can be so old, all tumbledown and rotten and apparently dead, and yet when April comes there will rise out of those black, crumbling ruins the most tender and youthful green wands, holding new leaves high in the air in great, round, soft, billowy bouquets, more expressive of spring than any other tree.

Because of this wonderful mingling of agedness and tender youth willows seem to belong to a race of trees apart, one that is ancient and magic and lorn.

KATHARINE BUTLER HATHAWAY

Lord, purge our eyes to see
Within the seed a tree,
Within the glowing egg a bird,
Within the shroud a butterfly.
Till taught by such, we see
Beyond all creatures Thee,
And harken for Thy tender word,
And hear it: "Fear not; it is I."

CHRISTINA GEORGINA ROSSETTI,
1830–1894

If life is a tree, joy is the leaf.
Leaves bud; leaves grow; leaves fall.
If life is a tree, its roots are sorrows.
Long after the leaves are fallen,
After the boughs are bare,
The roots cling in the Earth Mother's
bosom.

KWEIN CHEN

Leaves seem light, useless, idle, wavering, and changeable. They even dance. Yet God has made them part of the oak. So He has given us a lesson, not to deny stoutheartedness within, because we see lightsomeness without.

LEIGH HUNT, 1784–1859

DEBONAIR DANCER

Use a magnifying glass to discover how excitingly all of God's minutest details have been thought through toward the sole end of feeding the children of men.

On the under side of any apparently carefree leaf, the glass will show several thousand pores, arranged to catch carbon dioxide out of the air and to let loose on the air ("transpire" is the word) the water sent up to the leaf from the roots.

Here is a chemical process so complicated that no human chemist could make it work. But each debonair dancer-in-green up there on the bough just tosses off the coolness with such quiet ease that John Keats could be lost in wonder, love, and praise:

And then there crept a little noiseless noise among the leaves
Born of the very sigh that silence heaves.

THE PINE-TREES IN THE COURTYARD

Below the hall
The pine-trees grow in front of the
    steps,
Irregularly scattered,—not in ordered
    lines.
Some are tall and some are low:
The tallest of them is six roods high;
    The lowest but ten feet.
They are like wild things
    And no one knows who planted
    them.
They touch the walls of my blue-tiled
    house;
Their roots are sunk in the terrace of
    white sand.
Morning and evening they are visited
    by the wind and moon;
Rain or fine,—they are free from dust
    and mud.
In the gales of autumn they whisper a
    vague tune;
From the suns of summer they yield a
    cool shade.
At the height of spring the fine eve-
    ning rain
Fills their leaves with a load of hang-
    ing pearls.
At the year's end the time of great
    snow
Stamps their branches with a fret of
    glittering jade.
Of the Four Seasons each has its own
    mood;
Among all the trees none is like an-
    other.
Last year, when they heard I had
    bought this house,
Neighbors mocked and the World
    called me mad—
That a whole family of twice ten souls
Should move house for the sake of a
    few pines!

Now that I have come to them, what
    have they given me?
They have only loosened the buckles of
    my care.
Yet e'en so, they are "profitable
    friends,"
And fill my need of "converse with
    wise men."
Yet when I consider how, still a man
    of the world,
In belt and cap I scurry through dirt
    and dust,
From time to time my heart twinges
    with shame
That I am not fit to be master of my
    pines!

PO-CHÜ-I, 772–846

A tree is a nobler object
than a prince
in his coronation robes.

ALEXANDER POPE, 1688–1774

AMIENS' SONG

Under the greenwood tree
Who loves to lie with me,
And turn his merry note
Unto the sweet bird's throat,
Come hither, come hither, come hither.
    Here shall he see
    No enemy
But winter and rough weather.

WILLIAM SHAKESPEARE, 1564–1616
From AS YOU LIKE IT

INDISCRIMINATE

The tree casts its shade upon all, even
upon the wood-cutter.

SANSKRIT PROVERB

FOREST VETERAN

Not far down the hillside is a Sequoia tree famous for its record. It is more than one hundred feet around where its clumsy elephantine toes grip the ground. It is perhaps two hundred and seventy feet tall.

One can only guess how many times it has been attacked by forest fires, lightning, the violence of wind. The thick bark is virtually insect-proof and heat-proof.

Conscience dawned in the Nile Valley only three or four thousand years before this veteran set out on its patient effort to stand against disaster.

First the bundle of possibilities scarcely bigger than a mustard seed working through the snow and at last reaching the waiting soil. Then the green shoot pushing aside the exploded hull, exploring its foothold with tiny roots, pricking the air with eager, sensitive cells, and somehow escaping the appetites of chipping sparrows, red squirrels, and black ants.

After that the full-grown tree.

There is something strangely exuberant about the erect fluted trunk glowing in the afternoon sun as brightly as that breast of the robin flashing past.

In terms of its own rhythm of existence it is as alert and responsive as the two white-spotted fawns that just now in sudden panic bounced off on elastic legs.

The indestructible Sequoia keeps groping for and finding enough contact with sun and soil to maintain an invincible faith in life.

John Muir spoke of the strength of these Sierra giants as "so perfect it is invisible."

There are people in the world like that. They have seemingly made a total response to some mysterious principle which eludes the classifications of the scientific mind. Their adjustment to environment is not so narrow or imprecise as ours. It is terribly far-reaching and exact. They are "secretly armed against all death's endeavor."

ALLAN A. HUNTER

⚜

SYMBOL

My faith is all a doubtful thing,
　Wove on a doubtful loom,
Until there comes, each showery
　　spring,
　A cherry tree in bloom;

And Christ, who died upon a tree
　That death had stricken bare,
Comes beautifully back to me,
　In blossoms everywhere.

DAVID MORTON

⚜

LOVELIEST OF TREES

Loveliest of trees, the cherry now
Is hung with bloom along the bough,
And stands about the woodland ride
Wearing white for Eastertide.

Now, of my threescore years and ten,
Twenty will not come again,
And take from seventy springs a score,
It only leaves me fifty more.

And since to look at things in bloom
Fifty springs are little room,
About the woodlands I will go
To see the cherry hung with snow.

ALFRED EDWARD HOUSMAN,
1859–1936

FOREST SCHOOLTEACHER

What I know of the divine sciences and Holy Scriptures, I learned in woods and fields. I have had no other masters than the beeches and the oaks.

ST. BERNARD OF CLAIRVAUX,
1091–1153

From THE PLANTING OF THE APPLE-TREE

What plant we in this apple-tree?
Buds, which the breath of summer days
Shall lengthen into leafy sprays;
Boughs where the thrush, with crimson
    breast,
Shall haunt, and sing, and hide her
    nest;
    We plant, upon the sunny lea,
A shadow for the noontide hour,
A shelter from the summer shower,
    When we plant the apple tree.

WILLIAM CULLEN BRYANT,
1794–1878

JOHNNY APPLESEED

In the early 1800's there was a strange figure to be seen among the frontiersmen of the Ohio Valley. This man was recognized by his ragged dress, by his eccentric ways, and by his religious turn of mind. His name was John Chapman.

Chapman had started a nursery in Pennsylvania. He visited the cider presses, and there he gathered the refuse, sifting out the apple seeds and sorting them. He urged the people going west to take the seeds with them.

For forty years he himself went up and down the estates in the Ohio Valley and planted apple orchards. For this reason he was called "Johnny Appleseed."

One can hardly imagine a man doing that kind of thing if he believed the end of the world was coming in the next decade.

That willingness to provide for generations yet to come represents the kind of confidence in the future that we need in spite of the threats that are present among us.

ROLLAND W. SCHLOERB

STOPPING BY WOODS ON A SNOWY EVENING

Whose woods these are I think I know
His house is in the village though;
He will not see me stopping here
To watch his woods fill up with snow.

My little horse must think it queer
To stop without a farmhouse near
Between the woods and frozen lake
The darkest evening of the year.

He gives his harness bells a shake
To ask if there is some mistake.
The only other sound's the sweep
Of easy wind and downy flake.

The woods are lovely, dark and deep.
But I have promises to keep,
And miles to go before I sleep.
And miles to go before I sleep,

ROBERT FROST, 1875–1963

WOMEN

ABOUT ANTHUSA, MOTHER OF
ST. CHRYSOSTOM (A.D. 360)
*Good heavens! What women these
Christians have!*

SAID BY HIS PAGAN TUTOR, LIBANIUS

From WOMEN AND ROSES
Round and round, like a dance of snow
In a dazzling drift, as its guardians, go
Floating the women faded for ages,
Sculptured in stone, on the poet's
    pages.
Then follow women fresh and gay,
Living and loving and lovely today.

ROBERT BROWNING,
1812–1889

PLEA IN 1845
Gentlemen: I come to present the
strong claims of suffering humanity.

I come to place before the Legisla-
ture of Massachusetts the condition of
the miserable, the desolate, the outcast.

I come as the advocate of helpless,
forgotten, insane, and idiotic men and
women, of beings sunk to a condition
from which the most unconcerned
would start with real horror; of beings
wretched in our prisons and more
wretched in our alms houses.

DOROTHEA LYNDE DIX,
1802–1887

AFTER-SUMMER FACES
In the faces of women who are naturally serene and peaceful, and of those
rendered so by religion, there remains
an after-spring, and later, an after-
summer, the reflex of their most beautiful bloom.

JEAN PAUL RICHTER, 1763–1825

MISSION
Hannah Tubman, born a slave in
Maryland (1821), "who never learned
to sign her own name, but whose name
is in the *Encyclopaedia Britannica*," led
300 Negroes up from slavery to freedom, saying: "And I never lost a pas-
senger on my Underground Railway!"

ONE WOMAN
It takes a hundred men to build an en-
campment, but it takes one woman to
build a home.

CHINESE PROVERB

THE WOMEN AND THE MASTER

Perhaps it is no wonder that the women were first at the Cradle and last at the Cross.

They had never known a man like this Man. There never had been such another.

A prophet and teacher who never nagged at them, never flattered or coaxed or patronized;

who never made arch jokes about them; never treated them either as "The women, God help us!" or "The ladies, God bless them!";

who rebuked without querulousness and praised without condescension;

who took their questions and arguments seriously;

who never mapped out their sphere for them and never urged them to be feminine or jeered at them for being a female;

who had no axe to grind and no uneasy male dignity to defend;

who took them as He found them and was completely unself-conscious.

DOROTHY L. SAYERS, 1891–1957

EARLY AMERICAN EPITAPH

On the banks of James River a husband erected a tomb in memory of his wife, one of those hundred maidens who had come to Virginia in 1619 to marry the lonely settlers.

The stone bore the legend:
She touched
the soil of Virginia
with the sole
of her little foot
and the wilderness
became a home.

BIBLICAL VIEWPOINT

The Bible is the only literature in the world up to our century which looks at women as human beings, no better and no worse than men.

The Old Testament writers considered them just as impartially as they did men, free from prejudice and even from condescension.

What historian of any other nationality writing of a general's great victory, Barak's over "Sisera with his chariots and his multitude," would set down how he cried out to a woman when she bade him go fight, "If thou wilt go with me, then I will go; but if thou wilt not go with me, then I will not go." And Deborah answered, "I will surely go with thee."

EDITH HAMILTON,
1867–1963

CHARM TO CHARM

A wife's charm delights her husband, and her skill puts fat on his bones.

A silent wife is a gift of the Lord, and there is nothing so precious as a disciplined soul.

A modest wife adds charm to charm, and no balance can weigh the value of a chaste soul.

Like the sun rising in the heights of the Lord,
so is the beauty of a good wife in her well-ordered home.

Like the shining lamp on the holy lampstand,
so is a beautiful face on a stately figure.

Like pillars of gold on a base of silver,
So are beautiful feet with a steadfast heart.

ECCLESIASTICUS 26:13–18

From THE PRINCESS

The woman's cause is man's; they rise
or sink
Together, dwarf'd or godlike, bond or
free.
For she that out of Lethe scales with
man
His nights, his days, moves with him to
one goal,
Stays all the fair young planet in her
hands—
If she be small, slight-natured, miserable,
How shall men grow?

ALFRED TENNYSON, 1809–1892

At Anglo-Saxon weddings in the early
part of the Christian era, the bride
promised, among other things, to remain "buxom and bonny," and the
bridegroom promised to take her for
"fairer or fouler."

You ask me, what is civilization? I
reply: it is the power of good women.

RALPH WALDO EMERSON, 1803–1882

THE GREATEST WOMAN

When asked who is the greatest of all
women, Ida M. Tarbell replied: "The
woman nobody knows."

CAPACITY

When I see the elaborate study and in-
genuity displayed by women in the pursuit of trifles, I feel no doubt of their
capacity for the most herculean under-
takings.

JULIA WARD HOWE, 1819–1910

PORTRAIT

A woman said: "She disappointed me.
I'd seen her picture, read about her
work,
Looked forward so to meeting her—
and then
To find her such a frowsy little thing
With such a bonnet!"
        Thus a journalist:
"She wasn't worth my time to inter-
view;
Nothing to see, nothing to say for
print."
        A poet mused: "How simple and
        how pure
The soul that speaks in every word and
look,
That knows itself the priestess of God's
beauty.
And gives for love what others grudge
for praise!
What courage and what patience in her
eyes!
What music of true feeling in her
voice!
How every feature kindles with the
light
That burns upon the altar of her faith!
How beautiful, how beautiful she is."

CHARLES WHARTON STORK

INSCRIPTION

Donald Culross Peattie put on his
mother's tombstone the inscription:
"She ate of life as if it were a fruit."

If it was woman who put man out of
Paradise, it is still woman, and woman
only, who can lead him back.

ELBERT HUBBARD, 1856–1915

A WOMAN'S WAY

In the year 1900, when Chile and Argentina were actively arming to go to war over a disputed boundary line high up among the snows of the Andes, a Christian woman down in Chile started going from town to town, collecting cash or copper cannon to be melted down for a statue of Christ which would be placed on that disputed spot.

What Señora de Costa succeeded in doing in Chile, Bishop Benevenute copied across the Andes in Argentina.

From these metal materials of war a great statue of Christ was made and carried by muleback to the mountaintop.

At the time of the dedication, a symbolic gesture of peace was shown when the people from Chile lay down to sleep on the Argentine side, and the people from Argentina slept on the Chile slopes.

The words carved on the base of the statue state what any woman can bring to pass in any dispute:

"Sooner shall these mountains crumble into dust than shall Argentineans and Chileans break the covenant which at the feet of Christ, the Redeemer, they have sworn to maintain."

TWO WIVES

Every man has two wives:

The first is the one he thought he was getting when he married her and she had been on her good behavior.

The second is the one she turned out to be forever after.

AUTHOR UNKNOWN

QUEEN GUINEVERE'S LAMENT

Ah, my God,
What might I not have made of Thy fair world,
Had I but loved Thy highest creature here?
It was my duty to have loved the highest;
It surely was my profit had I known;
It would have been my pleasure had I seen.
We needs must love the highest when we see it.

ALFRED TENNYSON, 1809–1892

A WOMAN'S DAY

Twenty-four hours to do the one thing needful, instead of ten or twelve to do a dozen.

There will be time to place ourselves at the disposal of anyone in real need; no time to waste at the street corner.

There will be time to play with the children; no time to be devising schemes for our own amusement.

There will be time to read widely, deeply, generously; no time to waste on trivialities.

There will be time to pray long and passionately for the coming of the Kingdom; no time to question its present security or its ultimate triumph.

NATALIE VICTOR

SERVING A GREAT CAUSE

Nothing bigger can come to a human being than to love a great cause more than life itself and to have the privilege of working for it.

ANNA HOWARD SHAW, 1847–1919

MY WIFE

Trusty, dusky, vivid, true,
With eyes of gold and bramble-dew,
Steel-true and blade-straight,
The great Artificer made my mate.

Honor, anger, valor, fire;
A love that life could never tire,
Death quench or evil stir,
The mighty Master gave to her.

Teacher, tender, comrade, wife,
A fellow-farer true through life,
Heart-whole and soul-free,
The august Father gave to me.

ROBERT LOUIS STEVENSON,
1850–1894

✣

LARGER HOUSEHOLD

The invasion of our private lives by the
larger destinies of mankind.

GEORGE ELIOT, 1819–1880

✣

TRUE GREATNESS

Once there was a woman that had done
a big washing and hung it on a line.

The line broke and let it all down
in the mud, but she didn't say a word,
only did it all over again, and this time
she spread it on the grass where it
wouldn't fall.

But that night a dog with dirty feet
ran over it.

When she saw what was done, she
sat down and did not cry a bit.

All she said was, "Ain't it queer
that he didn't miss nothing?"

That was true greatness, but it is
only people who have done washing
that know it.

SCHOOLGIRL'S ESSAY

Man's virtues are chiefly those of
power; woman's of patience.

LEON HARRISON

✣

A PASTORAL LETTER

When woman assumes the place and
tone of a public reformer, she yields
the power that God has given her for
her protection, and her character has
become unnatural.

If the vine whose strength and
beauty is to lean upon the trellis, thinks
to assume the independence and over-
shadowing nature of the elm, it will
fall in the rust in shame and dishonor.

We, therefore, regret the mistaken
conduct of those who encourage fe-
males to bear an obstrusive and osten-
tatious part in measures of reform, and
we do not countenance any of that sex
who so far forget themselves as to itin-
erate in the character of public lecturers
and teachers.

GENERAL ASSOCIATIONS OF CHURCHES
OF MASSACHUSETTS (c. 1841)

✣

From THE GOSPEL ACCORDING TO THOMAS

Jesus said: The Kingdom of the
[Father] is like a woman who was carrying a jar full of meal. While she was
walking [on a] distant road, the
handle of the jar broke. The meal
streamed out behind her on the road.
She did not know [it], she had noticed
no accident. After she came into her
house, she put the jar down, she found
it empty.

PROVERBIAL LORE

Memory is the mother of the muses.
                    GREEK PROVERB

*

Wonder is the mother of philosophy.
                    PLATO

*

Obedience is the mother of success, the wife of safety.
                    AESCHYLUS

*

Jerusalem is the mother of us all.
                    HEBREW PROVERB

*

"Would to God" is the mother of prayer.
                    DUTCH PROVERB

*

Eve: the mother of all living.
                    HEBREW PROVERB

*

Religion is the mother of the arts.
                    LATIN PROVERB

*

Borrowing is the mother of trouble.
                    HEBREW PROVERB

*

Cowardice is the mother of cruelty.
                    FRENCH PROVERB

*

Diligence is the mother of good fortune.
                    FRENCH PROVERB

*

Limitation of aim is the mother of wisdom and secret of success.
                    JOHANN WOLFGANG VON GOETHE

*

Devotion is the mother of obedience.
                    ENGLISH PROVERB

*

Necessity is the mother of invention.
                    ENGLISH PROVERB

*

Sincerity is the mother of knowledge.
                    JAPANESE PROVERB

*

Opinion is the queen of the world.
                    BLAISE PASCAL

*

Truth is God's daughter.
                    SPANISH PROVERB

*

Theology is the queen of sciences.
                    ENGLISH PROVERB

*

A woman without religion is as a flower without scent.
                    GERMAN PROVERB

*

Women's wishes are God's wishes.
                    FRENCH PROVERB

*

Wherever women are honored, there the gods are pleased.
                    THE CODE OF MANU (C. A.D. 100)

*

Men have sight; women insight.
                    VICTOR HUGO

MOTHER EARTH

Why was Jane Addams called "Mother Earth"? Undoubtedly because she began adopting "the world and they that dwell therein" when she was only six years old and saw her first slum.

Haunted by its hideous ugliness and deafened by its noise, she cried, "When I grow up I'm going to have a big house down here in this horrid place, with a yard for children to play in."

When she grew up, she did have just such a big house in the worst corner of Chicago. The words "Hull House" now stand for a woman with enough natural neighborliness to want everybody to be as comfortable as herself.

One night a burglar climbed up to her bedroom window. She startled him by saying gently that that was a desperately dangerous way to get into a house. She asked him if he was jobless and poor, and needed something she had?

If so, why not walk down the front stairs on tiptoe, close the front door quietly, and come back in the morning to talk over some simpler scheme for supporting himself?

He was astonished at her friendliness and disarmed by her interest, and by her calmness in a crisis.

Eventually Sweden awarded to Jane Addams the Nobel Prize in recognition of her endless efforts for peace among men and nations. But first she had Christianized her own nervous system into something brave and beautiful.

When she was asked what on earth was the secret of her tirelessness, for actually she was always in very poor health, she replied, "My devotion to unpopular causes!"

She appealed to the heroine in all women by saying in a public speech: "A great world purpose cannot be achieved without women's participation and widest sympathy, its very success depending upon a conscious change and modification of her daily habits."

THE CAMBRIDGE LADIES

the Cambridge ladies who live in furnished souls
are unbeautiful and have comfortable minds
(also, with the church's protestant blessings
daughters, unscented shapeless spirited)
they believe in Christ and Longfellow, both dead,
are invariably interested in so many things—
at the present writing one still finds
delighted fingers knitting for the is it Poles?
perhaps. While permanent faces coyly bandy
scandal of Mrs. N and Professor D
. . . the Cambridge ladies do not care, above
Cambridge if sometimes in its box of
sky lavender and cornerless, the moon
rattles like a fragment of angry candy
     E. E. CUMMINGS, 1894–1962

MADAGASCAR BIRTH NOTICE

"We have the honor to announce that Mrs. X lives anew."

EVERYBODY'S MOTHER

This little Scottish woman said of herself, "I'm a wee, wee wifie, no very bookit, but I grip on well, none the less!"

Mary Slessor never lifted up her soul unto vanity, yet the King of Glory kept her safely among savages in Africa for thirty-nine venturous years.

Alone in the jungle, Mary Slessor built herself a two-room hut of bamboo, daubed it with red clay, made a fireplace, a dresser, and a sofa all of clay, took in a number of little black girls for her family, lived in mortal danger all her days in the midst of primitive people.

Yet wrote home to Scotland: "In a home like mine, a woman can find infinite happiness and satisfaction. It is an exhilaration of constant joy. I cannot fancy anything to surpass it on earth."

When the Governor himself decided to visit her and to inform her that she was to be named magistrate to rule the turbulent tribes who called her their "Great White Mother," he arrived in a drenching downpour. She greeted this glamorous gentleman with the words, "Hoots, my dear laddie—I mean, sir!" He immediately understood why she fascinated all the Africans by her winning naturalness and simplicity.

Much later, when old and ill and literally worn out by a long lifetime of loving everybody for miles around, the King of England bestowed on her the distinguished Royal Order, awarded for her success in changing savages into law-abiding citizens, she escaped into her little hut and away from the adulation and ceremony, murmuring, "I shall never look the world in the face again until all this blarney and publicity are over."

When she died, up and down those jungle trails the call drums sounded their sad message: "Everybody's Mother has died!"

RUSSIAN PROVERB

The Russian peasants have a proverb that says, "Labor is the house that love lives in."

TO HER MOTHER

Your love was like moonlight
turning harsh things to beauty,
so that little wry souls
reflecting each other obliquely
as in cracked mirrors . . .
beheld in your luminous spirit
their own reflections,
transfigured as in a shining stream,
and loved you for what they were not.

You are less an image in my mind
than a luster
I see you in gleams
pale as star-light on a gray wall . . .
evanescent as the reflection of a white
    swan
shimmering in broken water.

LOLA RIDGE

SYMBOLIC LINK

A child is tied to our heartstrings as the spheres are linked to their Creator. We cannot think of God except as a mother's heart writ large.

HONORÉ DE BALZAC, 1799–1850

THE TRUE MOTHERS

Many women, whose energies would have been, under former conditions, inevitably monopolized by home-keeping duties, are today giving their strength and special gifts to social service.

They are the true mothers—not only of their own little brood—but of the community and the world.

The service of the true woman is always "womanly."

She gives something of the fostering care of the mother, whether it be as nurse, like Clara Barton; as teacher, like Marion Lyon and Alice Freeman Palmer; or as social helper, like Jane Addams.

The service of these persons is that which only women could have given to the world.

MARY R. PARKMAN

MARY SLESSOR'S MOTTO

God can't give His best
till we have given ours.

ENORMOUS INFLUENCE

No thoughtful persons can fail to appreciate the enormous influence which women are constantly exercising for good upon the destinies of the world.

The charms and graces of existence, whatever ennobles and embellishes life, we owe mainly to them.

They are the natural guardians of morality, and from age to age the mothers of households have preserved the sacred fire on the domestic hearth, whereat every virtue is kindled.

FELIX ADLER, 1851–1933

THE IDEAL AIM

We have told the story of our mother's life, possibly at too great length; but she herself told it in eight words.

"Tell me," Maud asked her once, "what is the ideal aim of life?"

She paused a moment, and replied, dwelling thoughtfully on each word: "To learn, to teach, to serve, to enjoy!"

LIFE OF JULIA WARD HOWE,

1819–1910

A GOOD WIFE

A good wife who can find?
  She is far more precious than jewels.
The heart of her husband trusts in her,
  and he will have no lack of gain.
She does him good, and not harm,
  all the days of her life.
She seeks wood and flax,
  and works with willing hands.
She is like the ships of the merchant,
  she brings her food from afar.
She rises while it is yet night
  and provides food for her household
  and tasks for her maidens.
She considers a field and buys it;
  with the fruit of her hands she
    plants a vineyard.
She girds her loins with strength
  and makes her arms strong.
She perceives that her merchandise is
  profitable.
Her lamp does not go out at night.
She opens her mouth with wisdom,
  and the teaching of kindness is on
  her tongue.
Her children rise up and call her
  blessed;
  her husband also, and he praises her:
"Many women have done excellently,
  but you surpass them all."

PROVERBS 31:10–18, 26, 28–29

WORSHIP

We praise Thee, O God,
We acknowledge Thee to be the
Lord;
All the earth doth worship Thee,
The Father Everlasting.

TE DEUM LAUDAMUS

PRIVATE DEVOTION

Every man can build a chapel in his
breast,
himself the priest,
his heart the sacrifice,
and the earth he treads on, the altar.

JEREMY TAYLOR, 1613–1667

SIGHTLESS

The man who does not habitually worship is but a pair of spectacles behind
which there is no eye.

THOMAS CARLYLE, 1795–1881

INNER TOUCH

Such is the heat of this inner touch
and of His love, that it would seem to
burn us up; and His touch cries in the
spirit without ceasing: "Pay your debt.
Love the love that ever loves you."

JAN VAN RUYSBROECK, 1293–1381

Let any true man strip himself of all
pretence, selfishness, and sluggishness
of soul, lift off thought after thought,
the inmost depth of all, and it will be
passion after passion, till he reaches
strange if he does not feel the Eternal
Presence as close upon his soul as the
breeze upon his brow.

JAMES MARTINEAU, 1805–1900

It is quite possible to be Christian in
head and pagan in heart; to have
learned much in theology, and yet be
sadly clear that one stands in no close
relation to God Himself.

HENRY CHURCHILL KING,
1858–1934

The great use of life is to
spend it for something
that will outlast it.

WILLIAM JAMES, 1842–1910

DIVINE VIGILANCE

Do you wake? God too is awake. If you arise in the night time, if you anticipate to your utmost your earliest awakening, you will already find Him waking.

You will never anticipate His own awakeness. In such an intercourse you will always be rash if you attribute any priority, any predominate share to yourself, for He loves both more than you love, and before you love at all.

ST. BERNARD OF CLAIRVAUX,
1091–1153

OUR INNER NEED

The great want of modern Christians is deep vigorous inward repentance, and life goes too fast for that. Rapid lives and rapid thinkers make rapid worshipers, and rapid worshipers are rapid penitents, and the spirit of inward penitence fares ill with all this.

FREDERICK WILLIAM FABER,
1814–1863

ROAD TO HOLINESS

In our era the road to holiness necessarily passes through the world of action.

DAG HAMMARSKJÖLD, 1905–1961

BY THREE MEDICINES

By contrition we are made clean, by compassion we are made ready, and by true longing we are made worthy. By these three medicines it behooveth that every soul should be healed.

JULIANA OF NORWICH, 1343–1413

GOD OUR REFUGE

If there had anywhere appeared in
    space
    Another place of refuge, where to
      flee,
Our hearts had taken refuge in that
    place,
    And not with Thee.

For we against creation's bars had beat
    Like prisoned eagles, through great
      worlds had sought
Though but a foot of ground to plant
    our feet,
    Where Thou wert not.

And only when we found in earth and
    air,
    In heaven or hell, that such might
      nowhere be—
That we could not flee from Thee any
    where,
    We fled to Thee.

RICHARD CHENEVIX TRENCH,
1807–1886

From OUR TOWN

I don't care what they say with their mouths—everybody knows that *something* is eternal. And it ain't houses, and it ain't names, and it ain't earth, and it ain't even stars—everybody knows in their bones that *something* is eternal, and that something has to do with human beings. All the greatest people ever lived have been telling us that for five thousand years and yet you'd be surprised how people are always losing hold of it. There's *something* way down deep that's eternal about every human being.

THORNTON WILDER

TEN RULES FOR WORSHIP

I

Worship begins as I close the door to my home. On my way, I pray for my church, for the minister, and for those who worship far and near.

II

Before I enter the house of God, I pause a moment that I may cast off and leave outside all things and thoughts unbecoming to a child of my Heavenly Father: hates, grudges, frettings, worldly cares, and sinful thoughts.

III

The moment I enter the door of this sacred house I cease all conversation. I come in silence, for great things arise out of quietness and minister to me and to those about me.

IV

As soon as I am seated, I bow my head in prayer. I pray for others as well as for myself. I pray for my church and its great causes. I ask God to be near me now.

V

I join in singing the hymns and bow my head during the amen. I think about the words of the sermon and let their meaning and spirit go down to the roots of my soul.

VI

As I lay my offering on the plate, I say a prayer of thanks for my money, and I ask God's blessing on its use here and in the uttermost parts of the earth.

VII

Throughout the service I think of God objectively. As power, peace, strength, and love, He is all I need for life as it should be.

VIII

I listen as my minister preaches from God's Word, and I seek to apply his message to my life. I pray for him as he preaches.

IX

When the service has ended, in Christian friendliness I speak to those whom I know and also to those who are strangers to me.

X

As I pass through the outer portals, I dedicate my life to walk this week the high road with Christ.

AUTHOR UNKNOWN

⚜

In what thing soever thou hast thy mind's reliance and thine heart fixed, that is beyond doubt thy God.

MARTIN LUTHER, 1483–1546

⚜

CALAMITY! CALAMITY!

What greater calamity can fall upon a nation than the loss of worship! Then all things go to decay. Literature becomes frivolous. Science is cold. The eye of youth is not lighted by hope of other worlds, and age is without honor. Society lives for trifles, and when men die we do not mention them.

JOHN RUSKIN, 1819–1900

MORTAL PREPARATION NOW

None can become fit for the future life who hath not practiced himself for it here.

ST. AUGUSTINE, 354–430

FADELESS

Activity is only beautiful when it is holy, that is to say, when it is spent in the service of that which passeth not away.

HENRI FRÉDÉRIC AMIEL, 1821–1881

THE ETERNAL OTHER

In his history, "A Raw Youth," Dostoevski puts these profound words into the mouth of an old saint: "A man who bows down to nothing can never bear the burden of himself."

God is not a luxury; He is a necessity.

When man loses faith in God he worships humanity. When faith in humanity fails, he worships science, as so many are trying to do today. When faith in science fails, man worships himself, and at the altar of his own idolatry he receives a benediction of vanity.

Hence the tedious egotism of our day, when men are self-centered and self-obsessed, unable to get themselves off their hands.

Only God, the eternal Other, is equal to the need of the human soul.

Dostoevski himself found liberty, at last, in a final prostration of his soul, stripped and humbled, before God.

JOSEPH FORT NEWTON, 1878–1949

EUCHARISTIC LIFE

The beginning of that Eucharistic life, which is the true life of the Church and of each of her members, is a free and unconditional self-offering of the created life to that transforming energy which is even now at work on us.

We are to offer in simplicity what we are and what we have to the external purposes of Gd, without any self-occupied attempt to determine its precise quality and value.

The soul, says St. John of the Cross, is like an unopened parcel. Only God knows what He has put in it, and wherein its ordained perfection consists. Self-scrutiny at its best hardly gets beyond the paper and the string.

The meek, adoring, self-oblivious attitude, the generous gesture, the cost, are the things that matter.

EVELYN UNDERHILL, 1875–1941

WHAT IS FAITH?

Do you ask, "What is faith in God?"

I answer, "The leaving of your way, your objects, yourself, and the taking of His and Him; the leaving of your trust in men, in money, in opinion, in character, in atonement itself, and doing as He tells you."

I can find no words strong enough to serve for the weight of this obedience.

GEORGE MACDONALD, 1824–1905

If personality is the highest known thing, must not God be at least that highest thing?

CHARLES GORE, 1853–1932

WHERE IS GOD?

"Oh, where is the sea?" the fishes
  cried,
  As they swam the crystal clearness
  through;
"We've heard from of old of the
  ocean's tide,
  And we long to look on the water's
  blue.
The wise ones speak of the infinite sea.
  Oh, who can tell us if such there
  be?"

The lark flew up in the morning bright,
  And sang and balanced on sunny
  wings;
And this was its song: "I see the light,
  I look o'er a world of beautiful
  things;
But, flying and singing everywhere,
  In vain I have searched to find the
  air."

MINOT J. SAVAGE, 1841–1918

I believe in One God, Creator of the
Universe.
  That He governs it by His Providence.
  That He ought to be worshipped.
  That the most acceptable service we
render Him is doing good to His other
children.
  That the soul of man is immortal
and will be treated with justice in another life respecting its conduct in this.

BENJAMIN FRANKLIN, 1706–1790

Fear God, and next to God, fear him
who has no fear of God.

POLISH PROVERB

"YOUR WORTH-SHIP"

In medieval days, when all land was
held by an overlord, any man wishing
to live on a portion of that land went
through an ancient ritual.

Such a vassal, holding between his
two palms a bit of actual earth, would
kneel and place these two clasped hands
between the hands of the overlord, saying, "Your Worth-ship!" Thus he
symbolized publicly his indebtedness
for being allowed to hold such property in trust for a little time.

From this the word "worship" grew.

We recognize our Heavenly Father
as the Over-Lord of all our earthly possessions, and we realize that any true
worship implies a quiet and confident
placing into His hands of some share
of the gifts He has bestowed.

FROM FEAR INTO FAITH

Father, do Thou this day free me—
  From fear of the future;
  From anxiety for the morrow;
  From bitterness toward anyone;
  From cowardice in face of danger;
  From laziness in face of work;
  From failure before opportunity;
  From weakness when Thy power is
  at hand.

But fill me, I beseech Thee, with—
  Love that knows no barriers;
  Courage that cannot be shaken;
  Faith strong enough for the dark-
  ness;
  Strength sufficient for my tasks;
  Loyalty to Thy kingdom's goal;
  Wisdom to meet life's complexities;
  Grace to meet life's perplexities;
  Power to lift men unto Thee.

AUTHOR UNKNOWN

SOUL AND FLOWER

The soul of a true Christian appeared
like such a little white flower as we
see in the spring of the year;

low and humble on the ground,
opening its bosom to receive the pleasant beams of the sun's glory, rejoicing,
as it were, in a calm rapture;

diffusing around a sweet fragrancy;

standing peacefully and lovingly in
the midst of other flowers round about,
all in like manner opening their
bosoms to drink in the light of the sun.

JONATHAN EDWARDS, 1703–1758

⚜

LIVING COMMUNION

The solution of all our troubles and
problems is, I maintain, to be found
in the recovery of more vital methods
of living communion with God. It
would be well for us to reduce the
amount of talk, of words, of argument, of question-asking, reduce also
what is formal and mechanical, and
greatly increasing the living, silent,
penetrating corporate activity of worship of which Whittier wrote those
great words of his—the meaning of
which he had experienced:

"Without spoken words, low breathings stole

Of a diviner life from soul to soul,

Baptizing in one tender thought the
whole."

RUFUS M. JONES, 1863–1948

⚜

OUR DAILY BREAD

For the Christian who loves God, worship is the daily bread of patience.

HONORÉ DE BALZAC, 1799–1850

WHAT IS WORSHIP?

It is always easy to make fun of our
necessary methods of worship.

Why should the Creator of a myriad
stars desire us to gather together and
sing songs about Him?

Truly our best expressions fall short
of our meaning, and our meaning falls
far, far short of the Reality.

Yet if God is love and our worship
is real, then worship is what God most
wants of us, and is the chief means of
gaining strength to serve Him worthily.

For what is worship?

It is the quickening of conscience by
the holiness of God, which finds expression in confession of sin.

It is the feeding of our minds upon
the truth of God, as we listen to His
Word and rehearse our belief.

It is the opening of our hearts to the
love of God, as His truth and beauty
come home to us in the Gospel.

It is the submission or surrender of
our wills to the purpose of God, expressed in intercession according to the
manner of prayer taught by our Lord.

It is the gathering up of all these
in adoration, the most selfless emotion
of which our nature is capable. "We
give thanks to Thee for Thy great
glory."

WILLIAM TEMPLE, 1881–1944

⚜

LIMITLESS WONDER

Worship is transcendent wonder;
wonder for which
there is now no limit
or measure:
that is worship.

THOMAS CARLYLE, 1795–1881

"HE THAT DOETH
THE WILL"

From all vain pomps and shows,
From the pride that overflows,
And the false conceits of men;
From all the narrow rules
And subtleties of schools,
And the craft of tongue and pen;
Bewildered in its search,
Bewildered with the cry:
Lo, here! lo, there, the Church!
Poor, sad humanity
Through all the dust and heat
Turns back with bleeding feet,
By the weary road it came,
Unto the simple thought
By their great Master taught,
And that remaineth still:
Not he that repeateth the Name,
But he that doeth the Will!

HENRY WADSWORTH LONGFELLOW,
1807–1882

SOME KEEP THE SABBATH

Some keep the Sabbath going to
church;
I keep it staying at home,
With a bobolink for a chorister,
And an orchard for a dome.

Some keep the Sabbath in surplice;
I just wear my wings,
And instead of tolling the bell for
church.
Our little sexton sings.

God preaches,—a noted clergyman,—
And the sermon is never long;
So instead of getting to heaven at
last,
I'm going all along!

EMILY DICKINSON, 1830–1886

HOLY COMMUNION

Those creatures that live amongst the
snows of the mountains turn white
with their food and conversation with
such perpetual whitenesses. So our
souls may be transformed into the similitude and union with Christ by our
perpetual feeding on Him, and conversation not only in His courts, but in
His very Heart, and most secret affections, and incomparable purities.

JEREMY TAYLOR, 1613–1667

RELIGIOUS UNITY

Yes, we do differ when we most agree,
For words are not the same to you and
me,
And it may be our several spiritual
needs
Are best supplied by seeming different
creeds.
    And, differing, we agree in one
    Inseparable communion,
If the true life be in our hearts; the
faith
    Which not to want is death;
    To want is penance, to desire
    Is purgatorial fire;
To hope is paradise; and to believe
Is all of heaven that earth can e'er
receive.

HARTLEY COLERIDGE, 1796–1849

REAL PRESENCE

Worship is the art of rising to a personal, experimental consciousness of
the real presence of God, which floods
the soul with joy and bathes the whole
inward spirit with refreshing streams
of life.

RUFUS M. JONES, 1863–1948

Eternity is the complete and perfect possession of unlimited life all at once.

BOETHIUS, C. 475–525

From PARACELSUS

Truth is within ourselves; it takes no rise
From outward things, whate'er you may believe.
There is an inmost centre in us all,
Where truth abides in fulness; and around,
Wall upon wall, the gross flesh hems it in,
A baffling and perverting carnal mesh
Binds it, and makes all error: and, to know,
Rather consists in opening out a way
Whence the imprisoned splendor may escape,
Than in effecting entry for a light
Supposed to be without.

ROBERT BROWNING, 1812–1889

From THE PROPHET

He to whom worshipping is a window, to open but also to shut, has not yet visited the house of his soul whose windows are from dawn to dawn.

KAHLIL GIBRAN,
1883–1931

REVERENT FIDELITY

When we observe the needle of the mariner, without visible organ, or sense of faculty, pointing with a trembling and pious fidelity to the unseen pole, and guiding, no one favored people only, but all nations, at all times, across a wilderness of waters, so that a ship sails forth from one shore and strikes the narrowest inlet or bay on the other side of the globe, why ought we not to be filled with awe as reverential and as religious as though we had seen the pillar of cloud by day and of fire by night, which led the children of Israel in their journey through the wilderness?

HORACE MANN, 1796–1859

From THE CHAPEL

Like one who leaves the trampled street
For some cathedral, cool and dim,
Where he can hear in music beat
The heart of prayer, that beats for him;

And sees the common light of day,
Through painted panes, trans-figured, shine,
And casts his human woes away,
In presence of the Woe Divine:

So I, from life's tormenting themes
Turn where the silent chapel lies,
Whose windows burn with vanished dreams,
Whose altar-lights are memories.

There, watched by pitying cherubim,
In sacred hush, I rest awhile,
Till solemn sounds of harp and hymn
Begin to sweep the haunted aisle:

*

Restored and comforted, I go
To grapple with my tasks again;
Through silent worship taught to know
The blessed peace that follows pain.

BAYARD TAYLOR, 1825–1878

INDEX OF AUTHORS AND SOURCES

The unsigned materials are from various books by the editor.

SUBJECT INDEX